SPIRIT BUILDERS

SPIRIT
BUILDERS

CHARLES CATTO, FRONTIERS FOUNDATION
AND THE STRUGGLE TO END
INDIGENOUS
POVERTY

JAMES BACQUE

RMB

RMB | Rocky Mountain Books Ltd.
rmbooks.com
@rmbooks
facebook.com/rmbooks

Cataloguing data available from Library and Archives Canada
ISBN 978-1-77160-136-8 (paperback)
ISBN 978-1-77160-137-5 (electronic)

Printed and bound in Canada by Friesens

Distributed in Canada by Heritage Group Distribution and in the U.S. by Publishers Group West

For information on purchasing bulk quantities of this book, or to obtain media excerpts or invite the author to speak at an event, please visit rmbooks.com and select the "Contact Us" tab.

RMB | Rocky Mountain Books is dedicated to the environment and committed to reducing the destruction of old-growth forests. Our books are produced with respect for the future and consideration for the past.

We acknowledge the financial support of the Government of Canada through the Canada Book Fund and the Canada Council for the Arts, and of the province of British Columbia through the British Columbia Arts Council and the Book Publishing Tax Credit.

Disclaimer

The views expressed in this book are those of the author and do not necessarily reflect those of the publishing company, its staff or its affiliates.

A note on the illustrations

Many of the photographs in the book were chosen by Charles Catto to illustrate his memoir, *Beavering*. I am grateful to Barbara Catto, Marilyn Gillis, many former volunteers and others for sharing their memories and pictures. Unfortunately not all could be used. Unless otherwise noted, the illustrations come from the Archives of Frontiers Foundation, Toronto.

This book is my labour of love for Charles Catto and the volunteers who followed his music north, south and everywhere to answer a call for help from people who deserved it and who then helped others.

CONTENTS

PREFACE

"In cases of emergency, it is folly to fold one's hands and sit down to bewail in abject terror. It is better to be up and doing."

— Catharine Parr Traill,
The Backwoods of Canada

Charles Catto, the founder of Frontiers Foundation, and I became friends in about 1948 when we were students at Victoria College in the University of Toronto. In the mid-1960s, when I was the editor at Macmillan of Canada, Charlie asked me to publish his manuscript about the founding and success of Operation Beaver/Frontiers Foundation. Although I liked the subject, I turned it down because the writing was full of preachy clichés. But Charlie kept after me. I donated money to Frontiers to help him along because I believed in the work, but I also wanted him to leave me in peace. A persistent man, Charlie rewrote the manuscript and tried me again in 1969, after I had become president of another publishing house, newpress, but the manuscript was still not viable. Finally, in about 2005, when I had finished some major projects and had free time, Charlie and I agreed that I would write the story myself.

Charlie was very helpful, giving me all kinds of useful research material, including his own manuscripts and full access to the foundation's records. Even as I worked on piecing together the book, I continued donating both money and work to Frontiers. Discussing the foundation's internal affairs, Charlie held little back. He invited me to join the board, but I wavered because I wanted my work on the book to remain objective. When he died in May 2014, having made no preparations for his successor, I was dumbstruck, and I said to myself, "Instead of grieving, I will try to help Frontiers continue Charlie's work by finishing the book," which I have now done.

— James Bacque, September 2016

A SOCIETY LIKE NO OTHER

As he stepped onto the gangway of the steamship *Keenora* on that warm July evening in 1954, Charles Catto felt that his life was just beginning. His years of schooling and apprenticeship were finished and he was a missionary heading out to Canada's true North. The missions superintendent of the United Church of Canada in Winnipeg had told him what the Church expected him to do once he had moved into the manse at God's Lake, Manitoba, and now he was going there to introduce himself and make friends with the people of his new "charge," as the United Church calls its congregational areas. The very name God's Lake seemed to be significant, underscoring the importance to Charles of both the mission he was on and the greatness of the land he was entering.

As Northern Fish Company porters loaded cargo into the ship's hold and passengers climbed aboard with their duffel bags, knapsacks, dunnage bags and one brass-clasped steamer trunk labelled "Reverend Charles Catto, God's Lake," he felt that the North was already changing him, influencing him with its own strong character. Back home in Toronto, what had counted were brains, money, talk and connections; here, you needed all that and more – strength, courage and humility. Here, the clothing was different, the food strange, the languages multiple. The weather was dangerous, but the air was unique, fresh, cool, so clear and fine that it was a pleasure to smell it as it entered his lungs. The tips of his ears were chilly, and strangers smiled at him as they did not in Toronto.

The passengers, mainly men, represented a unique mix of cultures and traditions. The ship's name was rendered in Cree, and its first pilot was one of the Cree people. The *Keenora* had been built of steel on the River Clyde in Scotland, the country of Charles's ancestors, and boarding it today were fishermen, trappers, traders, lumbermen, prospectors, tourists and one young Christian minister.

Though Charles had left the familiar places of his youth, he immediately felt at home as he travelled north. He was a true descendant of his Ontario ancestors who had designed a unique society of three peoples loyal to the British Crown. They had firmly planted their society on the Ontario shore in 1791. The founders were monarchist Canadians and a few white aristocrats from Britain treating with Ojibwa and Mississauga lords of the forests and lakes around them. Their agreements to share Ontario "like two boats in one river" were witnessed by Iroquois diplomats and adventurous Canadien traders. Their land – "Upper Canada" to the settlers, "Turtle Island" to the Aboriginals – stretched west to buffalo prairies and north to polar-bear seas. The capital was a wood-walled village named York.[1]

These founders' agreements, injured but not dead, endured in the people of Toronto, where Charles Robert Catto was born in 1929. Some 600,000 now lived in stone and brick houses where a few hundred

The Land and The Law

The changes from about 1830 to today in the escutcheon of the city of Toronto parallel an ignorant trend in Canadian society toward energetic philistinism. Britannia, prime source of Canadian government and law is lost along with the source of the land, aboriginal people. The resulting vacuum Catto sought to replace with enlightened spiritual power.

Imagery of the 2014 coat of arms courtesy of the City of Toronto Protocol Office.

THE LAW AND THE LAND COATS OF
ARMS OF TORONTO (YORK)

had built wooden York. By the time Charles was born, the Aboriginal peoples had been betrayed, robbed and driven into ghettoes in the woods, and the monarchists had been absorbed into a democratic Anglo-French Canadian culture now embracing many other European peoples but excluding the Ojibwa and Mississauga.[2]

Loyalty was an important word to all these people. They were loyal to their old traditions, as well as to their new country. There were Loyal Orders of Orangemen, the provincial motto was *Ut incepit sic permanet, fidelis* ("As it began, so it remains, faithful"), and in Charles Catto's youth there were still monarchist families who proudly signed their names along with the initials UEL. – United Empire Loyalist – dating from 140 years before. At the Church of England College, Trinity, the students shouted the college cheer:

We are the salt of the earth
So give ear to us
No new ideas will ever
Come near to us;

Orthodox, Catholic
Crammed with Divinity
Damn the dissenters
Hurrah for old Trinity.

Thus, the ruling class of the city into which Charles was born: British, expansive, monarchical, snobbish, ordered and churchy. But its people were also liberal, inventive, educated, prosperous, confident and productive. They believed in freedom for all, even if it inconvenienced them. Upper Canada in 1793 preceded the USA in passing a law striking down slavery.[3] And it was the first to establish universal free education for every child, in 1846.[4]

In the decade of Charles's birth, the spirit of Ontario's people was still energetic and pioneering. Frederick Banting and Charles Best were saving the first of millions of lives with injections of their discovery, insulin, for which they won the Nobel Prize in medicine. A future Nobel Peace Prize laureate named Lester Pearson, and two doctors soon to be famous round the world, Norman Bethune and Bob McClure, had all just graduated from the University of Toronto, whose campus had been a wooded wilderness only 70 years before their birth. A few years earlier, Alexander Graham Bell, sometime of Brantford, Ontario, had co-founded the Bell Telephone Company, whose wires were establishing the world's first mass instant-communication system. Members of the Massey family were building and selling their efficient Massey tractors in ten countries, while early-maturing Marquis wheat, hybridized by William and Charles Saunders, *père et fils*, was revolutionizing agriculture around the world. Canada's universal, compulsory school system, including high school, had been declared perfected by its founder, Egerton Ryerson.[5] Starting to learn her letters in that system was a certain Alice Laidlaw, who, as Alice Munro, would win the Nobel Prize for Literature in 2013.

Among the original society of three founding cultures, only the Aboriginal peoples were not prosperous. Although Ojibwa leader Wabbicomicot had agreed with Governor Simcoe that their two peoples would share the forests and lakes "like two boats in one river,"[6] by the 1920s, the Ojibwa had been severely reduced in both numbers and circumstance. The new education system was scarcely "theirs," and the pledges made to them to share the land and its resources had been dishonoured. The land and lakes where their ancestors had lived for thousands of years had suffered perhaps the most concentrated destruction of habitat that had ever occurred in one human lifetime.[7] The wild paradise was destroyed, and cities smoked in the ruins of ancient forests.

The Cattos were distinguished leaders among those British-Canadians who were building this destructive and creative province. They were prosperous, hardworking Scots who, like many of their kind, had immigrated to Canada in the early 19th century to escape the English domination of their own native lands. But in crossing the ocean, many of these people bent to the Roman motto *alterum caelum, alteri mores* (other skies, other ways), for they were a practical bunch. In their new land, new rules applied, so they joined the Tory establishment of Upper Canada. Some of them were farmers, some merchants, some religious, and some even joined the same British army that had driven them and their ancestors from Scotland. One, Douglas Catto, became a lieutenant colonel in the Royal Regiment of Canada, which led the Canadian attack on the German fortifications at Dieppe in August 1942. And in matters of religion, the immigrants honoured the established Anglican Church. Charles's Presbyterian great-grandfather John Catto visited his Anglican bishop every New Year's Day until his death in 1928.

Charles grew up with his mother, father and three sisters in a close, affectionate family. Their house, two storeys of red brick, stood on a big lawn behind huge old trees, some of them survivors from the oak savannah that had dominated the area in the days of the Ojibwa and the French fur traders. Educated and prosperous, the family dressed in fine clothes and went to church regularly. They were baptized, christened, catechized, instructed, married and buried by clergymen.

Like most of the bourgeoisie of Toronto, Charles and his family lived outdoors as much as they could: skiing, tobogganing and skating in winter; canoeing and swimming in the warm seasons at their cottage on Lake of Bays in the Muskoka district north of the city. In their canoes and on their tent sites, they were typical of the Canadians who like to holiday by reverting to the way of life of their ancestors and the Aboriginal peoples before them. They romanticized the forest that their settler ancestors had hated, cut down and burned as fast as they could to gain access to sunlight and farmland.

The famous naturalist and writer Ernest Thompson Seton, educated in Toronto, developed the principles of woodcraft that soon spread round the world in the Boy Scout movement. Basic to that new romanticism of the white people were the Ojibwa, Cree and Iroquois, the "noble savages" who were now more condescended to than respected as equals, mentors and friends of the first white Canadians.

British Canadians initially honoured their former allies, who had fought in their wars against the Americans, who had been reliable business partners in the fur trade that opened the country to both British and French immigrants, and who had guided them in their far-ranging explorations of the continent to the west. But their descendants gradually ceased to honour in full the pledges they had originally made.

Many of Charles's cousins were patriotic Canadians who fought in the two world wars. So, from his tenth year, Charles was taught to pray for "our men overseas," and to sing hymns imploring God to protect them on land, on sea and in the air. He looked up at the regimental flags in church, he read the memorials "to our fallen dead" and he listened to sermons or read books justifying Canada's struggle against her enemies, who included the Americans, the Métis of western Canada, Russians, Boers, Germans, Italians and Japanese. But after the death of George Bean – a war hero from his school who was killed in action in 1945 – Charles began to feel the contradiction that existed in his society between the army and the Church.

His mother Marion had taught him one important prayer: "I love thee, Lord Jesus, please help me to be / Always good, kind and loving, and grow more like thee." She encouraged him to read the Bible, which he did, every one of its some 800,000 words by the time he was 16 years old. But the teachings in the New Testament were in direct conflict with what he saw going on around him in his school, his city, his country and the whole world. The Church was blessing the men who were using atomic bombs, air raids, death camps and machine guns against human beings. In Montreal a United Church minister, Reverend Lavelle Smith, was forced from his pulpit because he preached against the Second World War, using words from the Bible supposedly revered in Canada: "Put up your sword for they that take the sword will die by the sword." This contradiction between peace and war within the Church was so strange to Charles that at first he felt his mind must be confused. Finally he realized that *his* mind was clear and it was the *world* that was confused. The death of George Bean forced him to understand what was going on around him. He thought, "The existing world system consciously and deliberately kills its best young people, and that is wrong. It must be righted. I may be only one guy, but I *can* make a difference."

His guide was Jesus's teachings, which showed him how to bring about the change that he now knew was essential – a change to which, in fact, he had, without entirely realizing it, begun to dedicate his life. He told a friend, "When I graduated from University of Toronto Schools (UTS), I knew there was something rotten in the state of Denmark, and the whole Christian world. And I wanted to do something about it."

He was a happy, smiling boy, ready with a joke, with lots of friends, but there was always something a little odd about him, some independent purity that set him apart. A good sport, he did not drink much, or smoke or swear or romance the girls. He had an explorer's far-seeing squint to his eyes. He was intelligent and musical, a good learner, but he could not stand music lessons and so failed his first piano lessons and quit. Later, he taught himself to play the piano in a rollicking manner, embroidering on the melody extra notes and trills wherever he fancied.

He was so obviously honest, strong and willing that he was chosen by a Royal Mail supervisor along with a school friend, Don Williams, to load some very heavy sacks into a mail truck in the post office where the two friends were earning tuition and pocket money at Christmas time. Suddenly, there were uniformed supervisors everywhere in the mail room, some of them armed, watching their every move. After the sacks had been safely shipped, Don discovered that they contained ingots of gold.

The older he grew, the more his spirit matured toward independence. He read *The Life of Christ*, by Ernest Renan, which chipped away the encrusted legends of two thousand years, to reveal Christ the man. Although Charles despised the hypocrisy of the Church for teaching God's love while supporting war, he could not abandon the faith of his parents and his childhood. By the time he was at university, this conflict was tense within him.

When he was 21, at Victoria University in the University of Toronto, Charles wondered – as youth must – how to live this precious life that has been granted to us. His friends were planning to spend their lives in the city, practising law or medicine, or teaching. Many were headed into business. One was preparing to write books, which came to include the one in your hands.

Considering his future, Charles looked far beyond the sooty drudgery of a big-city life. Teaching appealed to him, but it was too conventional. Nothing about the money-seeking careers among the downtown towers moved his spirit. He wanted something more soul satisfying, something more adventurous and yet more practical. Despite the hypocrisy the Church interested him because it opened broad prospects as no other institution did. It taught belief, and it was founded on belief. It reached to the end of the world and the end of thought. He saw that despite the failings of many members, some people in the Church practised the words of Christ: "Love your neighbour as you love yourself"; "Love God and love your fellow man." That the human mind can reason no further than these awesome words satisfied him; they defined limits by creating absolutes. The question to which his spirit sought an answer now became: can action follow where those words lead? As the moral purpose of his life was growing clear in his mind, the challenge opened up. He wondered, "Can *you* go as far as the thought demands?" And he thought seriously about Christ's words: "If you would be perfect, sell everything you have and follow me."

Studying divinity at Emmanuel College in Victoria University, he knew fairly soon that an orthodox career in the Church would not satisfy his ardent spirit. A turning point came one day while he was listening to his professor, Dr. John Line, drone on about the Incarnation of Jesus Christ as if it were a problem in geometry. Dr. Line's words, which Charles remembered for the rest of his life, were: "The Incarnation represents a vertical impingement on the horizontal plane of our Euclidian cosmology." This sentence was one that Charles refused to serve. If nothing else, his experience as a student taught him that there was no future for him in the halls of religious academe. He needed to get as far away from that sort of thing as he could. Charles was energetic, merry, gregarious and optimistic in spirit, healthy and quick minded. Now, with a degree in hand, he felt he was ready to carry out a mission for Jesus.

He was ready, but he was alone.

He had not been paying much attention to girls so far in his young life, but he was now thinking about a future in the ministry, which to his mind included family life. He had met Barbara Loveys, a student in the University of Toronto's dental nursing program and a Girl Guide leader at a camp in the forested Haliburton highlands north of Toronto, not far from the Cattos' family cottage.

Charles wandered into the school of dentistry one day in October 1953, in search of some cheap dental work and a date for his fraternity Phi Kappa Pi's dance that Friday.[8] "Being the ever-efficient person that he is," Barbara said, "he made two appointments with me that day." The more he saw of this modest student with the brilliant smile, the more he liked her, so he made sure she was informed when he was asked a few weeks later to fill in as a summer replacement preacher at her church. She sat in her family pew listening to his authoritative young voice pronouncing on world affairs and Christian behaviour, sincere in every word but free of excessive moralizing.

BARBARA LOVEYS, DENTAL
NURSE, TORONTO, 1954.

REVEREND CHARLES
CATTO, NEWLY ORDAINED
UNITED CHURCH MINISTER,
TORONTO, 1954.

Soon he was riding the streetcar home with her after school, a long way to the Jane Street loop and bus terminal, talking all the way about world affairs, always in the spirit of determining what could be done about them. The Second World War had finished only four years before, and the Berlin airlift of 1948 had barely averted another European conflict. Barbara was fascinated because he not only knew what he was talking about but also had the spirit to do something about the problems he perceived and deplored. That, probably more than anything else, convinced her that here was a young man who was worth living her life with. Her growing resolve was not broken even when toward the end of each long streetcar ride he began to conjugate Greek verbs aloud.

Charles and his classmates at Victoria had a lot of fun along with their religious learning. Their bedroom windows opened out onto St. Mary Street, across from the bedroom windows of the young Catholic students at St. Michael's College. On winter nights, the students taunted each other with snowballs and religious jibes – "There's no snow where Martin Luther is," or "Come on over here and read the Bible in English." Together with another free spirit at Victoria University, Alf McAlister, Charles founded the Interdenominational Committee on Vocations to Ministry, whose aim was to promote ecumenism among fractious and quarrelling Christians. They wanted to mobilize interdenominational teams to recruit for the ministry among their fellow students. The two young idealists were turned down right away by the Catholics and made scant headway with the Protestants. Most of the professors at the divinity colleges were not interested. "We got only grudging support from the ivy-covered Pharisees who were much more interested in perpetuating their own denominational turf than venturing into the ecumenical challenge," Charles said later. So he and Alf offered to speak about the ecumenical movement at high schools, where they finally received a warm response. The high-school students wanted to know more about what Jesus Christ had done and said, rather than what "any strangling sect" was preaching to the world. While Alf and Charles's little movement lasted three years, it eventually died of suffocation at the hands of the denominational Christian establishment.

Emmanuel College confirmed Charles in his existing convictions and gave him the tools he needed to act on them. In other personalities and in other times, Charles's were the impulses that had driven conquerors, crusaders or inquisitors. In this man, however, they became a fury of belief that pressed him like a fierce wind toward his firm goal: serving others who were in need.

PRAYING BOSS

Charles Catto was 25 years old when he embarked down the Red River to Lake Winnipeg, on his way to his new life. The *Keenora* entered Lake Winnipeg ten miles downriver and steamed north all day, and the next night and day, to Warren's Landing, where passengers transshipped to the little *Chickama* (Cree for "sure"), which hammered along Playgreen Lake and Little Playgreen Lake to the famous Hudson's Bay Company trading post at Norway House. There Charles was met by the Keeper brothers, Joe and Walter, members of the Norway House Cree Nation and faithful adherents of the Church.

Joe Keeper had raced for Canada in the 1912 Olympics at Stockholm, where he finished fourth in the world in the 10,000-metre run. Using only hand tools, the two brothers had built the manse at God's Lake Narrows, where Charles was soon to set up house. They pow-wowed for a few hours, and the next morning a single-engine Noorduyn Norseman of Central Northern Airways landed on the lake. Charles climbed in.

SS *KEENORA* TOOK PASSENGERS AND FREIGHT UP LAKE WINNIPEG TO WARREN'S LANDING, WHERE THEY WOULD BE TRANSFERRED TO THE SMALLER *CHICKAMA* TO CONTINUE ON TO NORWAY HOUSE.

He stepped out onto the pontoon and the shaky dock at the Hudson's Bay Company trading post at God's Lake an hour and a half later. He was met by the genial manager of the post, Lee McIntosh, a blond Scot who introduced him as the new *haymaykamow* (praying boss) to two church elders, Jacob Bee and John Trout. They said, "How wah tyeh." Charles did not yet know it, but he was hearing 17th-century English transmuted into Cree. The original English, "Hello, what cheer," now meant "Let's shake hands." He was meeting that peculiarly Canadian mix of peoples and cultures that had begun centuries before in many places, particularly in Nova Scotia when Samuel de Champlain and a few dozen other Frenchmen had wintered over near a Mi'kmaq village in Acadie. That early language mélange – a mix of Aboriginal languages, English, French, Scottish, Basque, Portuguese and African tongues – was even more varied than what Charles heard that day at God's Lake.[9] He revelled in it all. His religious training had fortified his upbringing, giving him the means, via language, belief and vocation, to do what he naturally did well: lead, inspire, inform and be a good friend to many kinds of others.

He already loved the North as well as the works of the community in which he found himself: the odd little steamboat, the decorated canoes, the white-painted clapboard of the Hudson's Bay posts, the dock built on log cribs filled with stones, the names of the people and places, the genial expressions on the hard-skinned, weather-wrinkled faces of the trappers, traders and guides. From the moment he first heard it, Charles especially relished the language, soft and continuous like the whisper of a loon's wings flying past.

As they walked up to the post for lunch, Charles noted what he described in his next letter to Barbara as "the savage beauty of the triumphant wilderness."

His second and definitive arrival with his new young wife occurred some months later, after he had finished his orientation and flown back south to marry Barbara.

On a sunny afternoon in late September (*nochitoowepesim*, "the month when deer mate") 1954, Barbara, aged 20, and Charles, 25, climbed aboard a Norseman, heading north from Winnipeg over 400 miles of forest toward God's Lake. They flew above lakes and rivers that striped the landscape to the horizon in every direction. They

REVEREND CHARLES AND BARBARA CATTO'S
WEDDING, KINGSWAY–LAMBTON UNITED CHURCH,
ETOBICOKE, ONTARIO, SEPTEMBER 25, 1954.

could not see a house, road, railway, boat or dock anywhere beneath their pontoons.

Dark clouds built up ahead of the little plane, obscuring the sky with snow. Halfway to their destination, they were forced down to the water at Deer Lake. The people welcomed them with great excitement as no *haymaykamow* had showed up there for years. Local Cree brides and grooms gathered around, asking Charles to perform *wigito* (marriage) ceremonies for them. Two of the newlyweds already had three children, so he threw in baptisms as well. Then they danced, listened to Cree drummers and watched as two straight-backed bridesmaids in beaded song-dresses performed the delicate steps of the wedding dance on their heels and toes. Afterward, they feasted on roast moose, fresh trout, fresh pickerel and bannock. Charles and Barbara joined in the celebrations, touched by the ready welcome and the interest displayed on every face. There were cheers and laughter when Charles announced that he and Barbara had just been married, that this was their honeymoon.

Next morning the sky was clear, and the pilot taxied them out onto the water. Deer Lakers stood in the brilliant sunshine on the white shore of the blue lake in parkas and buckskin, waving goodbye. Then the plane vaulted above the dark evergreens, now glittering with snow.

At last their pilot, banking the plane, shouted, "Down there!" pointing to the narrows of God's Lake, turbulent with powerful currents, named *manitouwapa*, Cree for "the place where the Great Spirit whispers." Here is where, on Charles's first brief visit three months earlier, he had begun whispering on behalf of the Christian God.

Energetic children shooed dogs off the dock as the pilot taxied the plane in. The kids escorted Charles and Barbara to Chief John Henry Ross, who welcomed them with a smile and introduced them to several councillors and church elders. Then they ferried the new *haymay-kamow*, his wife and their baggage in canoes across *manitouwapa* to the couple's first home: the two-bedroom clapboard house hand-built for the church by the Keeper brothers.

Right away, Charles and Barbara faced enormous problems. Nearly all the people they were meeting could not speak English. Although Charles and Barbara had taken Cree lessons in Toronto, their knowledge was insufficient even for arranging the distribution of the clothing they had brought with them – and in the North's fierce climate, those clothes were needed. The Church gathered clothing made by congregants down south and shipped it free to a railhead 150 miles away at Ilford, on the Canadian National Railway (CNR) line to Churchill. But the Church could not pay the expensive freight by tractor-train on the winter road from Ilford to God's Lake. For delivery of future loads, Charles would have to raise the money among people whose income was not much more than $30 per month (about $275 in 2015). Despite their lack of Cree, Charles and Barbara went at it happily from the first day, encouraged by the hundreds of new friends around them. In a country where people are scarce, strangers are welcome.

On his first morning, Charles encountered chaos in the church

CHARLES WITH GOD'S LAKE UNITED CHURCH
ELDERS, 1954. FROM LEFT TO RIGHT: THOMAS
OKEMOW, THOMAS CHUBB, CHARLES CATTO, JOHN
TROUT, CHIEF JOHN HENRY ROSS AND JONAS FLETT.

office. Dental forceps were entangled with umbilical tape hidden under ration lists mixed with church records, all weighted down with a broken rifle. On top of the bales of donated clothing sat a yellowing copy of an old radio-telegram to the Royal Canadian Mounted Police at Norway House, 150 miles away: SOLOMON OKEMOW IS SHOOTING STOP COME AT ONCE. Tacked to his desk so it could not blow away was a welcome note from his predecessor. "God bless you and God help you," it read. Charles added, "Amen."

Daily, and often during the night as well, every conceivable kind of problem arrived at the mission door: crippled Andrew Snowbird with running sores on his thigh; little Rosemary sobbing over her gashed nose; old Bella Bee, certain she'd seen enough winters to qualify for her old-age pension, so would someone please notify the *suniogemow* (Indian agent, or "money boss"); Elijah Duck, wanting a job, any kind of a job; Lillian Goose, wanting a job, any kind of a job. People also arrived with messages: "Jock Perch got a moose in the lake last night.

You're invited to a feast this afternoon at his grandfather's." And "Peter is very sick, so will the praying boss come and pray to the Great Spirit with him?" Teresa Marten, heavy with child, requesting one of the nice new layettes; a fat, freshly killed duck, arriving with the compliments of John Trout; Minnie Chubb, selling a very fine pair of moccasins.

When it was all over, and he was in bed at 3:00 am, there was a knock on the door from an anxious young man with a plaintive plea: "Please wake up. Cora Nazee's baby may be dying." Cora's baby did die.

And in the morning, it started again. Jim needed help to start his outboard motor, the only one on the reserve. Another two messages came: "John Jackfish has got Bill Beaver's wife. Come quick – they're drunk and fighting"; "Hey, can I borrow your canoe? I've lost my wife and I want to find her." And another: "Can you come, praying boss? I'm cold at night; my daughter's gone to Island Lake and she's taken the blanket." Amelia Kirkness and Laura Otter came to scrub the church – could they please have the brushes? Another telegram, this time by moccasin: "John Okemow shot 22 caribou yesterday; come and get some meat."

Charles could not know it as he began his ministry, but he was living among people who were part of a civilization that only a few hundred years before had been admired and emulated by most of the Europeans who had experienced it. It was impossible for him to know this at first, because the Christian mission in the North in the 1950s was based on a belief that Aboriginal society in general was weak, decayed, primitive and in need of superior Western technology, laws, language and religion. But it is now known and broadly accepted that in 1492, the Aboriginals of North and South America were, in many ways, more developed than the Europeans. They were an advanced and healthy group of peoples living in harmony with their environments, with excellent pharmacopoeias, some with libraries with thousands of books, some with well-developed agriculture and big cities – one of which, Tenochtitlan in Mexico, ranked with the most populous in Europe at the time, Cordoba and Seville. The first European visitors repeatedly described North America as "paradise." In those early days, North Americans produced all that they consumed and consumed all that they produced. And it was plenty.

One unnamed Jesuit missionary advised his superiors in France not to tell too much of the truth about North America because:

> It is not fitting that every one should know how agreeable it is in the sacred awe of these forests, and how much Heavenly light one finds in the thick darkness of this barbarism; we would have too many persons wishing to come here, and our Settlements would not be capable of accommodating so many... [10]

Such thoughts had also occurred to Father Pierre Biard in the early 17th century, after he met and began to understand the indigenous peoples:

> ... their days are all nothing but pastime. They are never in a hurry. Quite different from us, who can never do anything without hurry and worry; worry, I say, because our desire tyrannizes over us and banishes peace from our actions. [11]

The Europeans loved and adopted many things North American, including various foods, furs, medicines, tobacco, sports, clothing, canoes, new political ideas, place names and more. The Scottish, French and indigenous people loved and depended on each other so much that they created a new people, the Métis. And a new language, Michif.

Early European visitors and settlers also immediately adopted many Aboriginal habits and modes of thought. The belief in individual freedom, for example, which had only recently been propounded in Europe by thinkers like Voltaire, Martin Luther and John Wycliffe, was given new energy by the first peoples of North America. Particularly striking to the visitors was the idea of "the priesthood of all believers," common in Aboriginal societies but a radical notion in Europe until the Protestant Reformation. The new knowledge gleaned from Aboriginal societies caused European thinkers to reconsider their own attitudes toward slavery, personal cleanliness and hygiene, medicine, farming, childhood education and government. The Iroquois Confederacy inspired British-Americans such as Thomas Jefferson and Benjamin Franklin to shape the government of the original 13 revolting colonies into a loose federation. [12]

The Iroquois (Haudenosaunee) Confederacy adhered to the Great

Law of Peace, or *Gayanashagowa*.[13] Jefferson wrote in admiration of that Great Law of Peace and simultaneously plotted to break it by advocating revolution against England. Even if it were argued that he was justified in overthrowing a distant tyranny, what he feared for the new United States of America came true, as if in consequence, only a few decades later, when the states went to war with each other.[14] That war would not have happened if he and his fellow revolutionaries had heeded the tenets of *Gayanashagowa*.[15]

L'Ingénu, a satirical novella by Voltaire published in 1767,[16] documents the "true story" of an orphaned Huron lad born in Ontario and brought by English traders to France. The boy is found to be of French extraction, although he was raised from infancy by the Huron people. Voltaire uses the "Huron" character – called "Child of Nature" – as a vehicle through which to criticize religious doctrine in France, as well as French politics, society and culture. He presents "Child of Nature" as Jean-Jacques Rousseau's "noble savage": intelligent, ingenuous, amiable, humorous, resolute and extremely attractive to women. Voltaire later said that this book was his favourite in his whole oeuvre. He liked it even better than his famous *Candide* because it was truer to life.[17] Nearly a century later some Ojibwa dancers from Ontario touring England and the continent proved this point. One of the dancers, Maungwudaus, wrote a book, published in 1848, offering some interesting and funny observations of European societies. He wrote, "Like musketoes in America in the summer season so are the people in this city in their numbers and biting one another to get a living."[18] The travelling Ojibwa so charmed the English ladies that the ladies begged to be kissed by them. Maungwudaus and his friends kissed them on the cheek, causing the English ladies to laugh: would they please kiss them again, on the mouths. The Ojibwa obliged, and the ladies urged their men to invite the Ojibwa again because they liked them so much.

Voltaire's work was so influential that both the government and the church in France exiled him and banned his writing for many years. The French establishment believed he was successfully subverting the established order, which in fact was his purpose. The movement that issued in part from his writings came to be called liberalism, which directed the progress of most North American and European societies for the next two hundred years. It is not very fanciful to suggest that writing about the character of "Child of Nature" may have played a powerful role in shaping the thought of this great reformer who, in the opinion of many historians, brought down a corrupt monarchy and a Christless church.

Unlike the Europeans, nearly all North American Aboriginals disdained the idea that personal wealth conferred prestige; they thought it was normal to share the necessities of life. Thus jails, keys and money were unknown to them before Contact. Their ways of teaching and learning were familial and exemplary, so there was no need for schools, and their religions were based on the priesthood of all believers, so churches were virtually unknown among them.

The agronomy that supported the highly organized cities of the New World – Tenochtitlan and Teotihuacan, Kaan and Mutal – was possibly the most efficient in the world. Of the five most important food crops grown in the world today – wheat, rice, corn, potatoes and soybeans – two, corn and potatoes, originated in this agronomy.[19] The agricultural practices of the ancestors of the Olmecs, Toltecs and Aztecs of central Mexico were so advanced that modern scientists spent years on DNA tests, trying to identify the wild grasses from which corn was hybridized by the early Mexicans.[20]

Meso-American farmers developed a mixed-crop system called *milpa* which allows sustainable use of the same fields for hundreds of years without fertilizer. Eastern North American peoples harvested healthy, sustainable numbers of deer, turkey, moose and elk from the forests, which they treated like farms. Their plantations of corn, beans and squash were highly productive and disease resistant, partly because they mixed their crops and partly because they also planted species such as peas, which fix nitrogen in the soil.

And as Charles would discover, the ancestors of the Cree of God's Lake lived a religion that paralleled Christianity, with several sharp differences. It was monotheistic, but God was not a loving father as in Christianity. God was seen as the source of all powers operating in the world, good and bad. This meant that what men judged as evil came from God as well, and not from the devil. The ethic deriving from this conception was little different from the teachings that Reverend Catto brought in 1954. One of the Cree headmen, Chief John Ross, expressed this humorously to Charles one day after church: "You know,

Charles," he said, "before you came, we had all the teachings of Christianity except the Sabbath." Saskatchewan writer Maggie Siggins relates a similar story, this one told by Namegus from the Rock Cree in Saskatchewan, who joked about his wife becoming a Christian. He did not forbid her, but in typical Cree fashion, made fun of her decision. After she had converted, she came to dinner with him, and he asked for her new Christian name. She said, "Nancy," and he gave her a piece of meat, the toughest he could find. He said, "Let's see if your teeth cut better now that your name is Nancy."[21]

The Cree, like most Aboriginal peoples, suffered greatly from epidemics of strange diseases carried to them by Europeans. The enormous losses of their populations were intensified by the fact that remedies for these foreign plagues did not exist in their own pharmacopoeia. So when the people asked their medicine chiefs to help, they couldn't. The wider the epidemics spread – up to 96 per cent of some populations died – the greater the sense the people had that their whole civilization was disappearing.[22] The plagues were spread by explorers like the Spaniard Hernando de Soto, who in the early 16th century travelled from Florida westward past the Mississippi River, accompanied by herds of pigs as was the Spanish custom. His account speaks of thousands of Native peoples lining the banks of rivers, hooting and jeering at the inept Europeans trying to cross in clumsy rafts. He saw "…a land thickly set with great towns… two or three of them to be seen from any one."[23] But the French explorer Sieur de la Salle, descending the Mississippi 150 years later, said he travelled for 200 miles through the area where de Soto had been without seeing so much as a village.[24]

The Aboriginals were probably killed as well by zoonotic diseases transmitted by animals introduced by the Spaniards.[25] Jacques Cartier, visiting the St. Lawrence River in 1535, saw orchards and fields of crops covering the banks of the river. Seventy years later, Samuel de Champlain travelled up the river and wrote that these same banks were overgrown with trees.[26]

According to many current experts,[27] European diseases were the chief cause of the population collapse that preceded the various European conquests among the Inca, Maya, Aztec and other civilizations of the Americas. One estimate is that some 15 major epidemics killed off about 90 per cent of the population of these regions in 80 years or less after the first Spanish group arrived in the 16th century. These plagues were thus proportionately three times as severe as the Black Death that devastated 14th-century Europe. The epidemics in the New World were the "greatest demographic collapse in human history," according to Ronald Wright, who quotes a contemporary Mayan source, *The Annals of the Cakchiquels*:

> After our fathers and grandfathers succumbed, half of the people fled to the fields. The dogs and the vultures devoured the bodies. The mortality was terrible. Your grandfathers died and with them died the son of the king and his brothers and kinsmen. So it was that we became orphans, oh my sons... We were born to die.[28]

In the 1770s, a plague of smallpox, probably brought to the area by traders from Britain and Montreal, devastated the Cree on the Canadian prairies. Smallpox struck again in 1784, again in 1838, and then influenza killed thousands in 1908–09 and again in 1917–18.

Canadians like Catto belonged to a race whose ancestors had passed through a genetic bottleneck which meant death for most of those whose DNA lacked the protective genes against certain diseases. The Cree who survived the epidemics of influenza, measles and smallpox from the late 1700s onward scarcely knew what had happened to the larger Aboriginal societies of which they were the northern extension just as Catto's ancestors in Scotland had been the northern extension of the cultures of England, Italy, Greece and the Holy Land.[29]

In his role as missionary, Charles benefited from two priceless assets. First, he was, like many Canadians of his ancestry and period, culturally confident and not arrogant or condescending.[30] In fact, he was curious and eager to learn about other people, to understand their beliefs and speak their languages. Second, he had the deep religious assurance of his faith.

The Cree's first recorded contact with European people came in the late 17th century, when traders from England arrived by sailing ship to explore the shores of Hudson Bay. Henry Kelsey of the Hudson's Bay Company in London landed at the mouth of the Nelson River, where he met Cree people who allowed the company to build a fur-trading post on the Hayes River, called York Factory. The Cree helped Kelsey ascend the river hundreds of miles by canoe to explore and to search for furs. For hundreds of years after that, the preponderance of meetings between Cree and European people turned on the trade in furs: their price, their quantity, the location of the trading posts. The country provided a rich harvest of the staple beaver, but also of mink, otter, silver fox, red fox and muskrat. Furs were an object of international trade in the 17th century just as they are today, their beauty, warmth and durability making them prized and expensive among women who live in the northern hemisphere. The Cree people were strong, healthy and self-reliant, and were adept traders who immediately understood the value of·European goods and system of credit. They were ready to work hard to provide the food and furs that Europeans desired.

The first missionary to the vast Cree territory, as large as Europe, was the Methodist James Evans, who came by sailing ship to Hudson Bay in 1840, then paddled upriver in a metal-clad canoe, preaching the Word and also studying it. He invented the first Cree syllabics, into which the Bible and many hymns were soon translated. The system was so simple that most people conversant with spoken Cree could learn most of it in a day or two, and it could be written on birch bark with the point of a charred stick.

As soon as he arrived at God's Lake, Charles was making friends, sorting clothing for distribution, setting up lessons for the schoolchildren, opening an infirmary, learning to handle a dog team, using his wits to help police the reserve, and preaching, especially against alcohol. He was also thinking about better ways for Church and government to get along with one another and with the Cree. Having ministered here briefly during his preliminary tour the previous summer, he was aware of the problems caused by the lack of coordination among government and Church agencies. This lack was one reason for the firetrap shacks, the poor education, and the self-doubt and despair harboured by many of the people in the community.

Since most of the people coming to the manse door at God's Lake had only rudimentary English, Charles knew he had to learn to speak and write Cree. In Winnipeg the superintendent of the United Church Home Missions had told him, "You'll have an interpreter." But Charles said, "That will make me deaf and dumb. I'll learn Cree." He soon did so with the help of the elders at God's Lake, and he donated to the Church the funds set aside for the interpreter.

Charles realized that history was built into language, both Cree and his own. The Toronto society into which he had been born and that had sent him here had taught him a devotion not just to Christianity but also to the forms of government that supported Canada. His Canadian upbringing also imparted a certain wariness of Americans – and his new Cree friends were similarly equipped with this suspicion of our neighbours to the south. In the Cree language, Americans are *gitchi mookumana*, or "long knives," in memory of the experience of Prairie nations battling the US cavalry. But the Cree word for Europeans and "Canadians" is *mistagoosowuk*, "wooden boats," derived from the Cree's first contact with European people when traders from England arrived on the Hudson Bay coast by wooden sailing ship or inland up the rivers by York boat. Charles found a religious aspect to the linguistic history of Cree, as well: Catholic and French are synonymous, *pacwice*; English and Protestant are also synonymous, *agnice*.

The society Charles was entering had known not only *pacwice* and *agnice* missionaries and fur traders for hundreds of years but also, more recently, miners and businessmen. A new stage in the history of the area's Cree began on Jowsey Island in God's Lake on July 13, 1932, when Archie MacDonald, a prospector, shouted out to his partner, Bob Jowsey, who was frying bacon over a campfire, "Robert, we've found a gold mine!" Mining promoters at Sherritt Gordon Mines Limited in Toronto raised capital for a winter road so construction and mining could begin the next summer. Production started in 1935, and the God's Lake Gold Mine continued to operate profitably until 1943. At first the Cree and the mining company men got along happily because the young Cree men worked so hard and learned so quickly. A mining engineer for Sherritt Gordon wrote:

> Contrary to all commonly held opinions on the subject, the members of this tribe revealed a willingness to work and an adaptability little short of amazing in an Indian... [In the hauling operation] they proved more satisfactory than white labour... [which] we practically dispensed with... their adaptability and willingness to learn were of great value, and it was only necessary to train one man in the

system to be used. Further instruction was unnecessary because the principles of the work were relayed from man to man by the Indians themselves.[31]

This ready sharing of knowledge and goods among all the people was something Charles also noticed among the Cree at God's Lake, and which other missionaries described among the Iroquois as well. As one of the 17th-century Jesuits wrote:[32]

> ... there are neither mendicants nor paupers... among them. Their kindness, humanity and courtesy not only make them liberal with what they have, but cause them to possess hardly anything except in common. A whole village must be without corn before any individual can be obliged to endure privation. They divide the produce of their fisheries equally with all who come.[33]

Charles had been warned by another missionary, Don Scoates at Oxford House, to beware the linguistic thin ice ahead of him. Cree people do not speak of catching fish, but of killing fish, which are *kinusao*. One day, Scoates had mixed up *kinusao* with *kishaynoo*, or old man, so when he politely asked an old Cree woman about her fishing luck, he actually said, "Have you killed any old men lately?" The outraged old woman told him to get out of her house because in fact she had just killed her husband and the suspicion in the village was that it had not been an accident.

Barbara was not yet old enough to vote when she moved to God's Lake, but she immediately took on adult responsibilities at Charles's side. These two young idealists from Toronto took turns teaching 20 children in six grades in the one-room schoolhouse. They had a few old, tattered texts about white children in cities or on farms, which had virtually no meaning for these forest children and so weren't of much use to them. Barbara also painted the manse, added to her initial stock of 150 Cree words, and learned to bake bread in the woodstove. She scarcely had time to organize their own few possessions before she was busy helping other people.

Before she left Toronto, Barbara had ordered food for a year, but it would not arrive until February, five months distant, when the tractor-train could run on the winter road that extended 150 miles from the

GOD'S LAKE, THANKSGIVING DAY, 1954. EIGHTEEN-
FOOT CANOES MEET THE NORSEMAN AT THE UNITED
CHURCH DOCK. BARBARA WAS ABLE TO SERVE CHICKEN
TO HER GUESTS FOR THE DINNER THAT NIGHT.

CNR railhead. In the meantime, she would have to buy supplies at the
Hudson's Bay trading post across the narrows.

During the winter, Charles had to chop a hole in the ice and haul
water up in a 45-gallon drum on a toboggan behind his dog team. In
the summer, he built wheels for the toboggan. When a friend later in-
quired, "Lots of the Cree today are depressed by their lives; so how did
you two feel?" Barbara replied, "We were never depressed for a moment. Everyone made us feel welcome. Charles was always bursting
with energy, and there was always something to do." Even the remote-
ness did not bother Barbara. As she wrote to a friend in the city, "I can
hear the silence."

The first 300 years of trade, proselytizing and tourism that marked
relations between northern Cree and settlers had been very good for
white people but at best marginally advantageous for the Cree. With
the closing of the God's Lake Mine in 1943, however, competition
among the churches for the souls of the Aboriginal people and the
spread of alcohol rendered parts of northern Manitoba a moral slum.

The reserves were sloppily administered by the Department of Indian and Northern Affairs in a loose partnership with the competing missions of southern churches. Instead of decent housing, basic health and economic justice, rival "missions" on reserves promoted sectarian agendas, apparently oblivious to the tuberculosis that was killing children. The disease is treatable, and preventable, as Dr. Norman Bethune had shown 20 years before in Montreal, but it seemed that TB was conquered only in the white South. Only a winter or two before the Cattos arrived, three tubercular children in one God's Lake family had coughed themselves to death. On all the reserves in the area, the great majority of people lived in shacks where deadly tuberculosis and fire flared up every winter.

In pain and frustration, Charles wrote to a friend in the city:

> In the midst of this morally provocative scene should have stood the Church of Jesus Christ, the most practical human being who ever lived. For most of his life, he was a framing carpenter, building houses of wood and stone, and the tables, chairs, beds and shelves to match. And during his entire three-year ministry he urged his followers to build homes on lasting foundations, to heal the sick, to feed the hungry and to pray that our Father's kingdom would come on earth as it is in heaven. So what the hell happened on the Canadian frontier?[34]

He soon found the answer. The missions were treating Christianity like a board game with a score, and the Cree were their tokens. Priests and ministers were racing by canoe and dog team past those smoky shanties to baptize Cree babies. Families were bribed with sugar, lard or blankets if they allowed themselves to be added to the Protestant or Catholic conversion statistics. The federal government played along, wasting millions of dollars on duplicate denominational schools. "Instead of faith, hope, love, safe warm homes and meaningful employment," Charles wrote, "the northern clergy were generating deadly sins – hate, greed, pride, jealousy and lust."[35] For decades, in some residential schools, Native children were sexually abused and no one protected them. If children complained, hardly anyone believed them. If they were believed, hardly anyone exposed the crimes, and even if someone tried to seek justice for victims, the churches routinely denied any abuse. These churches represented about 75 per cent of all Canadians at that time.

The depravity of white men was also a well-known aspect of the Canadian fur trade. Alexander Mackenzie, the first person to cross North America by land and who travelled the frontier for many thousands of miles as a fur trader and explorer in the 18th century, wrote in his journal: "The Canadian missionaries should have been contented to improve the morals of their own countrymen, so that by meliorating their character and conduct, they would have given a striking example of the effect of religion."[36]

Modelled on the cities of the South, the slums and the rich sections of God's Lake were distant from each other. Up and down the shore from the Cree village were busy tourist lodges, a thriving commercial fishing industry, some of the most productive traplines in the region and, earlier, the God's Lake gold mine.

White Canadians and Englishmen owned and operated the tourist lodges, the airlines and the commercial and sport fisheries plus the Hudson's Bay Company store, whose chief clerk bragged about his affairs with Cree girls as he bought their fathers' furs. Named Duncan Pryde, the young man boasted that "every girl in the Arctic should have a little Pryde."

The prudish Charles could hardly bear to speak civilly to the horny young man, and he preached fiercely against libidinous behaviour. And after some considerable struggle, he also persuaded the community elders to ban alcohol on the reserve. This was so successful, and the resulting improvement in behaviour so striking, that the ban became widely popular (though not perfectly observed), and it was still in force 55 years later when Charles visited God's Lake in 2009. Pryde, however, had been transferred away by the company after only a short sojourn in God's Lake.

The prices for fur were declining in those years, cutting sharply into the tiny incomes of the trappers, so the end of employment at the mine in 1943 was especially bad news for God's Lake. As Charles observed, "In ten years the company got $5-million worth of gold, and the Cree got the shaft."[37]

There was not one Aboriginal resident who had hydro, running water or an indoor toilet. There was no hospital and no doctor. The Department of Indian Affairs did eventually provide doors and windows for homes on reserves. Annually, Indian Affairs also distributed $5 to every treaty man, woman and child; $25 to the chief; and $15 to each councillor, as well as assorted trifles.

There was no police service, so praying boss Catto occasionally had to use his fists to keep order between fighting young men. One cold night Charles came home wearing a torn, bloody shirt and missing his prized wristwatch after a fight with John Osborne. For the first time ever, Charles was glad of the boxing lessons he'd had at UTS. John was not.

The next day, John sobered up and looked penitent as he returned the watch to Charles. Almost without exception, the fights happened after young men drank too much homebrew, which the white gold miners had taught them to make from beans. The effect of alcohol on Aboriginal North Americans was remarked upon by settlers from the earliest days, and often exploited by them. Many fur traders in Canada tried to protect their Native partners from the "whisky" traders, many of whom came from south of the border with loads of cheap whisky used to cheat the natives out of their furs, land, horses – whatever they could get – leaving disease and poverty in their wake.

One day in 1954, good news came to God's Lake from the Catholic Church. A young, recently ordained Oblate priest, Father Leon Levasseur, took over the rival church and helped to change the terms of competition between the United and the Catholic missions. A good-looking, cheerful young man, Levasseur, like Charles, was pained by the plight of his parishioners, and he immediately set out to help them. He soon ran into the difficulties that had been created by competition between the churches. As Charles put it to him, "It is up to us to diminish the significance of the categories of white man's alienation" – a wry take on the bafflegab he had mocked at university.

Levasseur was interested in this irreverent reverend, fresh-faced and eager like himself, who had taken over in this difficult place. With deep foreboding about the reaction of the Church establishment, but also a sense of relief at doing what was plainly in the best interest of the Cree, the two young clerics co-operated at first on small projects – distribution of clothing, a combined Christmas party, purchase and sharing of a three-horsepower outboard motor for towing home rafts of winter firewood (essential for everyone during the –50° nights that were bound to come).

These projects led to the creation of a community club to help distribute the clothing according to need, not denomination. The aged chief of the God's Lakers, John Henry Ross, was all for it, but even at this low level, ecumenism was a dangerous game for both minister and priest. For 18 months, the two co-operated in raising funds to pay for other community needs, such as a chainsaw, a bigger outboard motor and a washing machine. Reverend Charles and Father Leon travelled, fished and even prayed together, which in 1954 – well before Pope John XXIII's ecumenical leadership – would have given the Vatican apoplexy.

CHARLES AND HIS ROMAN CATHOLIC FRIEND
FATHER LEON LEVASSEUR FISHING, 1955.

Levasseur had to report honestly to his superiors on what he had been up to, of course, and no matter how much he might emphasize the importance of co-operation, his superiors disapproved of what he was doing. They let him continue for 18 months, but then the boot crashed down on him. He was ordered out of Charles's neighbourhood, off to Oxford House, a difficult hundred miles away. The people of God's Lake were left with nothing but a warm memory of Levasseur's devotion to them.

Although Charles was busy with practical matters, he missed his friend's companionship and the sense that he and Levasseur were at God's Lake for the same reason: to promote God's love among all the people of the area. In order to do this, Charles had to accustom himself to a new name for God, known to his parishioners as the Great Spirit. He spoke of the Great Spirit's love and care on the trail, in the truth and life of His son, Jesus Christ. Using the Cree language, he spoke with individuals, families and among the community at large. In all the time he was there, only one other Protestant missionary out of about a dozen or more in northern Manitoba could talk to the people in their own language.

Language was especially important to Charles because through it he was able to understand at least something of a cultural tradition that has impressed visitors to Canadian First Nations for hundreds of years. Here is a 19th-century description of the influence of the Canadian landscape on language:

> ... there were good speakers among the Indians formerly,
> but I have too much reason to believe that there are no such
> speakers to be found among them at the present day. In my
> opinion it was chiefly owing to their deep contemplation
> in their silent retreats in the days of youth, that the old In-
> dian orators acquired the habit of carefully arranging their
> thoughts; when instead of the shouting of drunken com-
> panions, they listened to the warbling of birds, whilst the
> grandeur and the beauties of the forest, the majestic clouds
> which appear like mountains of white granite floating in the
> air, the golden tints of a summer evening sky, and all the
> changes of nature, which then possessed a mysterious sig-
> nificance, combined to furnish ample matter for reflection
> to the contemplating youth.[38]

Charles had lots of help with both his new language and religion. The Reverend James Evans in his shiny canoe had succeeded completely in his mission to invent a system of writing Cree syllabics, and to record in them what Charles called the "noble guidelines of Cree history."[39] Evans's oeuvre was the invaluable primer for Charles and Barbara as they ventured into a "foreign" language in their own country.

Charles's Cree parishioners, whom he soon came to view as partners, were teaching him by example about the love and care of the Great Spirit. On a 40-below January day in 1956, Charles was mushing over the ice behind his dog team toward Job Okemow's winter fish camp, located in a group of islands in the middle of the lake, which is 80 miles long and 30 miles wide. In the early twilight, out on the ice, he found Job jigging his whitefish net. What a welcome! Job embraced him happily, left his net and escorted Charles to his camp for more welcomes from his family, a meal for all and fish for the hungry dogs. This visit was supremely important for Job, as no praying boss had ever before visited his winter camp.

After dinner, they shared in the sacrament of the Lord's Supper, using Charles's portable Holy Communion kit. The wine was actually grape juice, which Charles kept from freezing by carrying it close to his body. The old holy thoughts expressed in Cree in Job's log shack made this a very meaningful Eucharist for all involved. Charles wrote later, "It is hard to imagine a harsher way to make a living than by net fishing through the ice in northern Manitoba, so I felt privileged to be the guest of such a brave breadwinner."[40]

In the winter, when game was hard to find, fish were an essential

CHARLES WITH SLED DOGS SMOKEY AND SILVER, WINTER 1956.

resource. But it was impossible to catch enough of them without a net, and how do you set a net when the water is covered with three or four feet of rock-hard ice? Okemow used an ingenious wood, bone and light-line device called a jigger. He would cut a hole in the ice and push the jigger into the water beneath, where its buoyancy would keep it pressed snugly against the underside of the ice. A sharp pick attached to a hinged thruster on the jigger would hold the device temporarily in place under the ice. Then Okemow, standing above the hole, would pull on the light line, which, by means of a pulley on the jigger, would vault the device forward a few feet under the ice, towing the net-setting line behind it. Doing this many more times would gradually move the jigger quite a distance. When it was far enough away, Okemow would attach his gillnet to the near end of the set line the jigger had dragged along and then walk over to locate the device beneath the ice, held in place by its pick. When he found it, he would chop another hole, retrieve the jigger and start pulling on the line it had towed, gradually hauling the weighted gillnet into place so that it hung like a curtain valance under the ice, spanning the distance between the two holes. Returning a day or so later, he would pull out the net along with any fish caught in it.[41]

Late the next day, as Charles prepared for the 20-mile trip home, Okemow, fearing his praying boss might get lost, insisted on leading Charles with his dog team for the first couple of miles. Although Charles was confident with a map and compass, he agreed and later said goodbye, once more, two miles closer to home. After another few miles, though, surprise! There was Okemow again, with his team barking excitedly. He wanted to be doubly sure Charles wasn't lost. And this happened a third time, with 13 miles left to go. A fortnight later, Charles found out that Okemow had tracked him in the darkness right to his house, through the maze of islands and bays, to make certain he arrived safely. Okemow didn't need to be told any parables about walking that extra mile with a friend – he went 40 miles, and over ice, that night. "He was a wonderful friend!" said Charles. "Like many at God's Lake."[42]

In 1955 Barbara flew out to Toronto to have the couple's first baby. While she was still in Weston Hospital, she received a CN telegram reading:

O HAPPY ANNIVERSARY
WITH DANIEL FOR THE NURSERY
THE ONLY THING ABOUT THIS LIFE
IS THAT I REALLY MISS MY WIFE
I NEED YOU SWEETHEART COME HOME QUICK
CAUSE IF YOU DON'T I MIGHT GET SICK
NOW HURRY DEAR I DON'T MEAN MAYBE
COME ON UP AND BRING THAT BABY
LOVE
CHARLES

She returned a few weeks later with their son, Daniel.

Winter was advancing like a glacier crawling toward them over the land, and Charles began his trips out to parishioners using his dog team. He refused to carry a gun, although wolves might easily have scented the frozen fish he carried to feed the dogs. He was never attacked. Sometimes the snow was unbelievably deep. On one trip on a winter truck road near Churchill, he stopped so he could pick up a mirror that had apparently fallen off one of the trucks. As he pawed away at the snow, he realized that the mirror was attached to the whole truck buried many feet deep beneath him.

That winter of 1955–1956 was the hardest and longest that anyone in God's Lake could remember. After surviving it, Charles wrote in his memoir:

> Once, on a bone-crumbling night of forty below Celsius, I
> happened to be only one of many rolled-up balls of hud-
> dling humanity coiled in tattered bedrolls and blankets
> on the spruce-bough floor of the old Muskrat Portage fish
> camp. It was just too cold to sleep and the steel zipper tog-
> gle of my parka front was rapidly becoming skin covered at
> the expense of the local Adam's apple. After hours of tick-
> lish torture, finally true inspiration: a coon's tail was requisi-
> tioned and stuffed cosily down the front of my neck. Sweet
> slumber ensued at last.[43]

Sometimes the wind scoured the ice clean for miles. One clear, cold day en route all alone to the northeast end of the lake, Charles noticed that his watch was gone. Next day, after visiting the camps at the east end of God's Lake, he turned the team around and set out on the return trail, a faint scribble on the deserted ice. And 20 miles away, there was the watch, telling the time to anyone passing by. During another cold winter he was trapped on the frozen lake at night, blinded by snow, so he spread his down sleeping bag on an island and slept well with the dogs curled close around him. When he got home, he found that the temperature that night had been 14°F, or about −10°C. The date was Victoria Day, May 21, 1956.

In 1957 Barbara, Charles and baby Dan left God's Lake Narrows, grateful to the Cree for their friendship and for sharing their culture, now aware of the white problem nearly all Aboriginals face. Father Levasseur too understood the plight of his parishioners better. He departed the Catholic priesthood after about 12 years in the North to work with Canada Mortgage and Housing Corporation, providing affordable housing in the North. He married and became the father of two children, and he helped to persuade the International Nickel Company of Toronto to offer jobs and job training to the northern Manitoba Cree at the new Thompson nickel mine, 350 miles from God's Lake.

A few years after the ministries of Charles and Levasseur, the God's Lake Cree regained control of virtually all social circumstances affecting their lives. They now own and operate all the tourist lodges as well as all the stores on the lake. For years, the churches have been served by Cree ministers and elders, and two of them are independent of southern control.

Since their years at God's Lake, Charles and Barbara have both experienced all kinds of different cultures, languages, disasters, joys, countries and continents, but they agree that their "life at God's Lake was beyond wonderful." It hardly seems possible, but they both say, "We loved every minute of our time there." They remember dog-team trips by sunlight, by moonlight and by Northern Lights; learning new hunting, trapping, fishing, craft and survival skills; banquets of fresh moose, freshly caught trout or pickerel any time; big-ice skating from October to mid-May; and hundreds of new Cree friends teaching them a beautiful language that expresses a genial society. Perhaps most important is that they learned the joy of a life in service, partly from the teachings of the people they had gone to teach.

By the time Barbara and Charles left God's Lake, they could speak fluent Cree, and they understood some Cree history, traditions and culture. They had also made dozens of friends and could cook Cree staples. Charles could paddle skilfully, camp out on a winter night, drive a dog team and build a fire in the rain. His face was browned by exposure to the sun and wind, his eyes narrowed against the glare of snow and water, and as he returned once more to the Canadian South, he was wearing a fringed buckskin jacket. Part of his character had changed as a result of seeing how his friends coped with their difficult lives. For example, one day at God's Lake, one of the trappers, Andrew Snowbird, told Charles that he had lost his whole winter's catch of furs to a wolverine that had broken into his cabin and destroyed them. "*ki-yem*" ("that's how it is"), said Snowbird, accepting the loss. He was not resigned, defiant or despairing. He accepted it "philosophically." He asked for nothing, he needed nothing – he just wanted Charles to know what had happened. Snowbird was going to keep on trapping regardless.

Charles once wrote that he was struck by "the savage beauty of the triumphant wilderness." Now, having lived with the Cree, coped with the dangerous wilderness and survived, he saw the northern lands as home, beautiful in every aspect and weather. Having learned that there is no triumph where there is no battle, he lost his white man's anthropocentrism. The Cree had showed him that in the wild, one co-operates or dies. His citified clichés had dropped away like a useless carapace.

Charles and Barbara had come like ambassadors from the South. They were returning to the South like ambassadors from the Cree nation.

A STEP IN THE DARK CONTINENT

In 1959 Charles and Barbara flew with their two children, Danny and Linda, to Africa en route to his new mission in the Copperbelt region of Northern Rhodesia, now Zambia. As in God's Lake, for the Native people, this was an impoverished outpost of the mighty British Empire, which had ripped up their lands like a tornado, twisting land, water and people into the air, then wringing them tight for profits. The basic problems were the same in Canada and Rhodesia: ignorance, sectarianism, corporate greed, white racism in its several forms, and governmental indifference and chicanery.

THE CATTO FAMILY IN MINDOLO: CHARLES AND BARBARA
WITH LINDA, AGE 1, AND DANNY, NEARLY 3, AUGUST 1, 1958.

As soon as they looked around, the evidence of racism and environmental disaster was clear to the Cattos. *Northern News*, the white-owned newspaper, boasted of the profits being made from the very productive copper deposits that gave the region its name. White people raised the capital, provided the expertise, found the markets and took nearly all the profits from the mines. Their colonial towns and houses were neat, spacious and healthy, their roads paved, their schools and hospitals well built and well staffed. The local black miners, however, without whose labour and land there could be no mine, lived in tiny steel-roofed hovels that baked in the sun and were frigid throughout the cold nights experienced on the 4,300-foot plateau. They lacked schools, paved roads and hospitals. The white people were the leaders of the mining operation, but their motive was mainly to take as much as they could while returning as little as possible. It scarcely occurred to these entrepreneurs that they might offer any of their expertise, capital and skills in a spirit of service to the Bantu people. The British were there in the name of capitalism, and their god was profit.

The very name of the country – Rhodesia – was an emblem of British attitudes. It came from white empire-builder Cecil Rhodes, who had only one idea in his British head: to expand the Empire and grow rich and famous doing it. Therefore, among the local whites whom Rhodes had led to the Copperbelt, there could scarcely be any thought that they might share equitably with the Native people, respect their culture and traditions, understand their mores or even like them at all, unless briefly, furtively, at night, in shame.

United Church policy recommended that missionaries know indigenous languages wherever they served, so Charles decided to learn the local language of the Bantu people, Bemba, by immersion, just as he had learned Cree. He arranged for a locum at St. Margaret's Church, said goodbye to Barbara, Danny and Linda, and on a cool June day in 1958 got on a bus for the 500-mile, two-day journey on the Great North Road, most of which was a bouncy, potholed bus trail. He was the only *musungu* (white man) on the bus, which was a rolling junkyard, concert hall and challenge to Christian faith as much as a means of transport. On the roof, tattered ropes pressed into heaps of baggage, mattresses, sacks of charcoal, and pots and pans, and bicycles dangled over the side with their wheels spinning just outside the cracked and

THE FORMER GARDENER'S THATCHED *RONDOVAL*,
A STRUCTURE TYPICAL TO THE AREA, USED BY
CHARLES AS AN OFFICE IN MINDOLO.

dusty windows. Inside there were people from a variety of nations, Bemba, Bisa, Lala, Ngoni, Swaka and Tumbuka, usually singing, chickens squawking at their feet and guitars playing even before the motor started with lots of blue smoke and threatening bangs. They stopped every few minutes to get food, for passengers to get on and off at towns or villages, to pick up firewood, to present papers to officials, to fix a puncture, to help stranded cars, and to deliver mail, babies and assorted goods. All through the journey, the people were singing and the guitars musicking; the melody never stopped.

Aching, tired but entertained, Charles left the bus thankfully in Chinsali, where he was picked up by a Land Rover sent by the Church of Scotland's Lubwa Mission. There he met Dr. David Wilson, who would be his first host – a great-grandson of the famous explorer and medical missionary David Livingstone.

Charles occasionally scrubbed up for operations with Dr. Wilson, giving anaesthetic with a rag soaked in chloroform. The operating room was a grass-thatched hut with no glass, doors or screens. He remembered for years one sentence the doctor spoke during surgery: "Give him some more chloroform, Mulenga, he's wiggling." The mission itself was a rare historical example of fruitful white–black co-operation, having been founded by the evangelist David Kaunda. Kaunda's son, Kenneth, who grew up in Lubwa, became the first president of independent Zambia after it succeeded Northern Rhodesia in 1964.

Although mission staff were alarmed by Charles's determination to live in a Bantu village hut, missionary Reverend John Fraser nervously escorted him to the nearest village, Mpyana Bwalya, where he met one of its eminent Bantu families. His hosts were Charles and Marion Bwalya, which linked them immediately because Charles and Marion were the names of Charles's own parents. They led him to his home for the next six weeks, a hut with three small rooms, each about six by eight feet. In one room was a gigantic rat trap, in another was a short bed. Presiding over this room was an enormous spider. (Having read up on African habits, Charles knew enough to leave this spider alone, and though he stayed there for six weeks, he was never bothered by fleas, mosquitoes or spiders.) In the third room were stored spears, axes and gardening tools, as well as chickens, which did not like the Canadian duckling that had been imposed on them.

As Charles wrote later, "A stay in a Bantu village is an enriching experience, but the greatest aspect of it is the feeling of belonging to the biggest family imaginable. By the first nightfall, I had collected at least fifty grandfathers, grandmothers, parents, uncles, aunts, nephews, nieces, sons and daughters. The family feelings that immediately envelop the newcomer instil a sense of peace that has to be experienced to be believed."[44]

Much of south-central African social relations and culture derives from these family feelings. The obligations and joys of what is now Zambian village life pervade each person's life, from the words of a baby's lullaby to the stern warnings of a mother-in-law.

In the morning, over his breakfast of cornmeal porridge, Charles could see rows of backs bared to the sun in a custom called *ukwontela kasuba*, or "receiving heat from the sun." Then, to earn his keep, he went to work in the fields with his host, Charles Bwalya, to weed, harvest and clear the brush that would be burned to make fertilizer. When he reached the clearing, the old man always knelt down in his ragged work clothes to praise God. Seventy years old and headman of the village, Bwalya was an Askari veteran of the British Army who had served in the fighting against the Germans under General von Lettow-Vorbeck in the battles for Tanganyika during the Great War. He received no pension. He was so poor that he saved embers from his wife's cooking fire from one day to the next, because a match cost 1/40 of a penny. Charles kneeled and prayed beside him.

Working beside Bwalya in the field, Charles noticed that his host was setting aside certain logs and sticks, so he asked why. The old man said, "For the new school."

The old school had been destroyed after a lion had charged in during a class to seize one of the children. The other children ran screaming from the schoolhouse into the village, rousing the resting men, who grabbed their spears and ran to the building. They surrounded the school, their spears pointing inward at the lion feasting on the child. One man ran forward with a burning torch and set fire to the school. The lion charged for the door, but turned back from the ranked spears. Again and again the trapped animal ran for the door, or the window, any fiery opening in the collapsing wall. Always the men were there with the spears jabbing at her. In a few minutes, the thatched roof roared down on the lion, and she died with her prey.

Once the pile of new building materials was judged sufficient, the women transported the logs and sticks, mud and thatch to the site where several villages under regional chief Nkula had decided to build. They were planning a schoolhouse and latrines, as well as houses and kitchens for the two teachers to be hired by the white district commissioner. The "DC" had been convinced to do this by the white missionaries, and by his good experience of the few natives who had been educated in white schools, some with the help of the churches or far-seeing white families.

Most of the men and women in the three co-operating villages assembled at the site and began to build, singing, joking and laughing. They had no insurance claim, blueprint, architect's rendering, site plan, zoning permission, building permit, environmental assessment, manufactured materials, mortgage, grants or funding of any sort. They wove the uprights together in a traditional mud-and-wattle design, framed in the windows and mat doors mainly by eye and memory of tradition, set up the poled roofs, and thatched all the buildings. Everything was done co-operatively, everything was local and much of it was recycled. Not a shilling was spent.

The result was not just a community school, handsome in the traditional Bantu style, but also a happy time that became a cheerful memory for everyone who participated. Building the community school also built the community.

On the night the new school was finished there was singing and dancing in the villages. As Charles saw the scene, "On that magic night, when the sun had plummeted into the jungle and the darkness had rushed in through the banana trees, the Mpyana Bwalyans[45] gathered around the headman's campfire. Shadows in flowing motion, the girls began to dance and the circle of boys and grownups started laughing and telling stories under the stars."[46]

One day Charles went with Mpyana Bwalya to visit Chief Nkula at his village seven miles away. Charles pedalled the bicycle while his headman perched on the crossbar. As they went through villages, the sight of a white man pedalling an African made the villagers stare. Mpyana Bwalya called out, "*Ee sungukeni!*" – "Yes, be astonished!"

Charles was impressed by the time he spent in Mpyana Bwalya. The school-building experience in particular captured him to such a degree that it became a model for something he might do in another place. There was no need for him to perfect the village's school-building process or adapt it. It was already perfect. It seemed that in this village, everything necessary existed and everything that existed was necessary.

On the way back to Chingola, the bus Charles was riding stopped for the night in a small town where there was a hotel run by a European. The manager came out to greet the one white passenger among the dozens of Africans, offering Charles a room for the night. Charles thanked him politely and said that as he was on a training mission to learn Bemba, he would sleep with the Africans in their three-pence a night camp. The white man stepped back and exclaimed, "Jesus Christ."

Charles and Barbara were so sick of the colonial attitudes that prevailed in Kitwe, the town where they were serving, that they decided to live as if they too were colour-barred, partly to set an example to their English parishioners but mainly to share in the lives of the Africans.

This had an immediate and drastic effect on their lives, and their pleasures. It meant no movies, because the theatres were segregated; no swimming, because black people were not allowed in the pools; no dinners out, because the restaurants enforced colour bars; no books from the whites-only libraries; and no professional barbering. As Charles noted, "It cut us off at once from some white friends, certain of whom thought we were just plain nuts. Some even considered the plan a deliberately hostile, provocative idea like ordering a pork chop at a Jewish wedding." They understood better the feelings of "those who from birth are made to feel as if an inescapable curse has been laid upon them – as if in fact they are not human and therefore not entitled to the rights and the life of full human beings."[47]

As recent graduates of the "University of God's Lake," they were certainly not hypocrites when they condemned racism. However, in comparison to the English in Northern Rhodesia, the Cattos found it easier to sympathize with the Africans because the racism of white Canadians was not as intensified and complicated by England's entrenched caste system. Racist attitudes toward Aboriginal peoples in Canada are somewhat mitigated by the history of the nation: a significant number of Aboriginals have distinguished themselves as leaders, partners and integral parts of settler families. As mentioned in the previous chapter, Scottish, French and Aboriginal men and women in fact created a new culture and people, the Métis.[48]

Charles's peculiar attitude soon brought him face to face with a white Rhodesian settler who was a prominent member of the Memorable Order of the Tin Hats, a veterans' club in town that excluded all black veterans but included all Europeans and white Africans who had fought in either of the two world wars. This chap, scarred from his battle wounds, sporting a big British regulation-issue moustache, planted his desert boots firmly apart as he told Charles to get ready to christen the settler's newborn grandson in the clubhouse. Charles, in his clergyman's white collar and black shirt, refused, pointing out that his role as a clergyman was to spread the words of Christ "Thou shalt not kill," and "Forgive thine enemy."

The ex-soldier exploded: "Good God! What the hell sort of church are you running anyway?!"

"The ideals of the Church are not the same as the Memorable Order of the Tin Hats," Charles said, "although there is a similarity in the respective hypocrisies of Church and club."

The settler went away dumbfounded, perhaps to drink with one of the ex-Wehrmacht members of the Afrika Korps, who *were* allowed into the club. Native Africans, some of them veterans of the famous British Eighth Army, which had fought the Germans in North Africa, were allowed to enter only by the back door as cooks or sweepers, to serve, in part, their former enemies, the German Tin Hats.

One ditzy young mother showed the baffling face of local apartheid when she admonished her son, Stanley who was playing with his young African friend Kalongo on the floor of her drawing room. "Poor Stanley," she told Charles. "He just doesn't understand why little Kalongo can't sit on the chair with him. I've told him *so* many times that the little kaffir must sit on the floor."

"Excuse me, Mrs. Van der Merwe, but why *does* Kalongo have to sit on the floor?" Charles asked.

She answered, "Well, Reverend, there's a terrible lot of racial prejudice around, you know."

At the annual general meeting of his white congregants at St. Margaret's, the members discussed the case of a young black African medical student, David Makulu, who had previously addressed the church's young people's group as a guest speaker. A woman rose to protest: "Mr. Chairman, several of the parents are very concerned that an African has been coming to the Youth Guild. I mean, we had thought that this was a nice Christian group."

So the Church in Africa was part of the problem. It was "apartheid at prayer." In fact, as Charles saw it, the Church *was* the problem because it had first countenanced racism, then sanctified it, then promoted it by masking it with smug hypocrisy.

The Cattos' liberal friend Jim Chigwedere had seen what was wrong with the detribalized boys in Chingola, the Copperbelt mining town. Loose in the city without the help of their families in their home villages, they were constantly in trouble with the police and their neighbours. Chigwedere soon realized that what they needed was a "big brother." The name and concept were typical of the liberal spirit common in the Big Brother movement in North America. He organized young volunteers who agreed to mentor these de facto orphans, acting like older brothers or young fathers and saving many youngsters from loneliness. Two and a half years later, when the Cattos left Africa, not one of the 70 boys in the program had been in trouble since being paired up with a mentor. All had been saved from the despair born of loneliness and from the prison sentences that would harden it.

During their years in Northern Rhodesia, Barbara was busy learning not only from Chigwedere but also from her great friend Margaret Hathaway, who belonged to the World YWCA. They conceived a project that would have tremendous consequences in Central Africa, Canada and beyond. Northern Rhodesia in 1959 was as racially segregated as apartheid South Africa; Barbara and Hathaway determined to tear

CHARLES, LINDA AND DAN WITH WORKERS AT THE MINDOLO
ECUMENICAL WORK CAMP ORGANIZED BY THE YWCA,
WHICH BUILT A HOSPITALITY CENTRE WITH THE HELP
OF LOCAL AND INTERNATIONAL VOLUNTEERS. IT WAS THE
PROTOTYPE FOR PROJECTS UNDERTAKEN BY OPERATION
BEAVER AFTER THE CATTOS RETURNED TO CANADA.

Barbara Catto (centre front), first chairperson,
with members of the executive of the Central
Africa–Copperbelt YWCA in Mindolo.

Members of the Chingola YMCA, including
Charles Catto (centre front) and Jim
Chigwedere (back, far left).

the segregation down. They organized an international ecumenical work camp to build a YWCA hospitality centre at the Mindolo Ecumenical Centre, which was the new embodiment of the earlier Mindolo Mission. Using the existing communication systems and contacts of the various churches and the YW/YMCA itself, they rounded up eager young volunteers from far away, including New Zealand and Japan. These young people in search of adventure and purpose came to dig the foundations, lay concrete blocks, install doors and windows, construct walls and roofing, and do all the wiring, plumbing, drywalling, taping, sanding and painting needed during construction. Local black people worked with local white people, a thing unheard of in the area until the American and Canadian YW/YMCA members began to churn the racial mix. The oddity and excitement of it provoked not a storm of protest but invitations from previously whites-only groups to black people involved in the project.

The young YM/YWCA volunteers were interviewed by local media and asked to tell how they had built the centre and why. In the new building, they created work and education programs that were so popular that other YWCA and YMCA clubs began to imitate them, setting up their own versions.

What they did at Mindolo "had a catalyzing and healing effect," Barbara said. That effect spread throughout the region, from Chingola to Kitwe, Ndola and Kalalashi. It finally spread across the Atlantic to Canada after Barbara was forced to leave Africa because she could not take medication against malaria. Had she stayed on in the region, she would have been risking her life and all her precious experience too.

So it happened that Frontiers, conceived by two women, was born in Northern Rhodesia, moved to Canada as a child and grew up there.

▲ ▲ ▲ ▲

"THIS PROJECT IS GUARANTEED TO FAIL"

In 1962 Charles and Barbara left Zambia with painful feelings. They had many friends there who were facing a dangerous challenge: to help guide their people through a transition that elsewhere had proven extremely difficult. The country might go from British rule, which as Charles saw it was "white tyranny," into the care of untested black leaders, who might do as most revolutionaries do: replace one tyranny with another. Their own. This is what has happened in many parts of the postcolonial world.

As Charles has said, the new Zambia was able to survive the worst of the changes because it had a "shining human vision in the desert of blind, bloody slaughter" that soon afflicted the neighbouring countries of Angola, Zimbabwe, Congo and Mozambique.

Throughout the Copperbelt, imaginative YWCA and YMCA programming had brought people together without racial tension, eliminating gaps that had never been bridged before. Perhaps Charles's favourite memory of his work in Mindolo was Big Brother Night in the YMCA, which rounded off the Big Brother project conceived by his friend Jim Chigwedere. Especially gratifying was that Big Brother Night was held in a church hall that had never before opened its doors to non-white people. In the tense atmosphere of Northern Rhodesian racial animosities, the Y had become hope and help for thousands of people.

Back in Canada, Charles was to take up his new position at a United Church of Canada regular parish ministry, in a village named Hampton, just northeast of Oshawa. As he and his family flew home, Charles wondered how people of international and ecumenical faith acting on the Zambian Copperbelt model might be brought together where they were most urgently needed, in the ecumenical disaster zone of northern Canada. He and Barbara would have to figure this out if their unique African experience was to yield further dividends and not to have been in vain.

The winter of 1962–63 was killer cold in Canada, so bad that sympathetic white Canadians rounded up heavy winter overcoats to send to the shivering Cree in and around Nelson House Reserve. For a moment, Charles was touched by the gesture, until he realized that the Cree men, whose livelihood depended on their dog teams, were probably laughing at the strange apparel given by the southerners. The coats were about as much use to them as snowshoes on a streetcar. Later, he wrote:

> How can anyone run behind a dog team in a winter coat?
> Our religious approach to the Cree has been remarkably
> similar to the overcoat operation. The white man has tried
> to button the cloak of a religion that suited him around the
> soul of the red man. Like the overcoats, it's old, it won't
> fit and it's not designed by or for the new wearers to have
> meaning in their existence. All but a meagre handful of the
> clergy ministering on Indian reserves are white, are living
> in homes far outclassing those of the people they serve
> and receiving much higher incomes. They are also saddled
> with a wide range of paternalistic responsibilities inherited
> from the past in which no other arrangement for works of
> mercy was possible. None of these things is necessarily bad,
> but taken together they have the effect of saying that Jesus
> Christ is a rich white man in an overcoat who might help
> you if you let him baptize your babies.[49]

This sort of wild humour sometimes got Charles into trouble with the staid ministers in the Canadian Church and government. The metaphor was bizarre, but it cut through the cant.

As the liberal-inspired idea of a foundation devoted to building infrastructure on reserves developed in discussions between Charles and Barbara, Charles resolved to ask the Canadian Council of Churches (CCC) to co-sponsor the approach, accepting the responsibility that he felt belonged to the whole of Canada. He wanted help to found a prototype international work camp in a frontier Canadian community, which he could organize during his 1962–1963 sabbatical year. The CCC responded by striking a Work Camp Committee, to be chaired by Charles.

In creating this committee, Charles, without realizing it, was living up to an age-old British concept called "the honour of the Crown." His work revived this honour after it had languished for many years, dusty and forgotten, buried in case law and ignored where it was most relevant – virtually everywhere on the ground.[50]

The honour of the Crown had been ignored for centuries by the very agents of the Crown in whose hands that honour had been laid. Simply put, the honour of the Crown enjoins the government of Canada to abide by all the Crown's original treaties with the peoples of the British Empire, in both the details and in the original spirit of those agreements.[51] Without ever hearing the phrase or seeing a word of the several legal texts on the subject, Charles had gone straight to the main point, guided only by his own personal sense of honour.

Charles had several relatives in the Canadian Army and he had grown up during the Second World War, so he was accustomed to hearing military terms applied to everyday civilian life. This early habituation to the strategies and vocabulary of war lent a certain aggressive urgency to his organization. Later, the very names Frontiers Foundation and Operation Beaver created an image of a battlefront within the wilderness/civilization boundary lands where most Métis communities and First Nations reserves are located.[52]

The name Charles picked for the effort to house and help people in need during the first phase of his mission was Operation Beaver, in the manner of a battle plan, a phrase telegraphing all the urgency that war implies. And the essence of the foundation was remarkably similar to a unique characteristic of the Canadian military: during both world wars nearly all of Canada's armed forces were voluntary, including the air force and the navy. Throughout most of the second war, service in the army too was voluntary; it was only toward the end that some conscripts moved from supply work to the battlefront. Similarly, nearly all the workers in Operation Beaver were volunteers. This meant that an extraordinarily large share of the money donated to the foundation went directly into productive work on houses and community centres, and very little to the organization itself to pay rent, heat, salaries, phones and all its other essential services. The proportion of donations and grants that ended up actually paying for the organization's frontline work was normally higher than 80 per cent.

One of the Métis volunteers who worked with Frontiers, Steve McPhail, said that the foundation's economic efficiency was one of the factors that made him decide to give so much of his time and effort to the work and eventually become a director on the Frontiers board. Many charities in Canada spend between 30 and 50 per cent of their income on head-office services, fundraising and expenses, whereas Frontiers usually spent 18 per cent or less. During one severe financial crisis in the 1980s, Charles took out a mortgage on his own house to pay Frontiers' operating expenses for most of a year. He was not paid back for ten months, but this didn't deter him from loaning his own money to Frontiers again and again.

The economy McPhail praised was possible not only because most of the workers were volunteers but also because the recipients of Frontiers' benefits themselves contributed their sweat equity to the work.

Frontiers appealed to the robust spirit Charles and Barbara had observed in their Cree and Bantu friends, when they began seeking volunteers for projects and when they expected co-operation from Aboriginal and Métis peoples who had hitherto been treated as helpless indigents or wards of the state. In Charles's view, there was no essential difference between a volunteer and a project manager, between minister and member, between someone with a European background and someone whose ancestors had lived in North America. This shared spirit of equality was the mainstay of the new liberalism Charles and his friends had found the world over, especially among young people, as thousands of volunteers from every religious tradition demonstrated when they showed up at Frontiers work sites wearing their hard hats, work boots and ready smiles.

Alongside his work with Frontiers, of course, Charles continued his ministry with the Hampton church. In one of his first sermons there, he explained some of the projects he had completed with Native peoples on two continents and why he wanted to continue them. The congregation approved and offered to help him raise some of the necessary funds for Frontiers.

This was not a rich congregation, so contributions meant a great deal to the donors. Many of them were factory workers dependent on weekly paycheques not guaranteed by anything except automobile sales. Charles delivered impassioned sermons describing the urgency of the needs the Church was trying to satisfy among peoples scattered over the Canadian North from Quebec to the Pacific Ocean. This included the same trading area assigned exclusively to the Hudson's Bay Company by HRH Charles II in 1670, which formed most of the land mass now called Canada. Thus the people appealing to the Church were descendants of the same hunters and trappers who had once helped to enrich Britain and then Canada from the resources of these lands. The autoworkers in Charles's parish did not let them down.

Before Frontiers began, Charles had tested some of his broad-based liberal theories with the help of a young Zambian student, Rod Chintu, who was studying medicine at the University of Toronto. On the face of it, this was a naïve idea. Chintu, a keen student and record-breaking runner, knew nothing of the Cree, nor of Charles's wild ideas about sending amateurs to help build churches in the wilderness. But Charles's spirit had been moved by his vision of a powerful fusion between a tribesman from Zambia and tribe members in Manitoba.

So he asked if Chintu wanted to come with him to visit God's Lake, where he would find group dynamics akin to those in Zambia and take part in an international ecumenical effort to build (and here Charles's thoughts grew vague, tending to unconventional spiritual ideas) "a co-operative effort to create warmth and satisfaction"[53] among the people, which in fact did appeal to Chintu.

Charles still was not certain how to use his African experience to help northern Canadians, although his memory of building the thatched school in Bemba territory gave him a sure hope that Chintu could help to find a way. Chintu immediately agreed, and soon the pair were co-operating.

As Charles suspected, the people at God's Lake had never before met or even seen a black person. The God's Lake Cree, often quite shy with strangers, were fascinated and curious about the good-natured Chintu, so they contributed money for his train- and airfare, plied him endlessly with questions about his people and the wildlife of Africa, and immediately agreed to be part of any new project that included him and Charles.

Significantly, although Chintu had arrived on the reserve as a friend of Charles, the Cree referred to him as *ininu*, meaning "Aboriginal person," rather than *mistagooso*, or "white person." The Cree saw that Chintu was not part of the white world because of his colour, therefore he must be one of them. This recognition sparked across a gap in Charles's mind. He realized that anyone in the human family with the right spirit could pass easily across artificial cultural gaps, be they race prejudices, national boundaries, language barriers or any variety of religious hatred.

Taking the Cree enthusiasm home like an ore sample and using it the way a prospector promotes a new mine, Charles began a year and a half of organizing, persuading and fundraising to get Frontiers' first project going, while at the same time performing his regular pastoral duties in his new congregation and helping Barbara with their two children. In late 1962 the dream was being shared almost before it had taken shape. A project had appeared which he believed would fulfill the ideals he was forming.

Frontiers' first project was in response to an invitation from Chief Adam Mayham of the Tataskweyak (Split Lake) Cree Nation, who asked the foundation to send an international volunteer work crew to Split Lake, Manitoba, 150 miles north of God's Lake. Mayham, in co-operation with Harry Hives, the bishop of Keewatin, and a young Anglican priest, Reverend Ted Scott, later the primate of the Anglican Church in Canada, wanted to build a new Anglican church to replace the old one, which was literally falling down. All the local Cree were Anglican, and the original building had been the centre of a wide range of community activities. They would start by setting up an ecumenical work camp to build the church.

Charles began to search for suitable team leaders to live on the site, as well as a construction supervisor and many volunteers to work with them. They needed money and building materials, not to mention the co-operation of two senior players: the Department of Indian Affairs and the Canadian Council of Churches. The CCC and government had never worked together on a church construction project before, and they had agendas and responsibilities that were sometimes contradictory. The Work Camp Committee had to report to two different departments of the CCC: the Department of Christian Education

(DCE) and the Department of Ecumenical Affairs (DEA). At one crucial point, the DCE forbade them to continue with the project, while the DEA directed them to proceed. Charles proceeded.

Working with Reverend Steven Beardy, a Cree Anglican priest, Charles seemed to be halfway out the door of the United Church on his way to some new form of Canadian wilderness church. But he was not leaving his ministry; he was changing the face of Christianity and dragging the Church along with him.

The ecumenical co-operation he had dreamed of at university and experimented with in his earlier missions to northern Manitoba and Zambia was about to be born in Toronto and on a wild frontier – at God's Lake and Split Lake, with the full co-operation of the Cree.

There were soon more than half a dozen players in the game, some of them extremely suspicious and, in true Canadian style, several opposed to the project. The Cree themselves comprised many bands, and some looked askance at building a church for communicants who lived in dangerous hovels. The federal and provincial governments, the World Council of Churches, the CCC, the United Church of Canada and the Anglican, Presbyterian and Catholic churches all had interests in supporting, regulating, opposing, managing and just generally hedging-in such an odd project. Finally, there were the questions related to money: how could the committee possibly raise the enormous sums required? And required to do what, exactly? In Charles's mind, the answer was growing ever clearer, like a distant shore emerging through the mist. The work would honour the oneness of all people in body and spirit, in city and country, in Africa and Canada, in poverty and wealth, in church and outside it.

Having already asked his congregation for help, Charles did not lily-dip his paddle; he rounded up private donors among friends who had been at university with him and were now prospering in Toronto and far beyond.[54] Charles often called upon old friends or strangers to help him answer for the need he felt almost personally obliged to fulfill. He was pained that his rich countrymen were neglecting the people who had given and done much to make modern Canada. Charles and an old friend were returning from lunch one day and walked across the parking lot next to the friend's office. "Is this your car?" Charles asked, indicating his friend's Jaguar. When his friend said "yes," Charles said, pointedly, "Very nice." The friend remembered that comment when he came to make out the cheque in an amount that included one zero more than he had intended before lunch.

Slowly but surely, the necessary ingredients fell into place. Reverend Beardy would be the co-leader for the volunteers on the first site at Split Lake, along with Doug Browne, a high-school teacher in southern Ontario. Doug and his wife Sheila had had previous experience as work camp leaders in Europe.

That winter and through 1963 into early 1964, the committee struggled with government and Church bureaucrats to organize and finance Frontiers and its volunteers, who had come from Canada and five other countries. However, Beardy and Browne were capable of organizing only the travel, food, accommodations and so on for the non-local volunteers. They knew nothing of safe building practices or codes. Without an experienced supervisor, the whole project was certain to be a well-meaning fiasco. Charles had already been warned by an experienced bureaucrat from Indian Affairs that he was heading for disaster: "Forget about these goddamned lazy Indians, Charlie. They'll sit there and laugh at you. This project is guaranteed to fail."

In the end, the bureaucratic delays helped ensure the success of the project. The group of volunteers exhibited good spirits and self-reliance. The Split Lake Native Anglicans and the fledgling work camp committee, seeing that help would be slow in coming, while their need was urgent, relied on their own energy and ingenuity to solve problems, mainly transportation. Although there were some building materials already on site, the rest would have to come in on the CN rail line, whose nearest access point was between Arnot and Boyd, 25 miles away from the site, across Split Lake and up the Nelson River. There was no station or official stop where the CN tracks crossed the Nelson, but with the help of a company engineer, the Cree volunteers noted the number of the telegraph pole nearest to the bridge and telegraphed that number to Toronto, whence it would be relayed to the CN engineer on the train.

By April 1964 the situation was critical: the 22 imported volunteers were due to arrive at Split Lake by Canso seaplane on July 1, and the only thing that would be ready for them was a welcoming feast

OPERATION
BEAVER

A CANADIAN ECUMENICAL WORK CAMP PROJECT

A CANADIAN COUNCIL OF CHURCHES PAMPHLET
SEEKING VOLUNTEERS FOR A WORK CAMP IN SPLIT
LAKE, MANITOBA, TO REBUILD ST. JOHN THE BAPTIST
ANGLICAN CHURCH. VOLUNTEERS PICTURED INCLUDE
MEDICAL STUDENT ROD CHINTU (LEFT) FROM ZAMBIA.

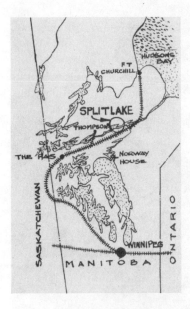

MAP OF SPLIT LAKE SHOWING
THE LOCATION ALONG THE
RAILWAY WHERE SUPPLIES WERE
PICKED UP FOR TRANSPORT ON
THE LAKE BY CANOE AND THEN
FERRIED TO THE BUILDING SITE.

arranged by Reverend Beardy, Chief Mayham and the band council. There was no on-site supervisor to arrange the myriad construction details, including tools and materials for the building itself, nor an engineering survey. Charles was ready to ask for leave to supervise the work himself, but his church building in Africa didn't qualify him to lead construction projects in northern Canada. In the nick of time the group's prayers were answered in the person of Charles's friend Bruce Edwards, a curly-haired 22-year-old University of Toronto engineering student who also understood construction, building sequences, carpentry and plumbing.

Edwards and Charles had become acquainted during a United Church meeting in Niagara Falls a few years before and had met again when they volunteered to help construct a new lodge for the United Church in Haliburton, Ontario. During that project, Edwards apprenticed himself to architect Bob Bradley, and there he learned some of the techniques one needs when building with unskilled volunteers out in the bush. Charles and Edwards made fun of the Council of Churches, calling it in their private lingo the Chouncil of Curses. They would also go swimming at "Leech Beach" on "Snake Lake."

Edwards had visited Split Lake in 1964 on a scouting trip. He surveyed the partially complete foundation and available building materials and ordered more supplies when he returned to Toronto. On the

SPLIT LAKE'S ST. JOHN THE BAPTIST ANGLICAN
CHURCH UNDER CONSTRUCTION, 1964. THE FLOOR
OF THE CHURCH WAS EXTENDED OVER AN EXISTING
FOUNDATION. (COURTESY MARION EDWARDS)

appointed day, the CN train slowed near the Nelson River crossing and crawled along until the loaded boxcar was next to the designated telegraph pole. From there, the Cree volunteers unloaded the heavy lumber and materials and slid them down the bank to the river, where 18-foot freight canoes were lined up and ready. From there the volunteers paddled tons of the heavy materials, in tippy, overloaded canoes, the 25 miles along the river and across windy Split Lake to the work site.

Edwards and his Cree partners, Reverend Steven Beardy, Chief Adam Mayham and other local volunteers, arrived just in time to make sure the subfloor of the new church was built before the international volunteers arrived. A foundation had already been built on solid permafrost, but Edwards recommended that it be extended.[55]

The new foundation and floor would be a challenge for the volunteer builders. Building on permafrost was a rare, evolving and difficult technique in 1964. Poorly laid foundations in this environment quickly endanger the buildings they support. If heat from the new church penetrated the earth and melted the permafrost, it could bring the roof down on the congregation at prayer. Edwards knew this, and he made sure the new floor remained sufficiently insulated from the surrounding soil in order to preserve the solid ice around and under the footings.

Edwards could not only design, direct and build, he could also innovate and motivate. The Split Lake Cree, particularly the women, charmed by the cheerful, curly-haired stranger, took him into their hearts and outdid themselves carrying sand and gravel from the beach to the site. On the busiest construction days, over a hundred local Cree volunteers hammered, sawed, hauled and painted alongside Mohawk, Blood, Salish, Métis and other Canadian and overseas volunteers. The work went on enthusiastically and constantly until the middle of August, when the Anglican bishop Harry Hives arrived. Hives was known all over the area as "Bee" Hives for his infectious buzz of cheerful energy. He blessed the work and rang the newly hoisted bell; the church filled with praise. The first hymn the people sang was "Praise God from Whom All Blessings Flow."

In Charles's words, Operation Beaver/Frontiers[56] aimed to "assist Canadians of all races to understand one another better through the comradeship of ecumenical work-camping so that lasting bridges of respect and affection may be built."[57] The aim was not to build something physical but to create something spiritual. He made this clear when he wrote later about the brief life of the Company of Young Canadians, an enterprise set up by the Canadian government to do many of the things Operation Beaver[58] had been doing for fifty years. "How and why did Operation Beaver survive on a fraction of the CYC's income? CYC was conceived, directed and exclusively funded from the top down. Operation Beaver on the contrary was self-help from day one. It said 'If you're interested, bring a hammer and forget money for a slice of your life; think of what you can give rather than get; honour the Great Spirit and work cheerfully on what Canada and the world needs most.'"[59] The CYC soon collapsed because it was well-funded but not well-founded. Charles's methods succeeded in the very first project at Split Lake, when the local Cree rejected the diocese's idea for a log church and chose Bruce Edwards's design for a white clapboard church like the old one. It was to be their church, so it was their choice. And they built it.

This was a revolution. Through Frontiers, Charles and the volunteers at Split Lake had begun to change the negative and discriminatory attitude that white people of his class and time all over British Empire had normally displayed toward Aboriginal peoples. The miners and prospectors; the oilmen, traders, politicians and soldiers; the road and railway builders; the lumber companies – all had one thought only: profitable trade. The gorgeous paraphernalia of imperial government, the might of the armed forces, were there only to protect that profitable trade. This materialism infected even the missionaries when they went to Canadian reserves or African villages. They thought much of physical structures in the shape of churches, schools and hospitals. The nearest that most of them came to the spirit of the people they "served" was to gain converts, but even these were merely added like profit to the bottom lines of the churches.

In addition to stating Frontiers' aim, Charles's description of the founding Frontiers document also speaks of "giving young people a true picture of Canada," sharing insights and experiences, bringing together young Canadians and youth from around the world, creating opportunities for service that would become "a personal ministry of reconciliation."[60] His was the first organized expression of the spirit that would later animate the Truth and Reconciliation Commission as it sought to heal the wounds inflicted by the residential schools of the 19th and 20th centuries

This founding document is an astonishing synthesis of the practical and the spiritual. Nowhere is there any mention of buildings, money, debt, trade, infrastructure, mortgages or land ownership. It was written at a time when bright young colonial men like Charles from all around the British Empire were still attending Cambridge University on government scholarships to learn how to rule and manage the profitable colonies. These students' brothers and fathers had given their lives in many wars to defend Britain's rule of that empire. Charles, whose family belonged to that class of people, ignored all that – in fact, when he saw those colonial precepts in action in Africa, he despised them.[61]

He was a revolutionary with a pulpit.

For all his righteous anger, his fierce determination and scathing scorn for hypocrisy, Charles was a healer, interested only in the health and happiness of everyone in his ministry – the volunteers and the donors as well as those who were temporarily in need of help. Years after Frontiers had grown into a big, solid enterprise with a worldwide reputation, a head office and a board of directors, the founder's radical principles were still in control, as Charles showed when he appointed a former bank robber to the board.

Mike McTague had just been released from prison, where he had served 18 years for bank robbery, when he met Charles. McTague wanted to get married, but he didn't think any preacher or priest would oblige because he was jobless and broke. Standing on the edge of the Bloor Street viaduct in Toronto, he was thinking about jumping when he decided to make one last effort. He went to Charles, whom he scarcely knew, and asked for his blessing. "He looked into my soul and made up his mind. He said he would perform the ceremony, but before he did he gave me a long exam in which he asked many questions. My wife and I have been happy with each other ever since, and always grateful to Charlie for his faith in us. I would do anything to help him. I'm the only director he ever had who had gone into a bank to rob it."[62]

In return for Charles's faith in him, McTague became Charles's "hitman." He once prevented a director of Frontiers from speaking at a board meeting because Charles had found him to be too self-assertive and disruptive. McTague, a big, strong man decorated in blue tattoos and coiffed in a prison haircut, sat down beside the disruptive director, and before the man could say anything, said, "Shut up. Stay shut up. At the end of the meeting, you're going to leave." The man obeyed. After this man was neutralized, Charles made sure the man saved face by allowing him to retain the title of director.

Charles always made sure that everyone who asked for a benefit from Frontiers was urged to volunteer. In some cases, he actually made volunteering a requirement. The principle of sweat equity that was taken for granted in African villages was also the norm among his white, liberal, middle-class Toronto friends, who had worked during holidays to help pay for their own education. And it was the norm among the Cree, where the principle was generously extended so that the work of each person also contributed to the welfare of all, and all benefited from each individual's labour.

Frontiers was never a charity; it was a co-operative that worked toward a greater common good, something that appealed strongly to Charles's liberal friends in Toronto. And to conservatives as well. Most of the conservatives Charles knew had achieved success on their own, so they felt instinctively that whatever was done for anyone in need should inculcate in them the same principles of self-reliance. In this manner, Frontiers' work would remove the stigma that "Indians" were helpless and always begging for handouts, a prejudice which cankered not only the idea of helping poor Canadians in the North but also the people themselves. The organization's self-help requirement also demonstrated to Aboriginal peoples that Frontiers needed them as essential partners in building their communities. The announcement of a project was always good news right away, even before a single volunteer arrived or a single tree was felled.

The participating young locals would end up with heightened self-esteem, new friends in greater Canada and new trade skills, not to mention a better knowledge of English. The young white workers and foreign volunteers would go home treasuring bonds of affection and a new understanding of the local religion, medicines, food and hunting practices. The point, as Charles saw it, was not the building but building the building.

Part of that "spirit building" was that all volunteers had to sign a pledge to behave responsibly. They had to promise to work hard, obey the orders of the group leader and avoid the use or possession of illegal drugs. Frontiers pointed out that it would offer full and immediate co-operation to the RCMP in enforcing the country's laws. Furthermore, every volunteer had to promise not to consume alcohol in an irresponsible manner. Drinking was forbidden on the work site and in the place of residence. As the Frontiers pledge explained, many of the "communities in which we work suffer severe social problems from alcoholism and our volunteers are expected to set a positive example in this setting." Finally, the volunteers were required to abstain from sexual activity outside of marriage – "This cannot be tolerated and is grounds for immediate removal from a Frontiers Foundation project."[63]

The building of the Split Lake church was Frontiers' first project, but it was the wrong kind of undertaking, according to Chief Stan Daniels, president of the Alberta Métis Association and a founding patron. Daniels was a voice of profane wisdom when he said to Charles, "Community centres and churches are nice, Charles, but, goddammit, we need housing! And you can start with my people in Wabasca and Conklin. Some of them have mud floors."

This comment stung Charles. Years of faith, effort and experience had gone into the project, and he looked on it with great satisfaction. He had literally prayed it up from the ground. The Split Lake project had barely been a start for Frontiers in the physical sense, but in the spiritual sense it had become an excellent model. It was co-operative, it was ecumenical, it brought together volunteers of many kinds, it was intensely local and it was fun. To hear it dismissed by Daniels as irrelevant pained Charles deeply, but when he got over the shock, he realized that Daniels was quite right.

The first help Frontiers received as it turned its focus on housing was from the local people themselves, who stepped willingly into leadership roles. Daniels had friends and allies who believed as he did and who pitched in right away to help: Clara Yellowknee at Wabasca, Dumas Tremblay at Conklin and Dave Starr at Peerless Lake. They shared what Charles called "a brave dream" of rehousing their people – brave because of the endemic despair that had been caused by the deep poverty in most reserves and Métis settlements. Charles got to work with a friend of Daniels, Lawrence Gladue, who knew the people, the area and the problem from bitter personal experience. Close to Wabasca, at Faust on Lesser Slave Lake in northern Alberta, Gladue's mother and sister had died in a fire, in a house very like the ones Frontiers was keen to replace. Once again Charles turned to Bruce Edwards, who by now was married to Marion Rattray, an adventurous young woman who threw herself enthusiastically into the project, and into Cree ways.

By this time, in 1968, Edwards had completed all the requirements for his master's degree in electrical engineering, one of the toughest courses at the University of Toronto: a thousand might apply and only fifty graduate. Now he was ready to graduate, but his supervising professor suddenly asked him to complete one more project before granting the final diploma. Edwards told him he had been asked to supervise an important volunteer job for the CCC in northern Alberta and that he and Marion had to leave right away. This decision probably determined their whole future because, at that time, companies were willing to pay a lot of money to attract such engineering graduates. Edwards

St. John's Anglican Residential School, Wabasca,
Alberta, closed to students in 1960 but reopened for
the Frontiers volunteers by Reverend Arthur Bell.
Bruce and Marion Edwards used the principal's office
and the volunteers slept in the dormitories on the
top floor. (Courtesy the General Synod Archives,
Anglican Church of Canada, P75-103-S7-270)

told Charles he would go and the professor relented. Marion, repelled
by the intense competition she experienced in the city, was looking
forward to a new life in the North.

The couple packed up their tiny car and embarked on a journey
through the wilderness north from Slave Lake, where they had taken
an orientation course. The drive seemed "interminable" to Marion.[64] If
she had been infatuated with Charles's initial "savage beauty of the un-
tamed wilderness," it began to wear away during the hours and hours
of driving through a landscape of water, rocks, sky and trees – a landscape unmarked by signs of human habitation. They finally came to a
lonely log cabin where they were welcomed by Nora and Wally Young,
both friends of Frontiers. The next day they made it to Lake Wabasca
and were welcomed and put up by Anglican priest Arthur Bell, who
lived across from St. John's, the old residential school that had been
closed eight years earlier.

From the high of travelling, Marion dropped down to her knees on
the school floor, scrubbing away years of dirt and maggots. Soon she
was taking lessons in bread making from Alice Auger, one of the Cree

GREENHOUSE IN WABASCA. DESIGNED FOR THE
NORTHERN CLIMATE BY VOLUNTEER ARCHITECT RICHARD
ISAAC, THE STRUCTURE HAD TWO LAYERS OF HEAVY
POLYFILM ENCLOSING AN AIRSPACE. PRODUCE GROWN
HERE WAS LATER SOLD FROM THE BACK OF A TRUCK.

women, and feeding 20 or more people at mealtimes. She cultivated a
vegetable garden, which soon grew enormous crops in the virgin soil.

Edwards started work with his 20 volunteers. At first, he thought he
might be able to supply the community's needed housing by renovat-
ing some of the existing houses, but the foundations, usually of spruce
logs set on the ground, were irreparable. Instead, he decided to build
new houses, employing a balloon-frame construction, with fibreglass
insulation – R10 batts in the walls, R15 in the attics – and solid-core
exterior doors. Edwards's friend Julian Cardinal found that when he
moved from his former cabin to a new Frontiers house, his fuel con-
sumption dropped from one cord of wood per week to two cords for a
whole winter. The work crew built 11 such houses, using three different
Edwards designs.

Edwards was a no-nonsense leader who knew exactly how to get
Frontiers-style results. At first, some of the prospective owners on reserves would sign up to work on their new houses and then think, "It
doesn't matter if I'm late to the site today, this is just another soft-touch

government handout. I won't bother." But each prospective owner had been firmly warned that they would be responsible for one or another aspect of the construction starting at a certain time on a given day. On that day at that hour, Edwards would arrive with his trucks, tools and volunteers. "If the prospective owner did not show up, we went elsewhere," Edwards said.[65] The missing man would see his friends and the volunteers working on another house, so the next day he would be on time.

Bruce and Marion Edwards made a lot of good friends in Wabasca. So good that when the project was finished, one of them – Francis Gladue – wanted them both to stay. He said to the couple, "If you like it here and you want to stay, I've got a piece of land for you, near the reserve. Stay and build a house."

At first the pair replied, "We have to go to Vancouver. Marion's sister is getting married."

They bid farewell to Wabasca, hopped into their VW Beetle and drove to the city, but the bitter competitiveness of urban life again discouraged Marion immediately, so the couple decided to return to Wabasca and take Gladue up on his offer. Edwards strapped a new toilet to the top of the car, and they set out to drive from the warm coast a thousand miles through the mountains into a northern winter.

Snow was falling just before they arrived on October 24, so they had not much time to build their house on Francis's land before hard frost would make it impossible. Reverend Bell offered to let them live on the third floor of the school while they were building. Many hands helped them construct the 16-by-34-foot cabin, lighted from above by clerestory windows designed by Edwards. The house was completed by December 24. When they moved in, Edwards joked, "The day we moved in, the temperature was 60 below, but it was colder outside."[66] Very Cree.

Later, while Frontiers houses were going up at Peerless Lake, north of Wabasca, the government agency Central Mortgage and Housing Corporation was also building several stackwall houses at Grouard, just 130 miles away. There was thus a chance to compare Frontiers' program with that of the CMHC, and judge its effectiveness.[67]

This led to a strange affray between, on the one hand, Frontiers

BRUCE AND MARION EDWARDS MOVED INTO THEIR NEW
HOUSE NEAR WABASCA ON A BITTERLY COLD CHRISTMAS
EVE, 1969. (COURTESY MARION EDWARDS)

Foundation and Ian Outerbridge, a successful Toronto lawyer and friend of Charles, and on the other hand, 27 blue-suited bureaucrats from Secretary of State, Indian Affairs and CMHC, all of whom had been dragooned into a meeting by Outerbridge. Outerbridge had phoned the CMHC in Ottawa and brusquely demanded an urgent meeting. He arrived at the meeting suited up like the bureaucrats but far better prepared. Charles was wearing his usual donated clothes, but he had dozens of statistics clear in his head.

Outerbridge said he and Charles wanted to discuss why it was that no government agency would write a suitable cheque for Frontiers' essential work. He pulled out some papers from his briefcase and told the 27 suits that they were going to hear the story of what had happened in Wabasca and Grouard when CMHC had sent commercial crews into a Métis community to put up stackwall houses. These houses were built but very soon had to be pulled down because the log sections of their walls had not been dried properly and so they had shrunk, which meant that outside air whistled into the houses, making them uninhabitable. Outerbridge, well aware that Charles had been fed essential information from inside the CMHC, asked Charles if he knew how much these houses had cost the Canadian taxpayer, and Charles said, "Yes."

"Then tell us, Mr. Catto, tell us."

"They cost 130,000 dollars each," Charles said slowly and clearly.

"And that was the unfinished cost, right?" said Outerbridge. "Because they were never used."

Charles said this was true.

"And now they have been taken down, isn't that right?" said Outerbridge.

The CMHC representatives agreed this too was true.

Outerbridge then said, "And how much did your houses in the same area, Peerless Lake, cost, Mr. Catto?"

"Thirteen thousand dollars each, finished houses," said Charles.

"I'm sorry I didn't hear that, would you repeat that?" Outerbridge's voice grew louder. "How much for a finished house?"

"Thirteen thousand dollars," Charles said very loudly.

"Did you say 13,000 dollars?" Outerbridge said even more loudly. "And the people are living in them as we speak, is that right?"

"That's correct."

Outerbridge looked at the uncomfortable suits and shouted, "And you tell this man that you can't give him any money. I say bullshit." He turned and stormed out of the meeting. A few minutes later Charles left the meeting with a promise for a cheque for $250,000. Which was honoured.[68]

The CMHC could not build as cost-effectively as Frontiers, in part because the organization did not bring in volunteers. The CMHC and the various Indian Acts, then dating back over a century, did not provide for volunteer contributions, neither by the contractors nor, perhaps even more important, by the beneficiaries of the housing projects.

A century or more earlier, for Canada to contribute "free housing" might have been seen as equitable under the treaties with the First Nations, but as time went on, the CMHC business model became both untenable and unstable, like the houses themselves. The Frontiers houses were still in good condition after 20 years and more.

The housing crisis on reserves resulted directly from the lack of employment for Aboriginal peoples, a situation described with eloquent patience by Chief Silas Wesley of the Albany North River reserve in 1962. In a letter to the Indian–Eskimo Annual Meeting, the chief wrote:

> First of all, we have a very hard time trying to earn a living. Trapping is the only kind of work we have, and we can only trap in the winter. There are hardly any jobs ever available to us at Albany [they were mainly reserved for white people]. We have an especially hard time in the summer when we cannot trap. Quite often in the summer, some of our people do not have enough to eat. Then we ask the Indian Agent at Moose Factory to help out those in need with rations. One or two are sometimes sent but that is not enough. Then too we often have to wait a long time before we get an answer from the Indian Agent. If we did not try to help out … someone might die before we get an answer. Sometimes we have had to wait a month for a reply.
>
> Then too … we get very little for our furs … The traders here make good profits, while we are paid very little for the fur we bring them.
>
> Another problem we have is housing. When we moved to the reserve in 1957, we thought we would get houses. In 1958 our Indian Agent had fourteen houses started for old people. Unfortunately he left before they were finished and even now some of them are not completely finished (the houses were provided with two doors but most of them are lacking door knobs for the back doors!). These houses are very small – eighteen feet by sixteen feet. They were built out of round logs, and since the logs were green when the houses were built, the logs have since shrunk and there are spaces between them where the wind gets through
>
> The houses mentioned above are only for the old people. Many of the other people have built houses of their own out of round logs but they have had to use old boards and old nails in their building. Then too, other families are living just in tents.
>
> So we do not have proper houses on our reserve. In the

winter we suffer much from the cold weather – the children especially find it hard – they catch cold and get sick.

So it is our hope that something can be done for us. Perhaps this our letter may bring some help – such is our hope.[69]

This dignified letter was written on behalf of people who had every reason to be angry about white encroachments on their lands. Their fishing was no longer their own. In more southerly areas, white trappers had moved in and were competing with Aboriginal peoples. Soon, First Nations would be flooded out by dams constructed for Manitoba Hydro. And finally, the railway and roads had not only taken land from the reserves but also interfered with the migration patterns and habitats of the animals on which the people depended: caribou, moose, mink, fox, beaver, birds and so on.

The words "we thought we would get houses" have a particular resonance with most Northerners, for it was almost universally true of Aboriginal peoples in Canada that they believed they would be receiving benefits from the promised treaties that the Crown did not actually intend, or the Canadian government had failed, to give them. In the words of Justice James Hugessen of the Federal Court, "In virtually all aboriginal rights cases, the honour of the Crown is at stake."[70] The white man's justice system, like the economy that was displacing the Aboriginals, had no room for Canada's first peoples, no matter how honest and diligent they were at fulfilling their parts of the agreements.

One Alberta judge, John Reilly, has said that both the Royal Commission on Aboriginal Peoples and the Supreme Court of Canada have confirmed that the Canadian criminal justice system has failed the Aboriginal people. He adds that after 33 years on the bench, he came to the conclusion that "these institutions actually fail everyone in our society and should be replaced by a system that emphasizes social development instead of punishment, a concept developed in the Dark Ages that should have stayed there."[71]

Yet many people living on reserves in Canada did not despair. At Moosonee, located along the shore of Hudson Bay, people who had been harshly treated by Canadian institutions were keeping themselves in good shape despite the incredible difficulties of life in a hovel. In 1966 a dear friend of Charles and Frontiers, Mrs. R.S. Mills, left her comfortable house in Rosedale to visit Moosonee and see the conditions for herself. She reported to Charles:

> Although there was a sea of mud everywhere outside their little hovel, I could have eaten off the floor, it was so clean inside. They had no idea I was coming to see them. Moreover, they have to carry every pail of water a quarter of a mile! How clean would my home be, or my clothes or my body, if I had to go so far for water? These people do not have electricity, their floor boards are rotten and last summer, the first in their "new" home, the water came up a foot over the floor so they had to move into a lean-to – not much good for arthritic knees. Their only stove has no oven, all food must be either boiled or fried and the water heated on this one-burner stove. Yet the house was clean and they were clean.[72]

The situation in some areas was even worse than Mills's letter indicates, despite many efforts at improvement made over 18 years. In Wabasca in 1984–1985, wood heat was so important that the new owner of a house built by Edwards moved the house closer to his own enormous woodpile rather than the other way around. Fires occurred often, largely because the houses were badly built and poorly insulated. The fire-death rate was often six times as high for Aboriginals as for non-Aboriginal people, 7.44 per 100,000 people, compared to 1.25.[73]

Bruce and Marion Edwards gave up their northern volunteer work at Wabasca in order to take up a teaching position in Africa, but new volunteers came north to replace them. Jamie Thompson, who had come to teach canoe building, and Frontiers' volunteer architect Richard Isaac planned the Wabasca–Demarais Recreation Centre, a big log structure to be funded in part by federal and provincial government grants. The local community was involved, as usual, when young, untrained people volunteered and learned new skills on the job.

The recreation centre was built over a two-year period in 1984 and 1985 by 45 Native workers and five Frontiers volunteers. They cut 700 spruce trees from lots destined for development in the local municipal improvement district. When a deal with a local mill fell through, the volunteers milled the logs with two Frontiers Wood-Mizer saw-mills. The 10×10-inch squared timbers were joined into bathrooms, an office, a kitchen and change rooms beside an outdoor hockey rink. A two-storey library was also designed for alternative use as a playschool. The large, 30×40-foot octagonal hall with an open ceiling and timber trusses had a state of the art air-handling system to clear the tobacco smoke, a necessity when it later became used for bingo nights. This being Alberta, the heat came from natural gas. A two-storey back wall had been designed to adjoin an indoor skating rink in the future, but in the end a new indoor arena was built on the reserve next to the Métis community.

Clara Yellowknee, who by this time was the coordinator for the NNADP of Wabasca–Demarais, reported that the finished centre was well used by the playschool program, Brownies, Girl Guides and four local hockey teams. It was also a site for the 1986 Peace Winter Games.

Under the Frontiers programs in the Wabasca area, local un-employment was reduced and sometimes even eliminated when a pro-spective house owner started helping on a new house because he was required to work on it as part of the agreement. If necessary he was also partially instructed in a trade on the job so that afterward he had a better chance at employment. His self-esteem rose with every nail he hammered in, and his spirit was cheered with every foot the walls rose toward the rooftree. It was also improved by the trust extended to him by his own people. In addition, his worldview expanded as he made friends with the volunteers who had come thousands of miles from the South or overseas to help him and his family. And because these people had come in response to his own invitation to share his experi-ence, he was not demeaned in any way, as many had been demeaned in the past by the white men who came to give a little but only after hav-ing taken much.

♠ ♠ ♠ ♠ ♠

FROM HOVELS
TO HOUSES

As the 1970s approached, Charles and Barbara saw a "new and unique ministry" beckoning them. There was little precedent for it and therefore little funding. The job description was both clear and vague – clear because the need for Aboriginal housing was stark, and vague because the way to fulfilling that need involved an exploration of the unknown. There was no organization yet in place to accomplish it. And Reverend Catto already had a mission with its own responsibilities, the Hampton Pastoral Charge, which offered a necessary and dependable stipend to support his wife and children, now numbering four. If he were to fly in the dark toward the shadowy figures in need in the North, he would have to leave that stipend, perhaps even his family.

Neither he nor Barbara hesitated long. In July 1968 Charles resigned the Hampton charge in favour of a full-time commitment to Frontiers Foundation. From the United Church Oshawa Presbytery and national United Church HQ in Toronto, he received these encouraging words: "Charles, you have our blessing." But he told Barbara that evening, "I was hoping for a more golden handshake."[74] Meanwhile, with the blessing of the Canadian Council of Churches, the newly incorporated and federally chartered Frontiers Foundation took over Operation Beaver, and the CCC recognized that it was in a "fraternal relationship" with Frontiers.

The foundation arrangement meant immediate good news for many reasons. In the 1960s the CCC was still frankly (and legally) a Protestant organization. As part of that organization Charles felt he could scarcely think of appealing to corporate donors in Catholic Montreal, where many of Canada's biggest corporations were headquartered then. But now, having set aside its original name (Operation Beaver) and free-standing in a new, arm's-length, non-profit corporate structure of its own, Frontiers could and did successfully approach Bell

Canada, Sun Life, Canadian Pacific and many others headquartered in Montreal for charitable donations. The foundation was now officially open to all Christians and to everyone else, including agnostics, atheists, Muslims, Jews, Buddhists, animists and in fact "everyone willing and able to serve our Creator and our fellow men and women."[75]

Charles's decision to leave his Hampton charge and fully embrace work with Frontiers had serious personal consequences for the Catto family. They no longer had a salary from the United Church of Canada, so they had to find a new source of income. Fortunately a beloved friend in the Phi Kappa Pi fraternity, Dr. Paul Rondeau, asked only one question when Charles told him about his hopes for Frontiers: "Charlie, how many thousands do you need?" The next day, thanks to Rondeau, Frontiers Foundation had all the start-up money it needed for its next building project, and then some.

By this time, Charles had become friends and good partners with Lawrence Gladue, a Cree man who had been deeply involved with the British Columbia Association of Non-Status Indians (BCANSI). When Gladue is feeling good, his smile fills his broad face, and that face filled with pleasure when he heard of Charles's new commitment to build houses, first in 1968 in Wabasca, Alberta, near Gladue's boyhood home at Faust and later in projects at Peerless Lake, Conklin and High Level. With Gladue's help and advice, plus the contributions of Annie House and her son Freddy and also of BCANSI and Métis Nation of Alberta (MNA), those projects succeeded quickly, and by the time Operation Beaver had morphed into Frontiers, the moccasin telegraph was busy with the news.

Frontiers staff and volunteers ensconced in their drab little building on Danforth Avenue in Toronto could feel the excited interest – they knew this was going to be a wildly successful venture. They were regularly invited to provincial, territorial and national Native conferences to tell the Frontiers story, and they were asked to respond to urgent requests for help, from Labrador to British Columbia to the Northwest Territories. All this meant that Frontiers very quickly became known throughout the Canadian North as the people who would help. In the six years immediately following the start-up, Frontiers built 171 houses, 18 community centres, schools, parks and one outdoor arena. By the mid-1970s more than 800 volunteers were helping strangers rebuild their lives, their houses and their schools, and not just in Canada but in Trinidad, Guyana, Anguilla and many other places. The foundation's volunteers now came from dozens of countries, and they worked in beautiful and dangerous places where they were in constant peril as they navigated heavy building supplies on small boats down rivers or across stormy lakes. On one work site in British Columbia they helped refurbish a tannery for the local trappers; in another, their office and command post was a plywood shed hardly big enough for the construction supervisor to sit down and work at an improvised desk. In other places, volunteers had to figure out all over again how to construct and maintain foundations for small houses sited on permafrost. And not all their challenges were physical. In Alberta, for example, they built houses on land the title to which was disputed as between the provincial government and its Métis occupants.

The young people on these sites not only worked on the housing and construction but also ran day nurseries, where they supervised children's games and taught English reading, speaking and writing. They cooked meals, managed summer camps, wrote reports for the Toronto head office, supervised public relations with the locals and kept the office accounts. These volunteers contributed to the new community centres in Lac Doré, Quebec, and Parry Island, Ontario, in 1966; at Montreal Lake, Saskatchewan, in 1967, and at churches in Whitefish Falls, Ontario, in 1965 and Mount Tabor, British Columbia, in 1968.

The variety of volunteers coming in from all over the world was amazing. During one year alone in the mid-1970s, Frontiers was represented by people from Australia, Canada, Central Africa, England, Greenland, Germany, Holland, Ireland, Israel, Japan, New Zealand, Scandinavia, Scotland, Syria and the USA. Most of them were young people with little experience, but joining the ranks was the occasional architect, businessman, cabinetmaker, carpenter, clergyman, dentist, doctor, engineer, musician, student, surveyor, teacher, truck driver, even restaurateur.

Before Frontiers' initial growth pangs had stopped in about 1980, its body of volunteers had built or largely renovated about 1,600 houses and 18 community centres, churches or schools at 50 locations in eight provinces across Canada. The foundation had rounded up and organized more than 2,000 volunteers from 25 countries.[76] Today the total number of volunteers who have worked on Frontiers projects has passed 8,000.

In one summer Frontiers could build a house that met the highest Canadian standards of construction and insulation for less than half the cost of a similar house put up for the CMHC by any local contractor. Not only that, but the participation of the prospective beneficiary of the project ensured that the new owners, usually the head of a family and its children, had a strong motivation to maintain the building. The employment of prospective owners and their friends also meant that apathy diminished. Local volunteers were trained on site in trades such as block laying, carpentry, plumbing and roofing, which prepared them for jobs off-reserve or for work building houses anywhere.

Because of what had happened in Canada's residential schools, the Frontiers educational system was especially important to the communities it served. Frontiers has built only two schools in Canada, but it has supplied volunteer teachers, supervisors and coordinators on request to community school boards. The volunteer spirit exhibited by these young people offered all kinds of extras that many professional teachers did not imagine. Many non-Frontiers teachers are adventurous young graduates with heavy student debts to repay, so when they consider work in the North, they rank financial interests first. Of their prospective employers they may request airfare paid up front, including fares for holidays in the South; a certain kind of (usually expensive) housing; and medical and insurance benefits, among other things. Frontiers volunteers, in comparison, cheerfully work long hours without pay because they are there purely to help, giving little thought to material reward, reflecting that spiritual impulse Charles recognized first in God's Lake and then in Rhodesia.

In his report for 1974, Charles wrote:

> The direct objective of Frontiers Foundation/Operation Beaver is to assist and encourage community self-development, in terms of both construction and personal interaction... Our funding enables us to send skilled and unskilled volunteers into small communities where they actively participate in self-help projects... which range from heavy construction to recreation leadership... Building within and without are of equal importance. The individual

community is thus assisted in the realization of its needs, and the volunteer is given an opportunity to accept his responsibility in the Brotherhood of Man.[77]

Given the nature of the organization and the climate of Canada, much of the work was carried out in summertime, but the volunteers were not just light-hearted adventurers hoping for a few sunny months to save the world and meet girls or boys. Many of them returned to the building sites in the winter or stayed all year long, teaching, building, whatevering. Jonie Leigh, for instance, went to Red Bay in Labrador in winter to direct a recreation program for the local fishing community. Neil Jefferson of New Zealand and his friend Boaz Tsairi of Israel worked for two years in central British Columbia. Garfield Bembridge of Jamaica saved lives and built houses for years in northern Alberta. Following a summer's work camp, others returned to communities during the skin-parching cold months after Christmas to put up, tape, sand and paint drywall, finishing the houses they had helped to close in during the sunny months.

The general staff of Frontiers, like the headquarters staff of an army at war, was focused, expert and driven, organizing supplies and volunteers from many parts of the country and the world, bringing in new recruits, raising money, responding to reports from the "front," allocating resources to the places where they were most needed. All this was done not only in a very efficient manner but also with imagination and sometimes desperate inventiveness.

One night, for example, Charles was pondering how to get a portable sawmill from a donor's factory in Indianapolis to a new work site in Labrador. The machine weighed more than a ton, and the cost of hiring a truck or shipper was far too great for the small Frontiers budget. Free transport was needed. On TV that night Charles saw a report about the Canadian forces about to send one of their Hercules heavy-lift aircraft to Goose Bay, Labrador, not far from the site of the new Frontiers housing project. Knowing that such aircraft often have to fly on urgent missions with half a capacity load or less, Charles took a chance. He picked up the phone and telephoned the colonel in charge of the mission at the Canadian Forces base in Trenton, just over 100 miles from Toronto. Later Charles admitted with a smile:

Perhaps I pulled my family's rank on him. Anyway, I told him what we do and that we needed to get a sawmill down to Labrador in a hurry, and the colonel said, "Sure, Reverend, we can do that. We got a Herc lifting off Wednesday at oh nine three oh for Goose Bay. Get that mill down here an hour earlier and we'll fly her in for you. Anything else we can do for you, Reverend?"[78]

Frontiers quickly crewed a truck to the Wood-Mizer plant in Indianapolis, picked up the mill, took it directly to the airplane on the runway, and it was delivered free of charge and safely to Goose Bay. Jonie Leigh, Frontiers' project manager there, picked it up on arrival, and it was up and sawing logs in the woods the following day. The total cost to Frontiers was a few long distance calls and gas for the trucks. The total cost to the taxpayer was basically zero.

One of Charles's favourite sayings was, "If you try, you may fail, but if you don't try, you've already failed."

Typically, while saying thanks, Charles would finish off a conversation like the one he had with the colonel with one of his terrible puns, something like: "Sir, before you go, maybe you can help me locate a friend, a real nut, went overseas, got shelled and came back a colonel." More often than not, he would get a groan, not a chuckle, but he always created just enough bonhomie so that he was welcome next time he showed up.

CANADIAN FORCES HERCULES AIRCRAFT AT CFB TRENTON, ONTARIO, ABOUT TO LOAD A FRONTIERS SAWMILL FOR DELIVERY TO GOOSE BAY, LABRADOR, CIRCA 1975.

Although Frontiers houses were sprouting up like mountain flowers in June, and the volunteers from around the world were spreading and building the good news for the foundation, Charles and the work camp committee were disappointed by the response to the foundation's appeals among Canadian Christians. They had hoped, even presumed, that after the inspiring success building the Anglican church at Split Lake, all denominations of Christians would team up for a national ecumenical work-camp campaign. It was not to be. Ironically, their member denominations missed the point of it all, retreating into their sectarianism and trying to imitate Frontiers without its unifying spirit. The United Church set up Operation Understanding, the Presbyterians mounted Operation Goodwill and the Anglicans devised Work Tours. Lacking the spirit of the volunteers who breathed the life into such organizations, all of these denominational offshoots expired soon after their birth. Despite this, Frontiers carried on ecumenically in co-operation with the CCC, working on church and community-centre projects, and many of the original project veterans like First Nations volunteers Nora Ross and Graham Everett returned year after year, often now as group leaders.

Charles soon realized that because Frontiers Foundation was defining and accepting a national responsibility, it would need national amounts of money. The volunteers, both local and international, were making up by far the most productive source of the foundation's energy and initiatives, but the Canadian government would have to begin to play a financial role in funding its operations and projects if it was to continue its work. However, since governments, as agents for Her Majesty in Right of Canada, had basically created the problem Frontiers was addressing by neglecting the honour of the Crown, it was inevitable that this necessary government funding would be hard to get.

One problem was that the government already had put ineffective and costly parallel programs in place, and they saw Frontiers as competition. Another was that funding the foundation would in effect admit that the treaties were valid and had been neglected, and that the government, ignoring the honour of the Crown, had cheated the original signatories and their descendants, raising all kinds of difficult and directly related questions: Who really has title to a piece of land if the purchaser has not paid the owner the full agreed price? Who has title if one party says they did not understand, because they were not clearly told, that the definition of ownership did not include mineral rights?[79]

Frontiers executives – Charles and later Marco Guzman from Bolivia – operating on trust, hope and sympathy, had to deal with government bureaucrats who needed budgets, receipts and triplicate copies with signatures in order to report on the results of their disbursement of public money.

Indeed, government was to some degree and for some considerable periods an impediment to the foundation's work. The few and wasteful programs that were in place had over the years developed into a bureaucracy that employed white people. Thus the people employed by government were bound to view with alarm any incursion on their turf by the non-profit sector that would derogate from their authority and affect the jobs and budgets for projects that had always been under their purview, built by private contractors.

Sensing all these complexities as he worked his way for the first time into these financing problems, Charles tried not to alarm government bureaucrats, while at the same time charming them into helping him. Money intended to flow from Canadian taxpayers via the Department of Indian Affairs and Northern Development to the reserves encounters severe turbulence at times, but when it is not paid, people actually starve. When transfers *are* paid, they often end up in the hands of the greedy, not the needy. But sometimes some band councils in Canada – entrusted with large sums of money or resources and unused to the task of managing them – also fail their own people. For example, Frontiers sent a Wood-Mizer to a reserve in Ontario with the firm understanding that the band council would pay $50 per month to rent the machine and issue a monthly report on its use (in the private sector, a realistic rent for the apparatus would have been around $50 *per day*). One payment arrived, then one report, then nothing. After two years Frontiers retrieved the machine, which had been seriously damaged. In other places the Frontiers coordinator had to take the wheels off the sawmills and chain them to trees to prevent them from being stolen. In these cases Charles would hear the mocking voice of the British in Africa, who said of the natives, "Give them the job and they will finish the tools." But in the experience of Frontiers Foundation, such cases were the exceptions that proved their rule. The major problem in the Aboriginal communities they worked with has continued to be a lack of education and organization among people who had scarcely graduated from high school and knew nothing about keeping accounts.

Until the late 1980s little or no government money was destined for Métis people, even in rich Alberta, so both the need and the opportunity for Frontiers became most evident among the Métis. The Frontiers focus thus began to shift toward them, as well as toward non-status Indians living off-reserve. Some funding for projects in these communities came from the federal government through the CMHC, but the major contributors to their housing programs remained the Aboriginal and Métis peoples themselves, assisted by the foreign and Canadian volunteers organized by and through Frontiers.

No matter where the Frontiers project was in Canada, however, problems with government funding were difficult and sometimes hilarious. The government administrators of course would ask Frontiers for detailed receipts so they could report to their cabinet ministers on completed projects. This was a problem for Frontiers because the government's fiscal and budget categories did not match exactly the system of recording and reporting on projects used by Frontiers. Of course, Frontiers already had a very reliable firm of chartered accountants and auditors who certified their books regularly in accordance with "generally accepted accounting principles" every year, so Charles knew their figures were "squeaky clean." He hated the tedious and mistrustful bookkeeping, but he knew that, even without any GAAP accounting, Frontiers houses were the best that could be provided with the money available. To be asked to line up his reporting with the government's accounting style seemed to him to be a waste of effort that could be spent on much more important work. The government also wanted proof of something far more nebulous, but crucially important: that the families receiving the houses were living happily in them and would stay there, forming a lasting human community.

So while the bureaucrats were all working for dependable salaries and generous pensions, Frontiers workers were either volunteers or working at half-pay, and most of the necessary supplies came in at a give-away price or free. It was impossible to put a "fair market value" on every donation in kind, because there were usually no competitive bids. For instance, who could define the fair market value for a used kiln dryer located in southern Ontario? If that dryer were airlifted gratis from southern Ontario to northern Quebec by the Canadian Armed Forces, that would increase the value of the dryer by at least the cost of shipping, but that value could scarcely be realized by a sale of the capital equipment, since there were no potential buyers other than Frontiers or their clients, who had no money. Frontiers was being asked to fill in a form with exact numbers for contributions of labour, materials and capital (plant) costs that were impossible to ascertain and therefore profoundly understated the "objective" value of contributions by and through Frontiers Foundation, a circumstance particularly vexing in situations where "matching funding" from government was the rule. This sometimes made Charles quite impatient with the very people he needed.

However, not all of Charles's encounters with governments were negative. For example, the programs of Ontario's Ministry of Municipal Affairs and Housing in the late 1990s and 2000s supported various Frontiers projects on land owned by Aboriginal peoples throughout the North. The province's bureaucrats were impressed by the combination of international voluntarism, local initiatives, private donations and the contribution of sweat equity from the prospective owners that the foundation projects generated. This combination seemed to promise that the tax money would not only benefit the homeowners and children, thus contributing to the economic and social stability of the province, but would also create other community benefits, whether on reserve or Métis-owned land.

It was challenge enough to build a physical community, let alone set up a structure or series of structures that would allow that community to thrive. First, the board of directors set an overall Frontiers Foundation budget for the year. That budget had to cover the program costs for individual projects to be carried out by the volunteers; it also had to pay for the rent on the foundation's simple offices and the modest staff salaries.[80] The organization was further complicated by the fact that the foundation depended on unreliable donations and grants, often promised but not as often delivered. Once a project was accepted, the many volunteers, who in the meantime had been writing in hopefully asking for projects in various parts of Canada and elsewhere, had to be organized. The work teams usually numbered six to twelve, men and women, mixed as to language, race, education and religion, but all driven by the same generous fervour.

Then the needs of the various applicants had to be received, judged and accepted or rejected. Start-up dates of each Frontiers project had to be matched to arrival dates of dozens of volunteers, who in any given year might come from 20 or 30 countries, five or ten provinces, speak six to 16 maternal languages, and offer many kinds of skills, including none. The variety in languages was handled easily enough by Charles, who spoke English, Cree, Bemba, some Spanish, German, Ojibwa and passable French – enough languages to handle most, if not all, volunteers. Once the application from the persons in need had been accepted, the local organizers had to agree with Frontiers head office about the total cost, accommodations for incoming volunteers, their transportation within Canada, trucks, availability of local volunteers and donations, woodworking machinery, kiln dryers, Wood-Mizers and other tools and equipment (including bundles of roofing and siding, cement, cement mixers, gasoline, hammer-staplers, hoses, oxy-acetylene welders, paint rollers, pipe, shovels, tongue-and-groove plywood, wheelbarrows and wiring), as well as food, first-aid kits, insurance policies and so on – and these had to be ordered, paid for, trucked or flown in, sheltered and distributed as needed.

As Frontiers' experience accumulated over the years, the organization was able to maintain and even better its phenomenal efficiency in construction. In one arrangement with the Ministry of Housing of Ontario, for example, Frontiers guaranteed to build 131 houses over three years (2007–2009) at a cost of $2.6-million. The cost for each house was an almost incredibly low $19,847. The cost breakdown for the whole contract was to be 18 per cent for Frontiers overhead, 32 per cent for mobilizing the volunteer labour and 50 per cent for buying building materials. Considering that commercial builders had in the past been charging the CMHC $40,000 per unit for houses on reserves, the Frontiers approach was clearly far more cost-effective.[81]

In order to assure two of this program's objectives – long-term family ownership of the houses, creating a stable, settled community – the

Ontario government asked each prospective owner to sign an interest-free, forgivable mortgage whose face value would decline by 8 per cent per year for ten years, then by 2 per cent per year.

Frontiers managed these mortgages in its typical way, by trusting the owners beyond normal banking practices. Most of them had no credit history and minimal employment prospects, but Frontiers knew that those things were likely to change through the achievement of home ownership and employment training, so the foundation asked for no paperwork beyond the signed mortgage. They trusted the owners to stay in the houses and keep them in good repair, and the results have been good: only two owners of the Frontiers houses have had to sell and move away, one for new employment and the other because of a death, and they both paid off the remaining amount owing on their mortgages.

The cost to the taxpayer of wiping the shameful lack of Aboriginal housing from the face of the province was phenomenally low. The cost of the houses to the province averaged only about $20,000 each, apart from the cost of the land. They were all standard three-bedroom bungalows, well insulated and well finished. For some, septic systems and wells had to be provided, while the rest were on municipal water systems. But every house had a furnace, a full set of kitchen appliances and bathroom fixtures, and each was pleasingly finished inside and out. The results were so cost-effective that when the government sent in the famous multinational accounting firm Deloitte & Touche to audit Frontiers, the accountants recommended to the government that "the ministry should give these guys more money."[82]

▲ ▲ ▲ ▲ ▲ ▲

THE DARK NIGHT
OF THE CREE

Many years ago, in the small-sticks forest of north-central Quebec, there grew a little town named Chapais. Inhabited mainly by hunters, trappers and itinerant prospectors, it was a good place for a man to live if he was a hunter and fisher, independent and self-reliant, like the Cree who lived in and around it. One of those self-reliant people in the 1930s was a trapper named Charlie Dixon, who provided the main support of his wife and five children.

Dixon and his fellow Cree had very little knowledge of white men and their society. Until floatplanes started landing on their lake during the 1920s, their land, several thousand square miles of bush located 600 air miles north of Montreal, was virtually unknown to white people, except for a few traders and prospectors who travelled there by canoe. There was no road or railway, and the Cree people in and around Chapais, who called themselves Oujé-Bougoumou, lived on their land and water as their ancestors had since time immemorial. They had never been at war with white people, so they had never been conquered and their land had never been sold. They were a part of the land as it was part of them, indivisible, like the sky, water, rocks and trees.

Dixon and others welcomed the strangers who were interested in their rocks, and showed them strange mineral formations, never imagining the consequences they were risking.

The white prospectors were searching for copper, gold, silver and other minerals, which in the recent past had made fortunes for businessmen from Toronto and Montreal. And it was there, in 1929, by Lake Opemiska ("meeting of the waters" in Cree) near what would become the town of Chapais, that prospector Leo Springer found a promising vein of copper. After six years of organizing, fundraising and promoting, planeloads of white men and their equipment began to drop from the sky onto Lake Opemiska. The miners built substantial warehouses and started to dig.

The price of copper began to fall and the vein proved unprofitable when prices were low. And then the war drums of Europe began to beat. Suddenly all the plans of the Springer Mine Company were cancelled, and in 1938 most of the white men flew away again. Their equipment was not worth the cost of shipping it out, but they would not abandon it. So the material would have to remain sheltered and guarded until the company could make new arrangements. On the last day of the project, just before the last floatplane out was due to arrive, the manager of the project approached Charlie Dixon with a proposition: would he take care of the buildings, with their valuable equipment, including canned food, blankets, clothing, dynamite, drilling equipment, hand tools and generators? The annual snowfall in the region was 11 feet or more,[83] so it was essential that someone clear off the roofs, or they might collapse and wreck the buildings and their contents.

Dixon agreed, and season after season for 13 years, as the snows came and went, Dixon shovelled off the roofs. No miners came to Opemiska. For 13 years, Dixon kept guard for the white men who did not know, or did not care to know, that the lake on which they landed their planes, the water they drank, the fish they ate, the land they built on and dug away, the trees they cut into lumber, belonged to Dixon and all the other Oujé-Bougoumou. The owners of the house were co-operating with the burglars. This bizarre situation was actually common in the colonial Canadian North.

For thousands of years before white people came, the Cree had lived throughout a vast area around Hudson's Bay that came to be known as Rupert's Land by a small group of white businessmen in London. In 1670 these men, calling themselves "adventurers," obtained from Charles 11 a royal charter guaranteeing a trading monopoly over the land from Labrador to the Rockies and north to the Arctic. Then, nearly two centuries later, another foreign document recorded the greatest land transfer in human history, purportedly conveying title from the Hudson's Bay Company to the Canadian government. In this document, which formed and continues to define Canada, there is only one brief mention of the actual historical owners of the land: "Any claims of Indians to be compensated for lands required for purposes of settlement shall be disposed of by the Canadian Government in communication with the Imperial Government; and the Company shall be relieved of all responsibility in respect of them."[84] These claims would be settled by the government "in conformity with the equitable principles which have uniformly governed the British Crown in its dealings with the aborigines."[85] In other words, the "Indians" specified in this document had no rights, only claims to rights.

In years to come, as white Canadians continued to exploit these vast lands, ruthlessly disregarding rights and treaties, the Crown, like the moon, remote and listless, shone down impassively on the doings of its subjects below.[86]

One spring day, after the Second World War had vanished like a season, a floatplane circled Lake Opemiska, searching for a safe place to land, and settled near the shore in front of Charlie Dixon's place. Standing on the pontoon, the new mine manager, Fred Cooke, asked for Dixon, who identified himself and took him over to the site. As Cooke said, "It was incredible." Half a million dollars' worth[87] of equipment, and the buildings were intact. Continued Cooke:

> Charlie and his family had hardly anything to cover them-
> selves at night, yet they hadn't even borrowed one of the
> company's blankets – and there were hundreds there. I had
> always believed that Indians were a shiftless, light-fingered
> lot, but I found they were honest and trustworthy almost
> beyond imagining. I don't know of anyone else who would
> have behaved with as much integrity. Charlie had done
> something wonderful for the company, so I decided the
> company owed him something in return.[88]

It was the company, not the Crown, who then treated Charlie equitably, giving him a pension, a house with two bedrooms, and hiring his two sons, Malcolm and Lawrence, to work in the mine. The boys could not speak English, so their first job was with two other Cree men who could, and they schooled themselves in the mine. One of them was named Fred Iserhoff, a sometime trapper, guide and prospector's aide, and the other was Harry Salt, Charlie Dixon's son-in-law. Iserhoff, newly married, got the chance to buy a company house on a rent-to-purchase plan, and the fruitful integration of white and Cree in

Chapais and in the nearby town of Chibougamau had begun. A railway from the nearest railhead, at Barraute in northwestern Quebec, was built, and soon, 11 Oujé-Bougoumou Cree were working at the mine, providing for their families, all working and living side by side with their white neighbours.

Clearly, in this case at least, it was the "backward" Cree who had shown the way and the light to the white men, whether company or Crown. And the white people had seen the light and realized what it meant. In Cree, it is *kwiusk mussunehikun*. In English, it is "equitable principles."

But as the news of the profits to be made at Lake Opemiska spread through the mining centres of Canada, more prospectors arrived and more deals were cut with parties of white men far away which ignored the rights of the inhabitants. These led to the seizure of land and the destruction of lakes, rivers, land, fish, game, forest and people. Over the ensuing years, from about 1951 to about 1970, the Cree were threatened and coerced many times into abandoning their village sites, which were then bulldozed and destroyed. As Freddy Bosum, a Cree from the region, wrote when he was a student at Trent University: "Through collusion among the mining companies and the Quebec and Canadian governments, we were forced to relocate our villages seven times over fifty years."[89] Freddy Bosum is the son of one of the Oujé-Bougoumou Cree elders, Charlie Bosum, who lived through many of these white invasions.

During these years, white men from the provincial and federal governments and the mining companies blew in like tornadoes from the South, devastating villages wherever they touched down. These men said things like, "You must move the village to make way for a new mine,"; and then, when it was done, "You must move to make way for a logging road"; and when that was done, "You must move to join other members of your band, the Mistassini." When the Oujé-Bougoumou showed that they had always been independent of the Mistassini, they were told, "You must move to conform with government policy, or you'll get no more social benefits." After this had happened six or seven times, the people were exhausted, afraid and bewildered. Some of them refused to live in the moving villages anymore because they had learned a terrible lesson: if they stayed together, they would be crushed together. Many of them went off into the forest to live alone or in family groups, in a wigwam or a moss house[90] or shanty, like refugees from a war zone.

The situation was most urgent in the shantytown of Lac Doré on the edge of Chibougamau, where a minority of the Oujé-Bougoumou had now settled. They were forcibly expelled again, and some of them returned to the bush to live on their family hunting grounds. Others took refuge in little shacks thrown up beside the gravel road where the trucks of the logging and mining companies roared by with their loads of equipment, sand and gravel, throwing dust over everything. As they drove through on their mission of construction and destruction, some drivers flung garbage out the windows in contempt for the "drunken Indians" of Lac Doré. Their huge tires fired stones like bullets randomly at the roadside shacks.

But by the mid-1960s, different kinds of white men began to take an interest in the Cree. They did not want Cree lands or minerals; they wanted to help because, like the Cree themselves, they placed a higher value on "equitable principles" and human life in general. In 1966 Oujé-Bougoumou chief Jimmy Mianscum asked an Anglican priest named Hugo Muller at the white town of Chibougamau to help his people. Muller approached his superior, J.A. Watton, the bishop of Moosonee and a friend of Charles, who put Charles together with Reverend Steven Beardy. Charles and Beardy were already friends, having co-operated in the construction of Beardy's Anglican church at Split Lake in Manitoba a couple of years before.

Charles and Frontiers were ready, willing and able to help.

Charles invited Barbara and their 2-year-old, Wanda, to come with him, and they set off from Toronto in their beat-up old station wagon in August 1966 to drive the 700-odd miles into northern Quebec to see the community and discuss plans with the chief and council. The last 200 miles of road from the Quebec boundary east were all gravel, so they travelled in a miasma of road dust, with Wanda asleep on the front bench seat beside Barbara, who kept her hand protectively over the baby. When they were about 50 miles from the village, a lumber truck roaring by fired a big stone into their windshield, spraying glass in little Wanda's face, including pieces near her closed eyes. Horrified, Barbara carefully wiped the glass away. Wanda did not even wake up.

CREE CHIEF JIMMY MIANSCUM (RIGHT) WELCOMES
THE ARRIVAL AT LAC DORÉ, QUÉBEC, OF
THE FRONTIERS VOLUNTEERS, WITH CHARLES
CATTO AND JIM CHIGWEDERE, 1966.

When they got to the reserve and told their hosts what had happened,
the local clergyman Reverend Glen Jackson said dryly, "Welcome to
the club."

The chief surprised Charles by asking not for houses but for something to draw his wounded people together and inspire them with confidence for their future. Charles offered assistance in design, money,
volunteer labour, machinery, materials and project leadership – everything necessary to help restore hope and shelter to the Oujé-Bougoumou. This was the start of l'Opération Castor, the first time Operation
Beaver had expanded into Quebec.

The people decided to build a new community centre with a library.
They would also need a laundry, meeting rooms, overnight rooms for
transient trappers, a kitchen, a convenience store and washrooms. With
volunteer help from across Canada, Africa and India, and no government funding at all, the eager Beavers and the Oujé-Bougoumou built
it all in a matter of weeks, at very low cost. In the town of Chibougamau,
the local Chibougamau project support and procurement committee,
mainly consisting of Anglicans, secured donations of surplus tents and
building supplies from the Canadian Forces base nearby.

Then, only four years after the new building was completed, the

BEAVERS VOLUNTEERS ON THE STEPS OF THE COMMUNITY
CENTRE AT LAC DORÉ. LEFT TO RIGHT: MARION
MCDOUGALL AND EVA LINKLATER (WESTERN MÉTIS),
MARION EDWARDS (BRITISH COLUMBIA), AND ELEANOR
RYERSE (ONTARIO). (COURTESY ROBERT JONES)

people were told once again, "Get out, we need the land" for the
Campbell Chibougamau Mines. The beginnings of their new life, including the big new community centre put up by the volunteers with
such help and hope, were once again smashed to bits by bulldozers. Even the cemetery was bulldozed, and Chief Jimmy Mianscum
might well have wondered as the drivers drove their blades into those
wooden crosses, "Is even one of the men driving the bulldozers here a
Christian?" As Freddy Bosum wrote in the essay cited earlier, "There
was a deliberate policy in place of attempting to make us disappear."[91]
The people once again sadly dispersed to shanties in the bush or built
little refuges along the edge of the gravel road. Jimmy Mianscum and
his people might have given up in despair; they might have thought,
'We have resisted and survived for generations; we have been starved
out, evicted, robbed, bulldozed and poisoned.' And every one of them

THE OPENING OF THE LAC DORÉ COMMUNITY CENTRE
IN AUGUST 1966. THE U-SHAPED BUILDING WAS
QUICKLY BUILT FROM PREFAB PANELS. THE CENTRE
WAS SUBSEQUENTLY DESTROYED WHEN THE CREE
COMMUNITY WAS FORCED OFF THE LAND AGAIN IN 1974.

might have thought, 'I am probably dying – my family is dying, my people are dying because of these invaders.' But although many of them may have thought this and some may have even given up in despair and died in the dark as truck wheels fired gravel at them, many more did not, because they were thinking, 'Our chief will not let us die, because he is the spirit of our people. He has always helped us and he will help us again.' And Jimmy Mianscum thought, 'We will survive because we have to, because our elders willed us into being and we will follow our elders with the help of our friends; and our friend Charles, who has helped us before, will help us again. Even among the white men killing us is a friend who has helped us.' Their building was destroyed, but the spirit that had built it survived and inspired Chief Mianscum through the darkest night of his people.

"With the last of these relocations in 1970," Abel Bosum wrote,

... our people dispersed throughout our territory and

established small encampments that consisted of crude makeshift dwellings, often just simple tent frames. We believed that if our villages could be destroyed so easily at the whims of mining companies and governments, then our territory was also in jeopardy. Our feeling was that we needed to demonstrate our continuing and total occupancy of our territory so that we would not be totally dispossessed of the very basis of our community, our way of life and our identity as Oujé-Bougoumou Eenou.[92]

By 1970 approximately 12 mines[93] were operating on their land, against their will and without any payment beyond the inadequate welfare payments of a grudging government. These welfare payments were scarcely better than hush money. The Cree and others have estimated that at least $4-billion in minerals and timber alone were taken from the Oujé-Bougoumou lands without agreements or royalties of any kind. The mines, the logging and the roads associated with them destroyed a significant amount of forest and, along with it, habitat for the animals on which the people depended for their living. White communities were thriving on the occupation, theft and destruction of the Aboriginal people's property. The companies exploiting the Oujé-Bougoumou resources were aided by governments that tried to subdue the natives as cheaply as possible while also paying with Canadian tax dollars for the roads, dams, bridges, hydro access and so on for the companies.

What was happening in Canada then, and continues to happen even today, are scenarios that Canadians as a nation have condemned and tried to prevent in other parts of the world. The seizures by a colonizing people, the Native resistance, the heroic determination to survive, the forced and illegal dispossession by colonial governments professing good intentions, the natives retreating into the surrounding forest, the starvation and squalor forced upon a normally self-reliant people – all are events in the lives of Native peoples today in the Brazilian rainforest or Chiapas in Mexico or in parts of Africa, Australia, Guatemala or New Guinea, anywhere in the developing world. "But not in Canada."

Or so Canadians think.

But it is very much the same here except that the highly polished hypocrisy of Canada's timid press, listless churches, greedy corporations and grasping governments reflect only Canadian citizens' self-interested colonial view of the situation, so we do not see through the shiny image they create to the reality of the situation. The churches that timidly supported Charles's work in the beginning have now largely abandoned their former sense of mission. He has said of them: "The churches of Canada are so timid and spineless it is a miracle that they can get out of bed and stand up in the morning."

Finally, in the spring of 1989, Chief Mianscum's successor, Chief Abel Bosum, said, "Enough." A still, thoughtful man, he had the skills and attitude necessary to deal like a diplomat with the many and complex levels of what was, to him, a foreign government. And he knew he had a spiritual ally in southern Canada. With the encouragement of Frontiers, he turned a desperate situation into a cause. In June of 1989, he led his people out to the highway nearby and set up a roadblock.

He chose the day wisely: it was the official opening of the Quebec fishing season. People in the stopped cars and pickup trucks on Highway 113 were angry and frustrated. Some turned around and went back to Chapais to phone the police; others returned 40 miles to Chibougamau and called their MPs and MNAs. The following day, not only the police were there, but the federal Minister of Indian Affairs and Northern Development (as the ministry was then called) as well as a Quebec cabinet minister, Raymond Savoie. The TV cameras and reporters turned up, and dozens of chiefs arrived, not only from the region but from all across Canada.

This was the beginning of thirteen years of complicated negotiations between the two governments representing 30 million settler Canadians in all, and the Oujé-Bougoumou, numbering around 500. The Cree were expertly advised by a community development adviser from Montreal, Paul Wertman.[94]

During these years, the Quebec and Canadian governments negotiated a $40-million settlement with the Oujé-Bougoumou Cree First Nation, based in part on the James Bay and Northern Quebec Agreement (1975). Oujé-Bougoumou was accepted as a distinct band with its own traditional territory on the same basis as other Cree First Nations. The mineral and timber rights in the band's area are defined by the same criteria applied under the James Bay Agreement. Chief Abel

Bosum and his band secured a new reserve on Lake Opemiska with all their mineral and timber rights guaranteed in perpetuity.

With legal title and lots of money in the bank, the Oujé-Bougoumou were a far different people when they began planning for new buildings this time. They hired a famous Métis architect, Douglas Cardinal, from Alberta. He sat down with the elders and band councillors, who told him what they wanted. Later on, several Frontiers volunteers from southern Canada, Africa and Bolivia arrived to help with the plumbing, framing, roofing and painting. The volunteers installed basement walls constructed of pressure-treated wood, as they had in many other Métis and reserve projects. These help retain inside the houses the heat that rises naturally from the earth all the time. They built more than two dozen big, widely spaced houses, each with the separate air-handling system necessitated by the unique heating system. Geothermal heat for these houses is supplemented by a central heating plant fired by wood and sawdust, which delivers hot water underground to every building, saving enormously on furnaces and fuel costs. This system means that the band is closer to self-sufficiency because it needs less money to buy oil, gas and hydro. In the mid-1990s, the total heating cost per year for the whole community was less than half of what a conventional white community of the same size would have spent over the same time.

New houses and apartments for 750 people were built. Roads, stores and a broad-winged new community centre were set up according to the elders' advice, employing a conventional circular pattern with the community buildings in the middle and housing forming the perimeter. In addition to the community centre, the common buildings included a hotel for visitors, a hockey arena, outdoor tennis courts, a church open to all faiths, an open-air dancefloor and bandstand, a gas station, garages, a convenience store and a medical clinic. The main doors of all the houses face the rising sun, as the elders specified. Each band member learned some trade so he could invest his own labour in his own house, according to both Cree and Frontiers traditions. The whole of Oujé-Bougoumou was much cheaper to build than a conventional reserve in the Canadian North, and it was, in Charles's words, "Virtually all done by band members."[95]

All of the new houses are grouped with plenty of space around each one, on a hillside that slopes toward the lake. On the far side of the lake rises the purple mass of Mount Opemiska, the first sight a visitor sees on entering the Oujé-Bougoumou reserve. The very look of the place inspires a feeling of calm, of being at home, to most people who visit. Even strangers from far away feel this allure when they first arrive, and it never leaves them. The memory of the village draws people back over long distances and long stretches of time.

In January 1993, Chief Abel Bosum invited Charles to the ceremony to celebrate completion of not just a new series of homes but a renewal of life for a whole people. To a crowd of young men and women fervently interested in the fate and the history of their people, the chief spoke very calmly and slowly about the recent events that had threatened all their lives. He said, "This building declares by its very presence that the days of our dispossession from our land are finished, and our alienation and marginalization from the economic and political life of the region are over and done with."

Chief Bosum also addressed the young Oujé-Bougoumou people directly: "You have every right to be bitter and resentful about the things which mining companies and loggers and government have done here. But I am asking you to be forgiving."

And it was precisely because of the healing work done by Charles and all the volunteers of Frontiers Foundation, Canadian and foreign, that Chief Bosum made this recommendation to the young people. As the chief said: "Charles, in 1966, when things were really bad for our people, you were here for us. We will never forget that. *meegwetch*."[96]

For Charles, this establishment of community was more than a sweet success. The independence of the Oujé-Bougoumou Cree was fulfilment of a goal to help injured people to recover and to live as they wish. With these thanks and with expressions of mutual esteem between Chief Bosum and himself, Charles retired from the scene. For many years afterward he would be wanted in the community, and welcomed there, but no longer needed. The building and the spirit that built it lives on, and on its own.

Chief Bosum cannot forget the experience, but neither can the governments of Quebec and Canada. Having been dragged "kicking and screaming" to the table, according to Paul Wertman, now an adviser to the Oujé-Bougoumou Cree Nation in Ottawa, the two governments are now resentful and on guard against similar "losses." That's how they continue to think of what happened here. The word in the Department of Indian Affairs and Northern Development Canada became, "Oujé-Bougoumou is the one that got away."

The friendly relations between trapper Charlie Dixon of Chapais and miner/prospector Fred Cooke representing the claims later taken over by Opemiska Copper Mines illustrate the way Canadians like to think the North of their country developed: in trusting trade that enriched Aboriginal and white people equally. But this is an illusion. The reality is that many of the natives of Canada, who were already short of food, began to starve once the land-hungry whites displaced the early traders.

Fred Cooke may well have been astonished that Charlie Dixon had not helped himself to the mining company's supplies during its long absence, but Dixon was not only honest, he was mainly indifferent to the things that white people value so much. Dixon was not thinking of what he might get from a white man's shed, but of what he might get from the enormous storehouse that the forest and rivers, the skies and the lakes, had always represented to him and his forebears. This is part of what the Cree mean when they speak of sharing an identity with the land, the sky, the animals and other people. The identification of oneself with the land was so intense in some cases that the individual Cree or other Aboriginal person could travel safely through their territory for many miles in winter or summer without referring to a map. When asked by a white man, such an Aboriginal person, untrained in writing or drawing, could easily create on paper accurate maps of huge sections of the world around him.[97]

White Canadians, at least in a symbolic way, have taken over this attitude, along with the land itself. Canada's anthem, after all, sings of "Our home and native land/*terre de nos aieux*," whereas in England the people ask God to save their king or queen, and in France *le jour de gloire est arrivé*. In the States it is all about rockets, bombs and the flag.[98]

♠ ♠ ♠ ♠ ♠ ♠ ♠

MOCCASIN FLATS

The story of building houses in Moccasin Flats starts many thousands of miles away in Poznań, Poland, where, in 1945 a determined teenaged boy named Franz Oberle was one among millions of German refugees fleeing the enemy armies. He was trying to reach a home he had not seen in years, in Forchheim in the Black Forest, hundreds of miles to the west. His parents had gone missing, so he was without any family on a refugee train stopped outside Dresden in February 1945. Thousands of British and American bombers now attacked the defenceless city in waves with incendiary bombs and explosives killing probably 100,000 refugees and locals. The only military target in the city, the railway assembly yard, was not hit, so Oberle and his refugee friends went by train through the burning ruins the next day, dumbfounded but alive.

Having lived off the land for months, Oberle was so thin when he reached home that his aunt, uncle and cousins did not recognize him. Their whole village was starving from the famine imposed by the Allies.[99] After the allies lifted the prohibition on German emigration five years later, Oberle left Germany for Canada. In Chetwynd, a newly incorporated village in northern British Columbia, he and his German bride Joan[100] set up a car sales and garage business that soon succeeded, and in 1968 Oberle was elected mayor of the town. One Christmas Eve, Joan told Frank she had promised to take a hot Christmas dinner to the cabin of Napoleon Blue and his Métis family who lived in Moccasin Flats, a depressed area just outside of town. Oberle wanted to stay at home with the children, so he objected, but Joan said she had promised they would all take some hot Christmas turkey to this poor family. Oberle later described the scene in his autobiography:

> Following some footprints, up to our knees in snow, we
> arrived at a scene that could have come from a horror
> movie. It was a little tarpaper shack, the walls not sheeted

or insulated in any way, but covered with soot and grime. A single low-wattage light bulb and the glow of a red-hot pot-bellied woodstove illuminated the place, giving it a cave-like appearance. There were six children there, the oldest perhaps 10, the youngest perhaps 2. Several were barefoot, running among puddles of spilled beer frozen to the plywood floor and stumbling over discarded bottles, the only sign that adults may have shared the space with them earlier in the day. I recognized none of the children as having been among those in the festivities in town earlier in the morning.

Anxious and frightened at first, the children quickly gathered around to explore what we were putting on the table, their dirty, groping little hands ripping the wrappings off the containers.

We remained only long enough to get them started on what might have been the only decent meal they had tasted in days. None of them even looked up as we went out to return to our truck. Both of us were too stunned to express our feelings. We could see a Christmas tree partly obscured by smoke as we passed the Ladies and Escorts door of the beer parlour, which appeared to be doing a roaring business. The parents of the children we had just left would be among the patrons. If they survived the hazards of the slippery highway they would have to cross in their drunken stupor and didn't freeze to death in a snowbank on the way home they would be greeted by the dull, dirty faces of their frightened children huddling together to protect one another from the abuse they could expect from their parents in their present state.[101]

Oberle and Joan got home safely and sat for a while in their truck outside the house, holding hands, and thinking of how conditions had been in Germany during the years under the Allied occupation after the war, which were called *die Hungerjahre*. (the Hunger Years). Now, here they were in one of those victorious Allied countries, seeing starving children again.[102] They were both fighting off tears, and they sat there until their own children came out to see what was the matter.

What they had just witnessed was the sort of situation that had impelled them to seek a new life outside Germany, and now, in the gloomy bush around Chetwynd, a new form of their earlier suffering was opening before them. Up to now they had been vaguely aware of the distress of the Aboriginal and Métis families in Moccasin Flats, where the sad children were "living," but like most people, feeling helpless and alienated from it, they had just tried to avoid thinking about the situation.

No longer. Elected just the year before, Frank Oberle was now the much respected and very popular mayor, although he still pronounced village as "willedje." Now he had influence, along with energy and friends. He knew he could do something about the horror he had just seen. Encouraged by Joan, who was not only a busy young mother but also a full partner in his demanding businesses, he followed her lead as she energetically organized the local women to help the unfortunate people of Moccasin Flats.

He began by talking up the idea of doing something for the children and families in their shacks around the edge of town. Up to now, when Chetwynd needed more space for its rapidly expanding population, the town simply annexed some more "Crown" land. Then the builders tore down the ramshackle cabins of the impoverished Métis, or bulldozed them back into the bush, out of sight – but no longer out of Oberle's mind.

One day in 1969, toward the end of his first term in the mayor's office, Oberle opened an envelope from the new Liberal government in Ottawa. The letter contained surprising news. The suits in Ottawa, led by Pierre Elliott Trudeau's cabinet, were appealing to small communities all along the northern Canadian frontier to ço-operate in a program to improve the living conditions for the poor on Native and Métis land. The municipalities would contribute serviced lots and the CMHC would finance homes for families on social assistance, with rental subsidies and housing allowances. If Chetwynd would administer the arrangement, collecting the money owed and doing the necessary repairs, it would be guaranteed payment of taxes and certain fees.

The bureaucrats in Ottawa would also guarantee payment of municipal taxes and services. As he realized the implications of the offer, Oberle was startled, then enthusiastic, despite his innate loyalty

CHETWYND MAYOR FRANK OBERLE, SEATED LEFT, AND
VILLAGE COUNCIL IN 1968. EMIL BREITKREITZ IS
SEATED AT RIGHT, AND IN THE BACK ROW FROM LEFT
TO RIGHT ARE ERNIE PFANNER, RON TARR AND MORRIS
HAYWARD. (COURTESY HERITAGE HOUSE, VICTORIA)

to conservative principles. This was just what he had needed, what the whole town needed, what the whole North needed. "How could we lose under such an arrangement?" he thought, and he took it to his council, who were much less enthusiastic than he and Joan were.

Oberle told one council meeting, "Not only will this plan solve the deplorable housing situation of a significant number of our people, but it will also help to make the Aboriginal people productive citizens by adding them to the tax base." As he later said, "Nothing produces sympathy in government quicker than a proposal to expand the tax base." But still there was opposition, which came, as he said, "From their most primitive instincts, prejudice and bigotry."

After several more council meetings, and talking it over with Joan, Oberle began to push some of the reluctant members a little harder, and he encountered face to face some of the causes of what he was trying to abolish. Until now, overt expressions of prejudice, like the recognition of the horrors it produced, had been suppressed. One of the councillors said, "Why should we help them? Nobody ever built me a goddamned house."

Another said, "How long do you think it will be before they take a chainsaw to the place and cut it up for firewood?"

The councillors feared that when and if the mortgage payments were not made, or rents were not paid, and the houses were repossessed, the village would be stuck with the ugly perimeter of Moccasin Flats II and encumbered with empty houses for which there was no conceivable market.

Right about then, Oberle had a flash of insight. The councillors' objections tended to coalesce around the fear that the Métis, lacking jobs and living largely on welfare, could neither pay rent nor sustain a mortgage. But the suits in Ottawa were guaranteeing basic welfare, as well as an income supplement sufficient to enable them to pay rent on just the kind of house that had been proposed. Oberle remembered the German saying "Every man needs a place no matter how small which he can call his own." He calculated that the total already being guaranteed by government in welfare plus income supplements could make more than a significant contribution to mortgage payments.

If the Métis families were allowed to apply their welfare payments toward a mortgage instead of rent, they would become homeowners like most of the other families in town. Much of the stigma of their social condition would thus be removed. But that would only be possible if the owners could make a down payment on the houses, either with their own capital – faint hope – or, and this was the stroke of genius, by working on the houses without cash payment, while their labour was counted toward equity, reducing both their down payments and their monthly payments. The potential owners' labour would be converted directly into capital. At a stroke they would be converted from semi-serf status to ownership. What Oberle had to do now was get the suits in Ottawa to agree, and to put them together with representatives of the Métis people to figure out how to implement the idea. He got in touch with Ron Basford, the minister responsible in Ottawa, and described the plan. Basford was intrigued and offered to consider launching a demonstration project along the lines Oberle had proposed.

This concept, so similar to the Frontiers spirit, was arrived at by Oberle separately from Charles Catto, but with exactly the same objective in mind: to make safe, warm, affordable houses available while reinforcing the self-respect and independence of spirit of the owners and their families and thus improving the whole community.

Thinking the project was well on its way, even though final approval of his council was still pending, Oberle went off to Toronto on business. There, he got an urgent phone call from Joan telling him to come home quickly because several of the opposition members of council had taken advantage of his absence to approve an order rescinding the town's application to redesignate the land for housing, which would wreck the project. The town clerk had signed the order and sent it to Dan Campbell, the minister of Municipal Affairs in Victoria.

The councillors did not realize that Campbell, a good friend of Oberle's, favoured the project because he thought it was a good model for the rest of British Columbia. Oberle immediately called Campbell, who said, "Well, we can do something." He told Oberle that the

FRANK AND JOAN OBERLE WITH ONE OF THEIR
SUPPORTERS, REVEREND EMILE JUNGBLUTH, IN FORT
ST. JOHN. (COURTESY HERITAGE HOUSE, VICTORIA)

provincial government could order a new survey of the land, which would delay matters long enough for Oberle to persuade the recalcitrant members of council. Oberle knew his enemies – several of the opposition were "rednecks afraid of publicity because it would show them up as the hillbillies that they are." He would play on that fear.

Oberle had already seen in Germany what such fearful people could do to a society. These people lacked *Zivilcourage*, meaning that they did not have the courage to stand up in public in favour of a controversial or minority view in which they privately believed. And by now, the work of Joan and Frank Oberle had converted enough of the people of Chetwynd to their ideas that their supporters seemed to be the majority. That was enough to frighten the ignorant and fearful who still opposed the plan.

Oberle put the project on council meeting agendas several times, and each time he invited, as observers, influential people with a broad knowledge of the world and a liberal spirit. One was Father Emile Jungbluth, the local priest, who spoke eloquently in favour of the mayor. Finally the council voted in favour – again – and the project lurched ahead.

Also aware of these community struggles were other friends in the British Columbia Association of Non-Status Indians (BCANSI), whose president, Freddy House, and vice-president, Lawrence Gladue, both of them Cree Métis, had been pressing for years for such a program in places like Chetwynd. House and Gladue had already helped Charles build houses on and near reserves, and here were white and Métis people, on their doorstep, planning to build more. As a member of the Frontiers Foundation board of directors, Gladue was eager to find worthy projects for its volunteers, so he called Charles, who immediately responded with offers of help, volunteers and advice.

Eighteen Frontiers volunteers, including Jim Chigwedere from Zambia, were in Chetwynd from the first day of construction in the summer of 1971, digging foundations. The first tranche of 16 houses got off to a fast start with the help of these volunteers who had flown in from six countries.

Under Oberle's guidance, a non-profit corporation was formed called the Chetwynd Housing Company. Most of the Moccasin Flats Métis agreed to become shareholders, each one responsible for working on his or her own house. A few days after the first bulldozer had begun working on site, a Métis shareholder named Harvey McFeeters, who as chief carpenter and straw boss had been putting in his share of labour, lamented to Oberle about the rest of his co-investors. "We won't get this done on time. We won't get it done in ten years," he said. This was the same kind of defeatist attitude the white bureaucrat had expressed to Charles at the beginning of the first Frontiers project, but it was worse because it was coming from a Métis participant. A little while later it began to seem that McFeeters might be right, because someone set fire to the new lumber piled up on the building site ready to be assembled into houses. But Oberle remained patient.

The Frontiers superintendent on the site, Don Swanton, was a highly appreciative boss with infinite patience in dealing with his wildly variegated crew. He was helped by the intense publicity the project generated across the province and even across Canada. Many visitors came to observe the novel sight of people used to living in leaky old shacks building themselves bright new houses, with the help of a variety of volunteers. Gradually trust spread, gradually confidence built up as people in Chetwynd saw that it could be done, because it was being done.

"It was heartwarming to see it turn around," Oberle said. "A joy to see the people coming in to work, sober, on time and enthusiastic, and to see the houses going up."[103] And then the spirit spread farther. Two of the non-shareholders who wanted to sign up were busy single mothers. They had neither the time nor the strength to take on the heavy labour associated with house building. Thirty of the existing shareholders asked Oberle if they could give their work to build the houses for the two women. And it was done.

In midsummer Oberle and Frontiers had thought the first tranche of 16 houses might be complete in two years, but the builders were so enthusiastic that most of the houses were done by mid-December. On Christmas Eve, as Oberle and Joan were closing their shop, he said, "I've got a Christmas present for you," and he drove her home via Moccasin Flats, where most of the homes were now brightly lit, occupied, with Christmas trees visible in the windows and strings of lights across the lawns.

Toward the end of the project, with the 32 houses all completed and occupied on time and below budget, there was so much money left over that the board of the Chetwynd Housing Company decided to build a recreation and community centre for the new neighbour-hood. Frontiers lent a hand. And so that too was done.

In the end the Oberle–BCANSI–Frontiers team had both accepted and improved on the original excellent Ottawa proposal. They had not only built more houses less expensively than first envisaged, but they had also guided the volunteer spirit through a multitude of spirit-ual challenges – pessimism, doubt, despair, arson, hatred and envy – to a conclusion that provided shelter and pride for people who had been homeless through little fault of their own. They had also brought together in a new amity people who, for generations, had been afraid of each other.

The Chetwynd project had ramifications far beyond the village. Frontiers Foundation brought the good will of one of the most famous filmmakers in Canada, Patrick Watson, a TV star who later became chairman of the Canadian Broadcasting Corporation. Watson, a friend of Charles and brother member in the Phi Kappa Pi fraternity in To-ronto, made a one-hour documentary entitled *Moccasin Flats*, which won a Canadian Film Award in 1973 and has helped the foundation raise money ever since.

Chetwynd also became a model for the very successful expansion of housing in the Canadian North undertaken by the Trudeau gov-ernment in the 1970s. At first the obstacles seemed to be beyond the CMHC's mandate because the corporation was limited by law to pro-viding loans for houses within municipal boundaries. But the Oberle–Frontiers solution approved by town council and the British Columbia government was applied and made to work nationally, even providing a precedent for expansion into education in the North, mainly because Oberle had succeeded in persuading both his council and the British Columbia government to allow the village of Chetwynd to incorpor-ate the extra land.

Not only had there been years of neglect, prejudice and despair blocking progress on this housing frontier, there were also these laws and entrenched bureaucracies jamming everything like ice in a spring river. To clear them away would take a dynamite blast.

One ice floe was the National Housing Act (NHA), the legislation defining the terms of loans for housing. To show their goodwill, the CMHC invited the Native Council of Canada[104] leaders to a meeting, at which CMHC president Herb Hignett stated that his staff would listen carefully to the arguments and would begin immediately working toward a solution. As Gladue began to speak to the crowded room, he noticed that a white-haired man sitting behind Hignett had his head back on the chair and was apparently asleep. Gladue asked, "Who is that gentleman and what is his role? It appears that he is not listening as intently as the president stated."[105] The question focused all eyes on the gentleman, who was the vice-president of policy at the CMHC.

Gladue pointed out that the CMHC's jurisdiction was strictly limited to housing within municipal boundaries. The people from the CMHC "were smirking across the table at us," said Gladue, "because as an Act of Parliament, the NHA was impossible for them to circumvent." Gladue said that the CMHC was not committed and was stalling, a government tactic to which they were accustomed. Gladue, thinking of his mother and sister burned to death in a shanty fire outside municipal boundaries, said that he and Tony Belcourt of BCANSI were willing to stage a sit-in unless there was a resolution.

Then he threw in a stick of dynamite disguised as a suggestion. "If you look at section 55," he said, "you'll see that the Act allows CMHC to undertake experimental projects." Since the CMHC had already said they were committed to addressing the housing crisis, he continued, let them start an experimental "Winter Warmth" program to fix the worst cases and prevent further deaths from fires in the Aboriginal shanties.

With that the CMHC groaned and the ice began to shift. The CMHC asked for time to consult with itself, and after convening privately it committed to giving a million dollars for emergency home repairs, "plus commitments to seek revisions to the NHA so that CMHC could offer help to Métis and off-reserve Indians." Walter Rudnicki, executive director of policy and planning, was appointed to start developing a Native housing policy, to which Belcourt and Gladue contributed Aboriginal knowledge and experience. The new head of the CMHC, Bill Teron, saw that Gladue's expert knowledge of the NHA would help the CMHC in its stated goals and appointed him to a senior position. The new plan was announced on March 7, 1974, by Ron Basford, under the title Rural and Native Housing Program. Basford committed the Canadian government to build 50,000 new houses for Aboriginal people in the ensuing five years.

Gladue was now working closely with the CMHC's sleepy, white-haired vice-president, who eventually became a good friend. They played golf together, and one day on the course he told Gladue, "I wasn't asleep that day, you know, I was thinking of a way out of the problem." Gladue wrote later, "Now, having worked with him for years, and feeling his support, I believe him."

Basford had promised 50,000 new houses and in the end actually delivered 114,000 of them, all safe, warm and efficient. The government suits did their work well, setting up a path to responsible ownership under which each prospective owner paid one quarter of his or her income for 25 years, at which time the mortgage was fully paid and ownership was transferred free and clear to the mortgagor.

A few years after the Chetwynd housing project, Frank Oberle left government and went to live in Nanoose Bay, near Victoria. In retirement he received a phone call from Father Jungbluth, who said the village council was demanding a large sum in back taxes from the Chetwynd Housing Co. for the meeting hall and recreation centre. When the sum was not forthcoming, the councillors had hired a flatbed trailer and boom crane, lifted up the building, moved it to the apron of a runway at the village's small airport and turned it into the terminal building.[106]

Oberle flew back to Chetwynd and advised the shareholders that the building was not subject to taxes because it was used partly for religious purposes; generated no income, as it was never used for commercial purposes; and should be treated as a non-profit entity like the six churches in the village. He asked the council for the documents showing the minutes of the meeting when the decision to threaten the company had been taken, and so far as he could discover, the minutes did not exist. He told the shareholders they should ask the council for a copy of the real-estate appraisal in order to determine if the value of the building exceeded the taxes claimed, in which case the village would owe the company the difference. And the company should also ask for proof that the building had been offered for sale by auction as was required before any power of sale or transfer could be issued. The

FACHWERK VOLUNTEERS FROM GERMANY SUPERVISED BY
FRONTIERS' NORTHWEST ONTARIO FIELD COORDINATOR UDO
STASCHIK, BACK ROW CENTRE. KENORA, ONTARIO, SUMMER
1995. (COURTESY *KENORA DAILY MINER AND NEWS*)

shareholders listened and one of them said quietly, "Frank, we don't want to make a fuss, we just want to get along with our neighbours." *kiyem.*

Despite the difference of opinion about the community centre, however, the Chetwynd housing project was deemed a success by all involved. The project is not over and never will be, because it is irrevocably part of the history of Canada. The suits from the CMHC came to Chetwynd to ask people about the results. They found out what Charles and Frontiers already knew – that it was a great achievement and that almost any self-help project driven by local initiative with volunteer help and significant sweat equity must succeed. From that day on, and for some years, led and prodded by Gladue, the CMHC had a different attitude. What formerly had been impossible became the norm.

Other measures of the success in Chetwynd were many and encouraging. Moccasin Flats children, now living in safe, warm, affordable houses with electric lights shining on homework, soon matched or excelled the performance of the white children in school. Far more of the men living there got jobs, kept them and kept their families. Alcoholism dropped significantly. Fewer children were born out of wedlock.

The residential schools of Canada may well have been designed by white men to get the "Indian out of the Indian," but it appeared that this housing program had helped to put some "Cree into the white man." And he liked it.

Unfortunately, the Conservative government under Brian Mulroney inexplicably abandoned a fundamental principle of the true conservative, that individuals should be responsible for their own livelihood. Mulroney imposed a sunset clause of December 31, 1993, on the CMHC housing program inspired by Moccasin Flats, which had originally been open-ended. Gladue resigned to rejoin Frontiers Foundation as vice-president and later became president.

Some years later, in northern Ontario, Frontiers Foundation volunteers worked on a project that once again united Germans and Canadians in a constructive way. Charles wrote, "For this particular project, I felt an immense personal satisfaction. There were 12 young Germans co-operating with Canada's poorest people." The German organization was Fachwerk, a vocational training institute, which sent nine carpentry apprentices and three supervisor/trainees to Canada. They were led by Udo Staschik, an architect who had volunteered for Frontiers projects many times before. On the job, he and his team displayed and taught the legendary German efficiency: in 11 working days three houses were framed in, and within another week or so they were ready for occupation. Charles said, "Just one generation before, my father and Udo's father and millions of others like them were denied the tools of mercy and humanitarian services and compelled instead to try to kill each other." The sorrow and anger he had felt when George Bean was killed in the Second World War were finally dispelled by his sense of gratitude for the kindness of these young Germans. By middle age, Charles had achieved one of his life goals.

♠ ♠ ♠ ♠ ♠ ♠ ♠ ♠

THE PROMISED LAND

One warm spring day in 1973, Charles received a phone call from Bob Lee, president of the Kenora local of the Ontario Métis and Non-status Indian Association. Lee asked him to send a team of volunteers to help build houses for them in Kenora. Charles knew very well that if he accepted, he would be sending his young volunteers to work among people weighed down by poverty, alcoholism, child abuse, slum housing and inferior education. He also knew that Frontiers volunteers would be accused of "siding with the Indians" in heated racial disputes with some of the white people living in Kenora. From the beginning, Frontiers volunteers faced the strong prejudice against Aboriginal peoples that is common throughout Canada. Many of the most prejudiced lived in Kenora, Ontario, where hockey fans routinely jeered Aboriginal players, even those playing on the Kenora teams. Such people hated "Indians" and would not hire them or rent rooms to them. Violence against Aboriginal people in the city came to include murder: Max Kakegamic, from the North Spirit Lake reserve, was beaten to death on a street in downtown Kenora in 2000, and one well-known Toronto human rights lawyer, Julian Falconer, agreed to represent Kakegamic's family in a suit against the Kenora police.[107] As the world-renowned human rights expert Dr. Alfred De Zayas observed in an email to the author:

> It is a grotesque and hypocritical irony that the Canadian
> government regularly sends soldiers to make peace among
> warring factions in violent places such as Hàiti, Israel, Cyprus and Rwanda, while it scarcely notices the violence
> within its own borders, to which it regularly contributes
> by neglect and by refusal to live up to the terms of its own
> treaties.[108]

A significant number of the 16,000 or so white citizens of Kenora, who were for the most part hardworking, provident churchgoers, viewed the Aboriginal people as shiftless, drunk and violent – a common prejudice in many parts of Canada. The white people thought the First Nations people had too much land, while they had none; they thought the natives got lots of handouts from government, whereas they were cruelly taxed and got little in return; and they thought the status Indians had an unfair advantage because they did not have to pay taxes. Most of the white people of Kenora disliked Native people without even knowing them.

Having secured a tentative agreement with Frontiers, Bob Lee now had to recruit as many local volunteers as he could from the very mixed citizens of Kenora. His presence meant a lot to the people involved in the project, because Lee is Métis from Dauphin, Manitoba, at the time married to Fran, a status Ojibwa from Shoal Lake. Lee would rejoin a young volunteer from Zambia, Jim Chigwedere, veteran of projects in Lac Doré, Quebec (1966), Wabasca, Alberta (1968), Auden, Ontario (1970), and Chetwynd, British Columbia (1971).

Charles later described the beginning of the Kenora project thus:

> [T]he choice of project leader might well decide the success or failure of the project. Somehow we had to find a person who would win the respect, confidence and hopefully the participation of both Caucasians and Aboriginals. Fortuitously we were once again able to secure our star African … Jim Chigwedere for the job. Immediately, charismatic Jim won the affection and support of all, even of the mayor of Kenora, and the project took off impressively. The only problem with Mr. Chigwedere was that all the female volunteers – of whatever colour – fell in love with him. One of them accosted me saying, "Charles, why did you select a guy that looks like Sidney Poitier and sings like Harry Belafonte?"[109]

Having grown up in Rhodesia, Chigwedere had learned a lot about colonial rule and how to cope with white violence. It was no surprise to him that the white people of Kenora despised the Ojibwa of Grassy Narrows and the local Métis while knowing almost nothing about them. For instance, probably not a soul in town knew that the very white Canada that Kenorans were now so proud to call their own could not have come into existence without the help of the ancestors of the Ojibwa around them.

In the 1970s the people of Kenora, generally unaware of the provisions of their government's treaties, but resenting them anyway, were angry about Native land claims and protests that they thought interfered with their jobs of cutting down trees, building roads and digging mines. The Ojibwa, led in part by the councils of various bands in the area, chiefly at Grassy Narrows 22 miles northeast of town, demanded enforcement of the land clauses of Treaty 3. The band, represented by the Treaty Three Grand Council, owned about 16 square miles of land at Grassy Narrows where they had built their village. This was the reserve proper, but under the treaties signed by Sahkatcheway and 16 other chiefs in 1871–1873, they also had the usufruct of another 1,550 square miles around the reserve. This area became known as the "Ojibwa traditional lands," because it was here that they planned to carry on their customary trapping, moose hunting, fishing for pickerel, lake trout and sturgeon, gathering of roots and berries for food and medicine, and hunting for game birds. These activities, which to many white people, are just pleasant seasonal games without economic importance, were to the Aboriginal signatories of the treaty absolutely vital interests that formed their economy and culture, much as mines, factories and cultivated fields on deforested land form the economy of "white" Canada.

Quarrels between the white and Aboriginal peoples of Kenora arose in the 1950s when the Ontario government, in defiance of the treaty, began to authorize logging companies to enter traditional reserve land to cut trees. This effectively betrayed Treaty 3 because it destroyed the Aboriginal people's ability to exercise their rights to hunt, trap and fish on their traditional land. Most of the game, fish and birds would be destroyed because their habitat would devastated by the logging companies cutting trees and making roads through the forest.

When white loggers armed with new Ontario government permits began to cut trees, the people of Grassy Narrows went to court to maintain the integrity of their land, but they lost at every stage of the process. The cost, more than $500,000 (probably over $4-million today), exhausted the financial resources of the band members, who had always managed frugally on small incomes. As they saw it, the income they needed to defend their rights, which should never have been reduced to "claims," had been taken away by one of the very governments whose duty it was to protect them.

Métis people have much the same history as the Ojibwa: starved out of their land and their customary way of life by the inrush of loggers, settlers, miners, trappers, railway workers and farmers. They saw that governments and big businesses were the main causes of the decline in their livelihoods. The Grassy Narrows people were not only being starved by the degradation of their traditional lands, they were also being poisoned by the effluent from industry, particularly the new paper mill at Dryden, Ontario, on the English River. From the early 1960s to the late 1970s, the English–Wabigoon River system was severely contaminated with inorganic mercury, when Dryden Chemical Ltd., a subsidiary of Reed Pulp & Paper, dumped more than 40,000 pounds of mercury into the environment, including the Wabigoon River at Dryden.[110] About 16 miles of the English River ran through the home section of the reserve and some Métis land settlements nearby. The mercury poisoning that resulted, known as Minimata disease, caused birth defects, insanity and suicide in anyone drinking the water or eating the fish. As Craig Benjamin of Amnesty International commented in 2010, the situation in Grassy Narrows was "utterly shocking… One can't imagine this kind of injustice going unaddressed for 40 years in a non-aboriginal community… It is as if this kind of severe health problems and chronic unemployment are more acceptable … on a reserve."[111]

The pulp mill at Dryden emitted such a repulsive stink into the air that some first-time visitors arriving by plane recoiled from the airplane's doorway as it opened, and had to be pushed off the plane to disembark – or so the local joke went.

Charles was fully aware of the history of white–Aboriginal relations in the area, and the threats that racism might impose on Frontier volunteers. He chose to mitigate them with a joke. "Well, it looks like we're going to Kenora. I hear things are so bad there that relations are frosty even in summertime." Not everyone laughs with him when he utters such threadbare witticisms, but his cheerful attitude usually dampens any fuse that may be alight near the dynamite.

But the volunteers were not at all afraid of stepping into the middle of this dangerous situation. In fact, as Charles said, "We went there *because* it was so bad. The people obviously needed our help."

Bob Lee was also well aware of the historical problems in Kenora. Raised a "strong Pentecostal" on the prairies, Lee took seriously his church's ideal of service to others. The ubiquitous racism of Kenora lived not only in his mind and memory but also in the serious expression on his face. He and his wife Fran had walked away discouraged many times from the doors of houses and apartments in Kenora where they had been refused accommodation by white landlords because Fran, a status Ojibwa from Grassy Narrows, was deemed an unacceptable tenant. He had tried to interest the people of Kenora through the city council, the mayor's office and the churches in doing something to solve the rental-housing shortage that plagued both white and especially Aboriginal citizens, but he had been discouraged at almost every turn. It was when he hit on the idea of helping the Métis and Aboriginal peoples to own their own homes on city land that his hopes revived a little, and that's when he called Charles Catto in Toronto to ask for volunteers.

For the struggling foundation, merely getting the Kenora project going was close to a logistic nightmare. The needs of Lee's various applicants had to be received, judged and accepted or rejected, and overall budgets had to be set months before, which depended on grants that sometimes were promised but often not delivered. Once the volunteers were accepted, they had to be organized into teams, usually consisting of 6 to 12 men and women, and usually mixed as to occupations and skills, sometimes as to language, race and religion, but all propelled by volunteer fervour.

Charles had phoned Chigwedere in Zambia to ask him to take charge of much of this work, but someone had to inform him of the aim and specific problems related to the project, persuade UNESCO to cover his airfare to Toronto, assure that his passport was up to date and fix any visa problems that might exist. Once he was in Toronto, Chigwedere had to be briefed on the purpose and organization of the Ontario Métis and Non-status Indian Association, and he had to be warned about the often violent systemic racism in the area. Chigwedere understood that part of the Kenora project easily enough. In his final project director's report, he wrote:

For years, the feelings between whites and Indians have been strained and bitter. Many despise the Indians as dirty, lazy drunkards and look upon them as second-class citizens. A good many Indians just do not communicate with the whites. Living on the outskirts of town on reserves where beer and liquor are illegal – i.e., liquor stores, pubs and clubs offering alcohol are prohibited – many Indians throng into Kenora or as the saying goes, hit town for a beer. Some say this is one of the reasons why Indians of Kenora drink so much when in town. Rather than walk back some thirty miles to their homes, many decide to stay in town on a drinking spree for as long as their purses can stretch. It is no wonder that many a tourist walking in downtown Kenora is shocked at the sight of so many Indians hanging about and shuffling through the streets in a drunken state. At night some of the Indians literally sleep on the pavement.[112]

While the project was still only a rumour around town, some local young white people nicknamed the city land that was to be purchased for the new Frontier houses Squaw Valley. They also formed a street gang to beat up Indians. This gang, like a similar one formed years later named the Kenora Indian Bashers, sprayed racist graffiti around town and brought drums to Anishnabe Park, where they hammered away on them all night as if they themselves were the "wilderness savages," calling their "white tribes" to war.

What Bob Lee was hoping to create were 29 new homes to be set up by Frontiers people working with local volunteers. The new houses would be turned over to those who had helped build them. These would be the first Métis- or Aboriginal-owned housing units in the city of Kenora. Lee arranged to finance the materials for this ambitious project with the CMHC under the leadership of the cabinet minister in charge of housing, Ron Basford. The Richard and Jean Ivey Foundation of Toronto covered the cost of transportation, food, insurance, tools and so forth for the non-local volunteers.

In that summer of 1973, a century after Treaty 3 had been signed, 12 Frontiers volunteers arrived in Kenora and Bob Lee met them outside the Presbyterian church. Seeing them, Lee broke down. "When I saw

12 volunteers coming from all over the world when you couldn't get anyone here in town to help, I started to cry."[113]

But Lee's generous efforts had been noted and appreciated in town, perhaps more than he realized. The Presbyterian Church had decided to help, as had John Fullmer, pastor of the Lutheran church. Elva Ross, a member of Fullmer's congregation, went to the building site to cut down trees and clear away brush beside the machete-wielding Africans and Jamaicans. She said, "The Beavers were marvellous people, absolutely lovely." Fifty years later she remembers with great pleasure that they sat around campfires in the evening, trading stories of their lives, "even though the mosquitoes damn near killed us."[114] The mosquitoes and other conditions were literally sickening: many of the volunteers came down with a bacillary dysentery, also called shigellosis, which laid them out flat for about a week, but everyone, young and hardworking, got better.

Although the mosquitoes were plenty, the volunteer accommodations were later described by Ann Hopkins, a volunteer from Quebec and co-leader of the project with Chigwedere, as some of the best that Frontiers ever had. The volunteers stayed in the basement of the Kenora Fellowship Centre, which had a big kitchen, a hall with a stage and storage room, a laundry room with washer and dryer, two half bathrooms and a shower room. The women slept on the stage and the men slept in the room next to the laundry room. The kitchen had two large stoves and a refrigerator, plus a freezer loaned by a local family. Hopkins organized the cooking and cleaning on a rotating schedule. This was not only to share the workload equitably but also to make sure "that everyone had a chance to get to know everyone else a little bit better."[115]

A recurring and charming part of the volunteer experience is making new friends among the people they are helping and with the other volunteers. In line with Charles's usual advice, one of the first things the Kenora volunteers did after arriving was to arrange a familiarization meeting. They borrowed a big tent from a friend in Kenora, Brian Sinclair, and went away together for a weekend. Jammed into the extended cab and clinging to each other in the bed of a three-quarter-ton pickup, they drove to Bird's Hill Park, 130 miles away near Winnipeg, where they held a retreat. There were 12 different nationalities in the party that weekend, all strangers until then.[116]

This first orientation program started with a discussion of Frontiers philosophy, including personal statements made by each volunteer about why they had come. They also talked about their accomplishments on other projects, since several of them were repeat volunteers. This led to a discussion of group dynamics where they discussed openly the differences that had already begun emerging among the members. For instance, right from the start language had been a problem because not everyone could speak English fluently. Several spoke French, several Dutch, and some stood up and openly criticized some of the others for not making the effort to include them in group discussions. After only a few days, people were already hiving off into little cliques that threatened the essential group spirit of the enterprise. Some of the introverted ones spoke up, asking the domineering ones to cool it. But the volunteer spirit was so charming that even these potentially disastrous difficulties were eventually averted, mainly by open, democratic discussions leading to mutual agreement. Democratic decisions were to rule, and the role of the project director was defined as the arbiter of whatever the group had decided. Thus, in true Aboriginal fashion and without any lessons, their leader was not elevated to power but appointed to serve. As Chigwedere said later, "The beauty of it all was that it was the group itself which had found and prescribed the dose that cured it."

On Sunday, Bob Lee and Brian Sinclair explained the history of the Kenora exercise. For two years, members of the Kenora Non-status Indian and Métis Association and its housing project had been trying to get the houses started. Once they had some funding in place via the CMHC, they had had to get permission from the city council to go ahead and clear the land. Once that permission was in place, the prospect of gaining permission to build the houses soon after was good. At first the very idea of building so many "Indian" houses in town stirred up such hostility that no headway was made at all. Often the prejudice had seemed so strong that Lee and Sinclair had thought of giving up. But after recent municipal elections the political climate had changed. The new city council actually backed the project and offered its Lakeside site. Further, the council was willing to authorize the sale of the necessary 25 building lots. They guaranteed to pay $51,300 toward the cost of sewer services. Up to 1974 the town had refused to permit any clearing on the land, but suddenly the way was open. Lee had arranged for his members and local friends to come after their regular jobs finished and work in the evenings and weekends to get the land cleared. He arranged for a friendly local contractor, Kelly and Son, to lend a bulldozer and to deliver sand and other fill to help dry up the boggy land. The local taxi association donated fuel to run the project's trucks, sawmill and chainsaws.

A white lawyer who lived in a house near the site was vehemently opposed to the project because he thought that "Indians" living nearby would depress the value of his house. Since he owned a second house farther away, he immediately sold the "threatened" house and moved into the other. Generally, however, Lee was able to mollify local citizens with the news that the project was not only generating jobs for local suppliers on the site but also would help a local industry, Canadian Instant Buildings Inc., who were under contract to supply prefabricated insulated panels for the house walls.

At last the work could begin. The volunteers oiled up their chainsaws, poured in the free gasoline, sharpened their machetes and started in. According to Jim Chigwedere,

> the site was a jungle…we soon turned it into an orchestra,
> the caterpillar zooming away, mowing the trees and steam-
> rollering them away to the dumping ground; the chainsaws
> whining away felling trees; the axes clattering with a bang
> as tree after tree came down; the machetes chewing and
> gnawing the underbrush; Gord Carmichael shouting, "Here
> comes Tarzan…!"

One young Jamaican wielding a chainsaw ogled Sabine Giesber, who was walking near him in her halter top and shorts. He was so intent on her that he cut off the toe of his boot with the forgotten saw.

Some locals had said it would take three weeks to clear the site; the volunteers did it in eight days. But there were many frustrating delays after that. Permission to build the foundations was not forthcoming. Then, when they did receive permission, the man they were paying to pour the foundations departed from the site with only half the footings poured. Bulldozers arrived to upgrade the onsite road, while the surveyors and engineers were still busy planning on paper and staking the lots. At that point, Charles and Barbara Catto arrived by car, en route to a Frontiers Foundation project in Alberta. This would have been summer holidays for other Canadians but for the Cattos there never has been a holiday from Frontiers Foundation – it is their life. They had their three children plus a volunteer going to work with them in Alberta. On his way through, Charles inspected and approved the Lakeview site and encouraged the volunteers.

While he was there, Charles also helped work out a unique arrangement that would help the volunteers fill their enforced downtime with useful work. Canadian Instant Buildings had a work site at Minaki, 34 miles away, where they were completing some renovations to a famous old resort hotel. The company was behind schedule with the project and late fines could cost them a lot of money, so the volunteers suggested that during the delay resulting from the missing contractor, they should go to Minaki and help the company finish on time. Frontiers would get credit for time worked at Minaki, which the company would pay back by assigning employees to help at the housing site in Kenora for nothing.

The volunteers also helped the people of Kenora and band members from the reserve to set up a centennial powwow in the city in August. The Native Women's Association needed construction help to put up a concession booth. The volunteers not only helped build it, they mostly ran it during the powwow. At the end, the association gave them a big cheque to help with the housing project.

During the summer, the cheerful young strangers charmed the local citizens with their open and friendly attitude everywhere they went in Kenora, and by playing pickup baseball games with the young men and boys. The volunteer women took local children for walks, sing-songs and picnics, and the locals responded by offering parties and a trip round the many islands and bays of Lake of the Woods on the famous old wooden tour boat *Argyle II*.

Kenora's mayor was amazed at the harmony that now prevailed on the work site. The provocative racist drumming was replaced by beery karaoke singing, the street brawls gave way to churning cement mixers on site, the Christians in the ultra-wary Kenora churches began talking comfortably to other Christians from churches on the reserve or on the Métis land nearby.

The main summer parties in Kenora include wiener roasts and barbecues, and very slowly, over the months as relations warmed up, the volunteers were invited to more and more of these. A few of them drank beer, wine or liquor, which according to Frontiers policy were forbidden on the work site and at the hostel. The few volunteers who had a drink or two also went to the bars and pubs, where they made friends with the locals. During the two summer seasons of the Kenora project (1973 and 1974), the citizens of Kenora, themselves descended from a mixed crowd of American, English, French, German, Irish, Polish and Scottish immigrants, frequently hosted and entertained their volunteer guests. There were picnics, dances, sing-songs, karaoke parties, barbecues, bingo and ball hockey. In the words of Chigwedere,

> By a combination of the above factors many felt that the volunteers were a useful vehicle of communication and to some small extent helped to defuse an explosive situation. But it would be idle to think that the situation is saved. The local people themselves have to find their own solution to the problem once they are on talking terms. If the volunteers helped some locals to be on talking terms, then some achievement was made.[117]

So the volunteers were not only helping a small number of people who were in need, in the larger community they were creating good will and happiness where there had been suspicion, ignorance and hostility. This kind of good will was assured by the spirit in which they approached Frontiers, which was expressed in its founding document: "assist Canadians of all races to understand one another better through the comradeship of ecumenical work-camping so that lasting bridges of respect and affection may be built."[118]

The houses Frontiers built in Kenora were generally 1,200-square-foot, three-bedroom balloon-framed bungalows on solid cement foundations with crawl spaces or full basements. They were insulated to the highest standards of the time, eventually to R28; each had a fully equipped kitchen, furnace, full bathroom and solid-core doors. The young volunteers, the new owners and their friends hammered the 20-year Brantford roofing onto three-quarter-inch tongue-and-groove plywood. Clean water was piped in via trenches dug below frost level, and the hydro system was 100 amps (later upgraded to 200 amps) with breaker panels and copper wiring. The plumbing was copper, and the kitchen and bathroom were connected to a septic system adequate for six to eight people.

The two-by-four and two-by-six lumber was kiln-dried spruce that had been cut, milled and dried by Frontiers machines. And – as a final touch – the happy new owner felt a boost to his pride as he showed his wife and children around the house he had helped to build himself. By the end of September 1973, four houses had been framed in and several new shells had been completed, while other houses were rising on nine more foundations.

Ray Polson, an Algonquin volunteer on a different project, expressed it for all when he said, "I was a shivering Indian living in a basket. I had to hold my hat on my head inside. Now I'm blessed – I got tight windows." There is such satisfaction in the Frontiers approach that whole families through several generations volunteer their summer holidays to help others as they were helped themselves. Members of the Polson family of Pikogan, Quebec, who grew up in a Frontiers-built house, joined the volunteers year after year. Glenn, Laura, Betsy, Ray, Virginia, Gloria, Sonny and Joshua all gave up their summer holidays in order to help provide a big, comfortable new house for other children of Aboriginal families like theirs.

The volunteers benefited too, of course. Every time three or four of the men joined strength to tilt up a section of wall, they were growing a bond they would never break and never forget. They were embarking on a way of life that would endure forever, beyond even their own lifetimes, because their experiences became pleasing memories they could tell their children. The good news that Lee and Chigwedere and Charles loved to promise and promote in these projects was coming true faster than any of them had dared to hope.

By the time the Kenora houses were finished, the Canadian press was beginning to recognize Frontiers' work, but incomprehension was still evident, even in the work of liberal writers published in popular journals. For instance, in 1974, Walter Stewart, known nationally for his attack-dog journalism, wrote a generally sympathetic report of the work that Frontiers did in Kenora and Prince Edward Island. He was sympathetic, but he completely missed the animating spirit of the young volunteers and of the organization itself. Stewart gave an accurate rundown of their material achievements, which were considerable. He even mentioned the benevolent side of the changes in the attitudes of the many Kenora citizens, and he did not omit the violence that was endemic to the area. But the closest he came to showing an understanding of the true aims of Frontiers was in his description of an oyster farmer in Prince Edward Island, John Fitzgerald, whom he quoted:

> The day I met the plane at Charlottetown and I got the first look at the volunteers, I said to myself, "What in hell have I done?" I was just like a lot of ignorant people when I seen the dark skin and the long hair… It took me about two days to crawl out from under my shell and do you know the first thing I said to myself? "John, you stupid bastard. Those are the kind of people that were back in Christ's days when they helped a poor man out. They don't stick out their hand all the time for money. They are here to help you, you stupid bitch." From then on, man, we were friends.

Stewart concluded, "The criticism may be made of Frontiers that, except for providing everyone a shining example, its works are nothing more than band-aid operations. That may be true, but at least it beats standing around watching the patient bleed to death."[119]

In the trivializing cliché "shining example," the story neatly exemplifies the bewildered embarrassment most of us feel when we are confronted with hard-driving, hard-believing Christians like the volunteers who are animated by the spirit of love. Charles wrote a laconic description of such people in his annual report of 1976, describing the St. Martin Welfare Association's work in Trinidad:

> [They are] busily engaged in social, voluntary and community action programs such as technical education, skill training, old age assistance, meals on wheels and serving catering co-ops. The number one priority of St. Martin is providing a second opportunity in life to those who feel helpless, lonely, shut-in and dejected.[120]

In 1974 the volunteers in Kenora completed the foundations for 29 houses, three of which were roughed in at the end of the season and were partly habitable before Christmas. With the help of local citizens, the road, water and sewerage facilities were completed the following year, along with the rest of the houses themselves. The ancient prejudices began to dissipate as the Aboriginal families settled warily into their new houses.

Speaking of the phenomenal success of the project, Charles said, "Credit for this success goes to their patient, courageous and determined fight."[121] By "their fight," he meant the work of the local Métis and band members. After the project he had helped start was finished, Bob Lee, a son of the prairie, realized he was "sick of water, rock and trees,"[122] and left for the broad land around Dauphin, Manitoba, where he had grown up.

That Frontiers and the volunteers were essential to the peace process in Kenora was shown later, more than 30 years after the building project was complete. A new mine to dig for platinum on traditional land was proposed, and band leaders of Grassy Narrows were jailed for protesting. Several of the chiefs, known locally as the KI6 ("KI" meaning Kitchenuhmaykoosib Inninuwug First Nation), were fined severely and jailed for their peaceful demonstration against the intrusion of Platinex mining on their lands. The case of the KI6 was briefly famous across the country and resulted in a moral victory for the chiefs and people of the reserves they represented, but it appears from subsequent events at Attawapiskat, Brantford, Fort McMurray and elsewhere that neither governments nor private interests have learned much from the outcome.

Bad habits die hard. There are 19 churches for the 16,000 people of Kenora, but a worldwide peace activist organization called Christian Peacemakers (CP) sent a team there in 2005 to educate the white people in the tenets of their own religion. The first CP team remained eight months. Another was there for a couple of months during 2005 and yet another in 2006. The CP teams comprise Christians who have decided to "get in the way" of violence so that they can, by example and by education, help to calm soldiers and terrorists in violent areas such as Israel, Palestine, Colombia, the US–Mexico border and Canada.

Soon after the houses were completed and occupied, Bob Lee summed up the project optimistically in a letter to Charles:

Here's hoping to find you and all your volunteers in good health.... The Kenora Metis and Non-Status Indian Association would be very pleased in having them return to Kenora for another summer.... In having them here, we all learned a new kind of working-together feeling which in turn was more fun than work.

This group is one of the finest that I personally have ever worked with. The Town and Council are quite happy to have them return to Kenora. As you know, Kenora has had a bad image from news reports and other happenings that take place here. But our group along with the volunteers, have created a new kind of image, one in which people are starting to work together instead of against each other. This is something we have all wanted to do for a long time and the volunteers took an active role in drawing people together. There remains a lot of community relations yet to be resolved. For this reason alone we find the volunteers a great assistance.[123]

Lee's optimism, however, was not fully justified by the final results. Thirty years after the paint had dried and the last owner had moved into the Frontiers houses, not one of the original occupants remained in the houses. In general, this was not a sign of the failure of the project: the people who had built these houses moved into them and liked them and lived in them. And then, as their lives changed, they sold them and left, just like Bob Lee himself, who ended up moving back to Manitoba. That's because just like millions of other Canadians, they were now free to choose where they live.

However, some of the houses that were built with such effort and faith were soon lost to the builder/owners because the CMHC ruled that the whole project was in default. Fewer than the projected number of houses had been built. This was because the local subcontractor who had guaranteed to supply building panels for all of the planned 32 houses absconded with the money for them, having delivered panels for only ten. By last-minute scrambling and innovating, the volunteers managed to complete 29, but the CMHC believed it had to live up to its own rules, and the organization repossessed sufficient houses to satisfy its bookkeepers. Now, none of the houses is occupied by a First

Nations or Métis person – all the owners are white people. Over the years, white owners bought their houses while Métis people were still living next door or across the street. But the value of the work and the integrity of the neighbourhood are attested by the price of the houses: the latest sales of Frontiers houses in the area, where properties were once literally dirt cheap, were for more than $200,000 each. Their value is high because the spirit endures.

Unfortunately the levels of mercury in the First Nations reserve near Kenora also endure. In the summer of 2012, the *Toronto Star* reported that "the latest report by Japanese experts in mercury poisoning – who have shown far more interest in this environmental disaster than Canadian officials ever have – found ongoing health problems."[124] Of the 160 persons tested in 2010, 59 per cent had symptoms of mercury poisoning. The *Star* has kept hammering away at the issue, not only mercury poisoning but at the general issues of white treatment of First Nations, and the reason may be that Charles himself, alone in his work-strewn office, picked up the phone and called them when there was news. In fact, what Charles saw as news often became news.

THE HONOUR OF
THE CROWN

A purple mountain falls from its cloud to the green Widzenkwa River, and the river falls to the sea past a high scaffold where a man dressed in a bark loincloth stands with a gaff pole in his hands. He feels the water with the hook, then jerks it up. A heavy fish, wildly flapping, pulls him toward the rushing water, but a spruce-root rope tied to the scaffold holds him as he flips the thrashing fish up to the wooden stage behind him, then kills it with one slash of his knife. He quickly guts it, throws it in a cedar-wood box and later carries it down with many others to Hagwilget village, where he shares it with his family and friends.[125] This scene repeats for many generations.

The first intimations of a mighty change to this scene were the iron pots, muskets, steel knives and blankets that these fishing people, the Wet'suwet'en-speaking tribes of north-central British Columbia, began to receive in trade from their neighbours, the Tsimshian-speaking peoples of the West Coast. Russian-speaking traders had arrived, seeking furs for the fashionable women of China and the court of St. Petersburg on the far side of the world. Then, down the green river from the east came a white explorer with Gaelic in his mouth, Alexander Mackenzie, from Canada, the first white man to cross the continent, and the first of the explorers, fur traders and missionaries to enter the region. Soon many more came overland from Canada and upriver from ships on the Pacific coast, seeking timber, converts to their particular brands of Christianity, and a route for a railway. One entrepreneur came with men, horses and huge drums of copper wire, building a telegraph line from North America to Europe.

Along with the plagues that spread into this valley from Canada came the residential schools program, which ruined the childhood of George Muldoe from the village of Kispiox. Residential school was so painful for him and his family that he has spent much of his later

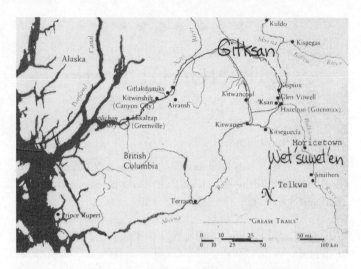

MAP OF THE BC BUILDING SITES, FROM A FRONTIERS REPORT
BY BOAZ TSAIRI. THE VILLAGE OF HAGWILGET (NOT MARKED)
IS ON THE BULKLEY RIVER JUST EAST OF HAZELTON.

life pursuing a lawsuit against his tormentors. When he became chief,
Muldoe, whose ancestry is Gitxsan, was a sombre-looking man. In his
strong-featured face you can see the inspiration for the heads in the
powerful totem sculptures of the coastal peoples of British Columbia.
Muldoe has a vision for his people: to raise them from the poverty, despair and ill health that came with white society.

When Muldoe heard about the work of Frontiers' volunteers, he
temporarily laid aside his research work into residential schools and
called Don Irving. Formerly a foundation volunteer in Ontario, Irving had been asked in 1974 to come on staff as the western coordin-
ator/supervisor for Frontiers. His first big job was supervising the
work at Kispiox and Moricetown, the foundation's first major, long-
term commitment in British Columbia. As is usual with Frontiers, Irving responded to a request from the Aboriginal people themselves,
and he has come, over the years, to view his job as assisting them to
realize their own plans. A good-natured redhead with a deep, rumina-
tive voice, Irving chooses volunteers so well that many of them come
round for second and third terms.

After Charles told me I should go to Kispiox, Moricetown and Hagwilget to complete the research for this book, my wife Elisabeth and I met Irving in Vancouver and we flew north to Prince George in late summer 2010. Huge tracts of standing dead timber reddened the mountains beneath our wings and all along the highway as we drove west in our rented car. These were the visible effects of global warming, which had enabled the mountain pine beetle to survive in areas where winter cold had formerly killed them off. As we travelled, Irving reminisced about his experiences with Frontiers and with Charles.

Irving was driving as we headed from Prince George toward Smithers, on the way to Hagwilget. We gradually left the despoiled region of dead trees behind and entered the broad, wooded valleys leading west toward blue and green mountains filling the windshield. Irving's stories of Frontiers made me laugh so hard I couldn't take coherent notes, so Elisabeth craned forward from the rear seat to write them down. As we drove past long trainloads and storage yards of red timber harvested from the devastated forests behind us, Irving told the very strange story of Charles in the parking lot. Charles and Irving had been on their way in a borrowed car to an important fundraising meeting in downtown Toronto. They parked the car, got out, locked it and then realized that they had left important documents in the trunk. And that the owner had neglected to include the trunk key with the ignition key.

Charles said, "Wait a minute," and then stood in the parking lot saying nothing, but looking around. After a few minutes while he seemed to be in a trance, Charles walked over to a car that had just driven in and parked. The driver was walking toward Charles, who stopped him and explained the situation. The driver sympathized and said, "You'll have to break in."

But Charles said, "Let me just try opening it with your key." The surprised driver, telling Charles that he was nuts, handed over his keys. Charles stuck one into the trunk lid and opened it.

Astounded, the stranger said, "How did you know that?"

Charles explained that he had read that this particular automaker had saved some money for that model year by making all the keys from a single pattern with few variations. This meant that each key would open the appropriate vehicle, but some keys might open two or even three. Charles had hit on the right key.

I was able to contribute another story that took place in Toronto. Charles had come to dinner at our house and I was serving wine as I normally do. He refused the wine as he always did, and I teased him about his aversion to alcohol by saying I was the president of the Reformed Teetotallers Association of Canada, although I had only just that moment dreamed it up. I said that the RTTA encourages the drier among us to enjoy life more by giving up their dry habit and taking a glass of wine when it is unnecessary, as Jesus and St. Paul prescribed. When I asked him to be chaplain to the RTTA, Charlie replied immediately: "I don't think the RTTA would ever make Charlie Chaplain." Irving and I agreed this was pretty nimble for someone with a dry sense of humour.

As we drove along, Irving topped my Charles story with his about the first time he met Charles at the Frontiers headquarters in Toronto. A meeting was about to start in the front office when Irving heard a timid knocking at the back door, which opened onto a broad parking lot, mostly empty. Two boys about 10 years old were standing there with hockey sticks in their hands, and the braver one said, "Can Charlie come out to play?" Irving turned and called Charles, who seized his hockey stick from behind the door and went out for one of his regular sessions of ball hockey. The meeting began after the hockey ended.

After an overnight stay in Smithers, we eventually rolled into Hagwilget at the foot of its enormous purple mountain just as Irving was telling an amusing story about Charles and the Frontiers accountant of years before, James Gesner, nicknamed Scrooge because he was always giving dire warnings about the foundation's precarious finances. Presenting the interim accounts, Scrooge liked to say, "Looks bad, I'd give you three weeks." Charles would just laugh. Gesner ran on money, Charles ran on faith, and the two don't meet, except on the books of Frontiers Foundation, where, somehow, faith continues to write the bottom line.

Charles once asked Gesner to come to Haiti with him to check the books of the volunteers there. Gesner said yes and immediately went to his doctor for the requisite immunizations. Charles took no special precautions. They flew together to Haiti, and when they arrived Gesner ate only what his doctor had advised. Charles, on the other hand, ate and drank everything he was offered. Despite the precautions

Gesner took, he got very sick, while Charles came home healthy and working. Finishing this story as we drove on to Kispiox, Irving said, "I figured in the end it was some vast, karmic God-joke." When asked about this, Charles just laughed.

Gitxsan chief George Muldoe welcomed us to Kispiox, whose history he has helped to record.

As a 3-year-old boy in 1951, Muldoe had been forced into a train car where he had to stand for hours with hundreds of strangers en route to a United Church residential school in St. Albert, just northwest of Edmonton. There had been terrible suffering among the bewildered children on the train and in that school. After he matured, he co-operated with former United Church minister Kevin Annett in creating a book called *Hidden from History: The Canadian Holocaust*, in which Annett charges all the Canadian churches and the federal government with collusion in committing genocide against the Aboriginal people by many means, including the residential school system. Muldoe has made it his mission to find and rebury some of those children's corpses. He has brought suit against government and churches for their transgressions.

Of all the white people he encountered in his years in residential school, Muldoe had never seen any like the 38 volunteers Irving rounded up for him and his Kispiox project. They were young, full of enthusiasm and received not a penny in pay. They were there simply because they had been invited and were needed. The whole thing to them was something of a lark. But these larks could not only sing, they hammered nails, carried cement and worked happily from dark to dark.

Eighteen frame houses and two made of logs were projected to be built for Kispiox. They would replace dilapidated shacks cobbled together from scraps of plywood and heated by dangerous home-built stoves. The new houses were built by foreman Andy Dennis and volunteers Andy Alfred, Clarence Dennis, Gord Holland, Larry Jim, Bill Mitchell, Henry Mitchell, Frank Naziel, René Tait and Larry Tom, all from the village and recruited by Muldoe himself. They were joined by 38 other volunteers from British Columbia, England, Germany, Ghana, Japan, Manitoba, Ontario, Quebec, the USA and St. Kitts and Anguilla in the Caribbean.

Among them were Boaz Tsairi of Israel and Neil Jefferson of New

Zealand, who had never met each other before. They were challenged to design and build a log house, so they bought the "how to" book of a well-known log-house designer/builder, sketched out their own version of it and put it up. When we saw it 30 years later, it looked only a few years old and was still warm in winter and weatherproof in all seasons.[126]

"Our people welcomed the first white men who came here," Chief Dan Michell said as he welcomed us to his house when we arrived at the village of Moricetown on the Wet'sinkwha (Bulkley) river north of Smithers. He was seated in the comfortable living room of his well-made three-bedroom house on the gravel Beaver Road, named thus because every house on it came via Frontiers and had been built by "Beavers." In gratitude for Michell's services to the people, primarily in getting these houses built, the other villagers gave this house to their chief.

Michell shows his visitors the talking stick, a symbol of his rank. It is an elegant pole of carved cedar, inlaid with copper and mother of pearl. Briefly he holds it, point resting on the floor as he speaks, while at the other end of the room a radio scanner broadcasts the conversations taking place in various trucks driving around the village.

The initial contacts between European and indigenous peoples here had been very like the early ones in central and eastern Canada: bewildered and dying white men encountered Aboriginals who saved their lives with food, medicines and maps. But very soon, smallpox and measles epidemics hit the people of the villages, bringing them so low that elder Thomy Namox told a village boy in 1920, "In ancient times, [when I was a] boy, lots of people. Now when white man come, all sick, sick ... Now just a little bit of people."[127]

Then lumbermen came, cut the trees and set up a sawmill, although there was no treaty governing this use of land and resources. Later on, the Canadian government "developed policies" to "handle" the Indians. "There were 14 floors of people working in Ottawa," said Michell, "but we didn't see them. We didn't know anything about them. Oh, we got a few rubber boots one time. I don't know what happened to the money." As far as he was concerned, the money poured out in Ottawa was a river that never got to the sea.

One day a few years ago, Michell had been informed by a man from the Department of Indian Affairs and Northern Development that he would have to move his cabin, which was located in good hunting territory a few miles away. The DIAND man said the cabin was illegal. When Michell protested, the stranger said that the government would burn it down unless he moved it. The man had a strong foreign accent, so Michell asked, "How long have you lived here in Canada?"

"Two months," the man replied.

Michell said, "You've only just got here and you tell me I'm trespassing?" He hired a lawyer, using government funds provided through the intelligently designed Test Case Funding Program,[128] and won his case against DIAND. On appeal by the government, he won again, in the Supreme Court of Canada.

After the chief went public with his story, a white writer asked, "Is there any hope for the white man?"

Michell's impassive face cracked a smile as he said, "You're a joker."

On the Bulkley River live the Wet'suwet'en people of the village of Hagwilget, where, on April 15, 1955, 40 elders gathered to draw up a petition that started a campaign to save their village and their lives. The Department of Fisheries and Oceans had been nosing around the village, and rumours reached the people that the government was planning to "improve" the salmon fishery, which constituted their main livelihood. The Wet'suwet'en people know the saying "the more you improve it, the worse it gets," which seems especially true when white people "improve" things for Aboriginals.

The Wet'suwet'en ancestors had built their village here precisely because of that salmon fishery, which depended on one big rock that narrowed the river, concentrating the salmon swimming upstream in late summer to spawn. This made the plentiful fish easy prey to a skilful man with a gaff, and so the people were satisfied with their lives.

The 1955 petition began: "We the Hagwilget people petition that the Hagwilget Canyon be left as it is." In reply, they got a letter from the department saying that it had "employed outstanding authorities on engineering and hydraulics to inspect the canyon" and decided that the fishery needed to be "improved." There would be a further decision later about the best way to do this, but they would not meet with the band until "such time as the decision is reached."[129] The rumour was that the government wanted to blow up the rock.

The experts, ignoring the huge thefts of salmon by the big Inverness cannery at the mouth of the river, along with the pollution of the river's spawning grounds by the white men's lumbering, had decided that the salmon runs were down because the big rock in the middle of the river had suddenly reduced the number of fish that spawned in it. And so the government bulled ahead, indifferent to the advice of the only people in the world with long experience of that fishery, which coincided, incidentally, with the advice of other outside experts hired by the villagers themselves. The government paid no attention to villager Phillip Austin, who asked, "The rock has been here a long time, fish know how to get through for a long time, why don't the fish still know how?" It appeared that the government was determined to improve the fishery even if that meant destroying it.

An access road was needed for trucks to bring in equipment and supplies for the workers to blast the rock. The villagers were not asked about this but were informed that there would be a meeting on July 29, 1958. On that date, eight bureaucrats from three departments of government arrived in the village, but suddenly all the able-bodied men of the village were called out to fight forest fires. Only four men, all old and sick, were left behind. The bureaucrats held the meeting mainly among themselves. At a later meeting the elders and the council voted unanimously against giving permission for the access road. Informed of this, the department threatened to get an order-in-council giving it the right of entry and access without the consent of the people of Hagwilget. Faced with the prospect of defying a legal order, and the RCMP, which was sure to follow to enforce it, the council reluctantly conceded permission for the road to be built.

On the morning of the blast, white engineers and workers began drilling the rock to insert the dynamite. Above them on the bridge to the reserve, the people lined up with rocks, protesting. One of the village girls standing there, carefully lobbing rocks not too near the workers, was Dora Kenni (later Wilson). How to resist the white man was part of the little girl's education. When she was 6 years old, the same people who had come for George Muldoe in Kispiox also came for her in Hagwilget. She and her mother Sadelalgex and her grandmother

Yaglahl, who had sensed in advance some of the horrors hidden inside the residential school system, stood in the doorway of their house and Yaglahl said, "She's not going." The police threatened her with jail. But she stood firm and the police went away, never to come back. As Dora said later, "She was a scary woman."

The rock was blasted with a tremendous bang. The following season, very few salmon came up the river, and, because the water was flowing much more slowly through the newly widened river canyon, they were virtually uncatchable at Hagwilget. The villagers would have to look elsewhere for their food, but as a result of logging, trapping and hunting by white people, there was now also less game in the woods than ever before. The government offered welfare, but it was grudgingly little, and it went against the independent spirit of these people to accept handouts if there was any alternative. Some of the villagers began to think of education as a stern necessity if the people were to survive.

Yaglahl did not object to education, of course, not even to white man's education, as long as it avoided the dangers of the residential school system. So she and Sadelalgex sent little Dora to a Roman Catholic day school nearby. Dora remembers some of her teachers there with distaste because they were so strict. One made her wash her mouth out with soap for uttering the word hell. But one teacher, a Mennonite named George Thiessen, encouraged in her a love of learning that lasted her lifetime. Her taste for education stimulated instead of destroyed by white teachers, she graduated, went to Vancouver to study accounting, then returned to help out in the village office.[130]

As the consequences of the blast expanded toward disaster, more meetings were held. The department, which had promised that the run would not be reduced, and if it were, the fish lost to the village would be replaced, now suggested that the people fish with nets from boats on the Skeena downriver, but this territory either belonged to others or was claimed by others. The Wet'suwet'en custom was to salt, dry and smoke the salmon, and the fish were in a superior condition for that processing when they arrived at Hagwilget because of the effort it took them to swim farther upriver. Besides, the runs were now much reduced since the establishment of the cannery and the "development" by dynamite: where 70,000 had passed in the canyon before, the runs were now averaging around 6,000. The department proposed to buy fish downriver to replace the ones they had blown away. Some few were delivered in cans, perhaps from the Inverness cannery downstream. Another year, a few fresh fish were delivered but not nearly enough. Present in the village one day in 1978, when more inedible government fish were delivered, was a young lawyer from the lower mainland named Peter Grant, who saw and smelled the rotting fish. Dora remembers him saying, "The government is not honouring its promise in good faith." Furthermore, for years the department did not satisfy claims by the villagers for property damaged or destroyed when the access road was built.

As the historian of the village, Maureen Cassidy, describes it, with the destruction of the rock, the relationship of the village people to the land and the river had been altered beyond repair. The rock could not be replaced.[131]

Dora Kenni Wilson had recently become the village manager of Hagwilget when Don Irving's Frontiers volunteers descended with a whoop on Moricetown and Kispiox to have fun building houses and save the world while meeting girls and boys. But partly as a result of the destruction of the fishery, apathy was spreading in Hagwilget. Many people thought, "It doesn't matter what we want or what we try to do, someone comes along and tells us to stop or takes it away, and there is nothing we can do." The old ways were being destroyed, the elders were seen to be more or less powerless, alcoholism was becoming rampant, young people were killing themselves, hardly anyone graduated from school, and the game in the bush was as scarce as the salmon in the Bulkley. But Wilson was not depressed. She could practically hear the cheers of joy from Kispiox when people finished a house and danced on the new floor, and she decided to act. She looked at the tumble-down houses, the fertile bench land where the only things growing were rusty old pickup trucks and she thought, in the spirit of Yaglahl and Sadelalgex, "We can do better than this." She campaigned on that belief and was elected village manager, then mayor. As soon as she could, she picked up the phone and called Don Irving of Frontiers Foundation. Irving immediately agreed to co-operate with her villagers.

Irving in Surrey, BC, Charles in the Toronto office and the band council of Hagwilget started in June 1976 to organize volunteers to fix up the houses in the village. The first four volunteers aimed to build new and renovate the old; they were joined by many other youngsters throughout the next 20 years. By 1996 the whole village of about 35 to 40 houses was either new or largely renovated. As of this writing, the houses rebuilt or extensively renovated by local and outside volunteers number about 90.

Here, as elsewhere, the first problem faced by the incoming volunteers was to find somewhere to live themselves while preparing a place for others. In Hagwilget they began a new house while living in one of the houses they had been sent to renovate, then as soon as possible moved into the house they were building to start on the next one. They had arrived strongly motivated, but this immediate challenge gave them an urgent new impetus. Beyond that, and as usual, the young foreigners and Canadians were enchanted by the village and the people who lived there.

On most Frontiers sites, nearly all the volunteers are young and healthy and share close quarters. All of them feel the tremendous gravitational force of youth, health, happiness and a shared enterprise uniting them, on site and at night. Charles, who was straitlaced about the public arrangements that young people make for private matters, adopted a hands-off policy toward their hands-on policy. However, as Wilson says, "We are all taught in this village to make strangers welcome." It is normal that this welcome may occasionally include the invitation "welcome to my body." The volunteer Lilija Stoeppler of Germany welcomed her friend Roddie and went back to Germany at the end of the season with his gift inside her, a son. Stoeppler returned many times to Hagwilget, always bringing her son Jesse, who in the end decided to live there. As head of the local fire department, Jesse (James) Stoeppler is perhaps the only chief in the world who can issue instructions to put out fires in both German and Wet'suwet'en. He not only protects the people in the houses built by his mum and dad, but he also takes nephews and nieces and young friends into the bush to hunt or fish, and he leads them in sports.

Charles commented, "When we asked them to foster creative and amiable relations among the group, the community and the organization, we weren't expecting them to respond quite so energetically."[132] Volunteer Boaz Tsairi, an inventive and self-confident youth from Israel, felt a tremendous force pulling him toward fellow volunteer Kyoko Shishikura of Japan. Although initially she did not like his participating in the local hunt, she was impressed by Tsairi's solution to a serious problem among the volunteers. Someone among them had been stealing money; Tsairi, suspecting the culprit, saw her proffer a Canadian $50 bill in a store and said, "How did you get that?"

The woman said, "When I came through Toronto."

Tsairi asked the storekeeper to show it to him, examined the bill's serial number and then said to the thief, "This is one the Mounties can trace. You stole it, didn't you."

The woman confessed and Tsairi became a momentary hero, especially to Shishikura. Tsairi and Shishikura married and went to Jerusalem, where they opened Sakura, a sashimi restaurant.

The village itself exerts that same tremendous gravitational pull that most volunteers feel among themselves, for it drew Tsairi and Shishikura back later on, long after they married. The couple have several times returned to Hagwilget with babies, not hammers. They came back again in 2009 with their four children in a convoy of three SUVs. Hagwilget is now a main stop on their trade route between Tel Aviv and Tokyo.

In about 1985, almost 30 years after the destruction of the fishery, the village became fed up with the delays and deceptions of the government lawyer, so they hired Peter Grant to prepare a formal claim. Grant was familiar with the area and with some similar problems involving other villages. He generously and perhaps daringly agreed to go ahead with only small interim payments, but he and the village were constantly stymied by repeated delays imposed by the government. When Wilson criticized the government's handling of the matter to one of the government men, he threatened her with court action. This could have been a serious danger to her, for she had years before lost her status in the band – she had married a white man – and had only recently regained it. Wilson, who is less than 5 feet tall, gazed up at the big man and said calmly, "You don't scare me."

In 2003, some 18 years after litigation had begun, and 44 years after the rock exploded, the government advised the people that even if litigation went ahead, there was another stage to be passed, which would take another 20 years and could not possibly be expedited. By then many of the litigants and witnesses would have died, just like the potential beneficiaries in the famously interminable inheritance case imagined by Charles Dickens, Jarndyce v. Jarndyce.[133]

Thus the Wet'suwet'en litigation had been formally placed in abeyance, but in 2005 Mr. Justice James Hugessen of the Federal Court of Canada was appointed as case-management judge. "My first active involvement with the case was to hear and dismiss a motion to strike the action brought by the Crown some 20 years after the case had been started," he wrote.[134] The Crown appealed that ruling, then discontinued the appeal two years later. Of these repeated delays Hugessen commented, "...I would above all note the quite extraordinary delays to which the plaintiffs have been put by the tactics of the Crown both before and after the launching of this litigation. Almost 50 years have passed since the blasting of the rocks and only a few members of the band remain who can remember the fishery that once was theirs. For over 25 years the plaintiffs were continuously put off by a series of unkept and broken promises that the situation would somehow be remedied."[135]

The claim was then quietly divided into two parts, as if by parthenogenesis. The government perhaps thought that since it had already screwed the Aboriginal people, there was no need for further intercourse and began to discuss how to end the affair quietly. Thus one part of the case became the exploratory settlement talks, while the other, in Justice Hugessen's words, was in "the pretrial stages of the action."[136]

Then suddenly it was over. In 2009 the phone rang in Wilson's office and a familiar voice said, "Are you sitting down?"

Diminutive Dora Wilson, who does not have far to fall, said, "I'm standing up." And the friendly voice of Peter Grant informed her that the government had offered to settle. They would pay the village $21.5-million to settle the claim and end the action. Only the amount of money to be paid would be revealed to the public; the village would have to agree to keep the other terms of the settlement secret.[137]

The villagers and their neighbours rejoiced, as did their volunteer supporters. The room where Wilson was standing to take the phone call had been built by volunteers. Every house in the village had been built new or been renovated by Frontiers volunteers. Through the 20 or more years the case had been going on, a total of over 70 volunteers had been at work repairing the houses and band offices in Kispiox, Moricetown and Hagwilget. The work done by them steadily, winter and summer, had also created warm, safe accommodation for the office workers and leaders in the Hagwilget case. Without that warmth and safety, all that clerical and negotiating work could not have been done. There is no point in putting a phone or a computer or a fax machine under a dripping ceiling in a house so cold that fingers stiffen and refuse to type or where a computer screen suddenly goes blank because the hydro bill wasn't paid, or storing files in a house that is likely to burn down because its dangerous wood stove overheats and the room suddenly explodes in flames.

The legal costs for the villagers in 2003 were over $83,000 spent plus another $140,000 in debts incurred by their council. In a village of only 35 to 40 low-income households during that time, those totals had become a crippling amount. Without the Frontiers volunteers, however, the village would have been impoverished long before. Its people could not have continued even to negotiate a settlement. The value of the volunteers' work on the village is probably on the order of $2-million,[138] but even that is not the true measure of their success. Beyond their decisive financial contributions in kind, there was also the steady encouragement that kept up the spirits of the people and their leaders through their hardest times.

There had been the singing, dancing, friendship and lovemaking; the marriages, births, birthday parties, games, swimming, fishing, hunting, skating, feasts and bonfires. There was the on-site training in construction skills, the return visits after young volunteers had departed for a season. There was the cheerful young Radar – Ewan Robertson – from the Caribbean island of St. Kitts, sliding down a snowy hill (8 feet fell that winter) with excited kids from the village; and Russell Lewis, also St. Kitts, sharing his big lottery winnings with family, children and friends in the Wet'suwet'en and Gitxsan tradition. There had been dancing and other celebrations when a new rooftree went up. And there was the two-storey log cabin, designed by Tsairi and Jefferson 25 years before, still looking handsome. And that street through Moricetown named Beaver Road after the volunteers. As Chief Dan Michell said to Charles, Irving and the many volunteers at the end of it all: "Bless you."

♠ ♠ ♠ ♠ ♠ ♠ ♠ ♠ ♠

THE KID FROM JAMAICA

After the Chetwynd houses were occupied and thousands more were on the way with federal help, all seemed well on both sides of the Alberta–British Columbia boundary that Charles was surveying from his cluttered office in Toronto. But Canada, together with the Alberta government, had its eyes on some Aboriginal land around Primrose Lake in northern Alberta and Saskatchewan which the Canadian military had decided it needed for a new training base and bombing range. That the land had been occupied since time immemorial by the Cree, and that the Métis of Canada had officially claimed for themselves this Province of Assiniboia starting in 1815, was of no interest to the Canadian military and apparently of no interest to the Alberta government (founded in 1905) either. Nor were the claims of the occupants of any interest to these governments – only the resources that the government, the military or a private company could take from the land for their own benefit interested them. "They just came in and booted them off their traplines and told them they would be trespassing if they stayed," according to Lawrence Gladue, representing the Métis Association of Alberta.[139]

One day in 1995 a Cree trapper, Bob Martin, was out checking his trapline behind his dog team when a Canadian Forces jet swept in low behind him and opened fire. One bullet smashed into Martin's wooden sled and lodged there, but none hit Martin or the dogs. Charles said, "Well, we knew the government was not always a straight shooter, but this was ridiculous. Were the Canadian Forces berserk? Or were our pilots so inept that they couldn't take out a toboggan?"[140]

Nor was it only the military and the government that had their eyes on Aboriginal and Métis lands in Alberta. Private companies and clubs also coveted their neighbours' goods. In the late 1960s, for instance, the provincial government, caving to the demands of a white people's fishing club, withdrew Aboriginal fishing licences from a profitable commercial fishery near Aboriginal communities on Winefred

Lake and Christina Lake near Conklin. The fishery was destroyed and people were thrown out of work, straight onto welfare, for which the government was, ironically, responsible.

This arbitrary attack on traditional fishing rights was not an isolated case in Canada. In New Brunswick Aboriginal fishers had been excluded illegally from their traditional fishing grounds as early as 1752. In Ontario, starting in the 19th century, Cape Croker fishers, who for centuries had fished the lake trout, pickerel, whitefish and perch of Georgian Bay, were restricted, prosecuted and virtually robbed of their catch through many decades by government fiat, although their rights to the fish, the water and the land itself had never been ceded. In Georgian Bay, where no treaty about fishing rights was signed, the provincial government in the 20th century passed an illegal law requiring all fishers to have a licence. The Aboriginal peoples were not exempted, so they were presented with a dilemma: either refuse to pay for a licence to do what had been their right since time out of mind, or else apply for a licence, which would lend a semblance of legality to the licensing system. By not paying, they would open themselves to prosecution. More than a century elapsed before the Federal Court rectified a little of the injustice done to the Nawash band at Cape Croker.[141]

Where there was no treaty the natives were most often robbed, but not even a treaty protected them. For instance, in 19th-century Ontario, despite treaties, once white settlers had taken possession, the provincial government passed a law permitting whites to hunt and fish on traditional land or cut trees or dig mines or build roads or whatever. The Ontario of those days even forbade individual "Indians" to own land, as we'll see in a moment.

Stan Daniels, head of the Métis Association of Alberta, who had heard of Frontiers' early housing work, told Catto in 1967 about problems at Primrose, Alberta. He said, "What are we going to do? My people can't hunt, we can't fish, we can't trap and we can't get title to our land. Can you help?" Some of the Métis and First Nations in the area were attempting to secure 25-year leases on land in Alberta where they wished to build houses. They believed the land and the fish belonged to them by historical right, a belief that Frontiers shared (and a belief that is increasingly shared by government and courts with regard to many other Aboriginal/Métis land claims now, though not in 1967).

The Métis and their ancestors among the Cree had been living on this land since long before the Canadian governments had been created, but the latecomers, in their new concrete towers in Edmonton, were denying them the right even to lease it, let alone have deeds to it in fee simple. This was nothing new; much the same thing had happened in Ontario more than a hundred years before when an Ojibwa woman named Nahneebahwequay, married to a white Methodist minister, was denied deeds to land that was given to her by the elders of a neighbouring band. She took her claim to Queen Victoria in person, but even the Queen was indifferent to the honour of her Crown. Nahneebahwequay's claim was set aside by the Queen's subject Canadians, and Nahneebahwequay was even refused permission to buy the land at auction, on the grounds that Ontario law forbade "Indians" to own land.[142]

At Daniels's request Charles stepped up and began to discuss the Métis claims with the Alberta government. At the same time, he called for volunteers and printed out the blueprints for Frontiers' Plan F series of three-bedroom houses and actually started construction. In co-operation with Daniels, his Métis association and a group of international volunteers, Frontiers had the houses well under way when an outraged and perplexed letter arrived from the Alberta Housing and Urban Renewal Corporation. In it the provincial government was complaining that the Foundation was illegally building houses for the Métis and/or Aboriginal peoples.

The Alberta government, denying the history of the ownership of the land, was saying that their own subsequent claim was superior to that of the Métis occupants, whose ancestors had been there for generations. At the same time, it was saying Frontiers could not build houses for these people because only the government had the right to do what the government refused to do, which prevented it from being done.

Frontiers continued the lengthy land dispute with the Alberta government until the Opposition in the House of Commons heard about the brouhaha and began to mock the whole ambitious Basford federal housing program, which, still in its demonstration phase in 1972, was proceeding at the rate of 12 dwellings per year. Opposition members were laughing at the program, which at that rate, would take 4,167 years to complete. Finally, some provincial bureaucrats saw the good sense in the Frontiers Foundation–Métis approach, gave up their opposition and actually joined in to help. The original project of 12 houses for Alberta was expanded after the Chetwynd success to 27 houses and then extended across the country through the CMHC. The Métis and Cree were happy to see that there were to be many more houses and that they would also be bigger and better equipped. Of course, they also cost a lot more than the Frontiers houses.

Then, in 1976, Frontiers received a letter from an organization whose very name made Charles smile for its juxtaposition of high-rise nomenclature with woodsy simplicity. It was from the Isolated Communities Advisory Board.[143] Gordon Auger of the board was appealing to Frontiers on behalf of the Cree and Métis people living on and near the reserve near Peerless Lake, approximately 93 miles north of Lesser Slave Lake. Auger needed five houses to be built either of log or frame construction.

Very soon the Peerless Lake project was approved, and a well-organized, detailed memorandum of understanding was issued in Toronto, outlining the responsibilities of each partner as follows:

> The community hosts [people at Peerless Lake] guarantee:
> - to ensure that sufficient materials and supplies for the work to be undertaken are on hand when the volunteers arrive and that they remain so during the project;
> - to supply mutually acceptable accommodation for the volunteers, and to ensure that all necessary domestic facilities and utensils are available when the volunteers arrive, and that they remain so during the project;
> - to organize the recruitment of local volunteers and workers;
> - to ensure that all necessary tools are available when the volunteers arrive and that they remain so during construction, or, if otherwise, to notify Frontiers Foundation/Operation Beaver accordingly, so that Frontiers Foundation can procure the required tools;
> - to provide the volunteers with a welcome meal July 8 and

with an opportunity to become acquainted with the members of the community;

- to ensure that the community of Peerless Lake is aware of the presence of the volunteers and the reason therefor;

- to work with the volunteers on the work-site and to provide skilled supervision when necessary;

- to arrange local publicity; and

- to reach an acceptable arrangement with the volunteers regarding the choice of a representative to be sent to the evaluation and planning session.[144]

Then Frontiers required Gordon Auger himself to guarantee regional orientation for the Peerless Lake volunteers on Wednesday, July 7, and Thursday, July 8 – including breakfast, lunch and supper on those days – to arrange accommodation for the volunteers in Slave Lake on the night of July 7–8, and to handle regional publicity, all in consultation with Frontiers Foundation Alberta coordinator Lee Anderson.

Frontiers guaranteed to find enough money for five log units, which it planned to get from the Alberta Housing Corporation. It also committed to: supply volunteers; arrange leadership training and general orientation sessions in Toronto and regional sessions in Edmonton and Slave Lake, in consultation with the Isolated Communities Advisory Board; pay for all living expenses incurred by the volunteers, including travel in Canada and insurance against accident and illness; and accept final responsibility for all actions of the volunteers.

As soon as they were accepted, the volunteers were informed that they were expected to supply themselves with work clothing and to arrange their working hours with their hosts, as well as use of tools. They were further asked to: put in an industrious five-day work week; ensure that no task was undertaken until all safety precautions had been put in place; maintain steady communication with the national office in Toronto; report on all work and community activities they would take part in and on the amount of work time spent onsite each week and account for all funds advanced to them by Frontiers. They had to agree among themselves regarding the nature of a retreat to be taken approximately midway through the project according to guidelines presented at the general orientation. And finally, although the volunteers' free time was their own, they were required "to present to the community as a whole a standard of conduct which will bring credit to Frontiers Foundation/Operation Beaver, and to foster creative and amiable relations between the group, the community and the organization."[145]

These memoranda of understanding are typical of the foundation's work in many ways. Certainly they are meticulous, well-organized and clearly based on long and fruitful experience. But the unusual thing about them is that they emphasize publicity, communication and amiable relations among all parties, including the retreat midway through the project. In effect, they convert the Frontiers volunteers into ambassadors of the foundation and uphold the neglected honour of the Crown. The memos reflect the original founding charter of the foundation as Charles had written it way back in the mid-1950s, which is quoted in the opening pages of this book: "to build bridges of respect and affection while building houses of wood and cement."

Once all the memos were signed, work got under way. Wasting nothing, the Frontiers volunteers reused the successful designs first provided to them in the 1960s by Bruce Edwards. But now, each Frontiers home was equipped with all bathroom fixtures plus fridge, stove and washing machine. Uldis Stoeppler came from Germany to help with this project. He was an able and hardworking supervising draftsman and architect in training, assisted by the cheerfully competent Anna Dunets of Toronto and Uldis's elder brother Jan, both of whom would later become engineers and architects. Their work, which started in that fall of 1976, went on through the winter and the following summer and fall right into the following early summer of 1978. The project took far longer than expected and it was harshly demanding, but they did not falter. They simply continued.

Not only were Frontiers project volunteers unused to the killer cold weather of northern Canada, but they also had never faced anything as distressing as the living conditions they had come to correct. The challenge at Fort Good Hope in 1981, for example, was particularly profound for one young volunteer from Jamaica, Garfield Bembridge. He was a physical education student at G.C. Foster College in Kingston,

Jamaica, when he saw a recruitment poster for Frontiers Foundation, which interested him. Bembridge talked to the recruiting officer – who was himself a volunteer – and liked what he heard about adventure, long hours, extreme climate, no pay, and strangers in need whom he could help – the description written by Charles, which attracted exactly the kind of adventurous young soul he himself had been when he first saw God's Lake in the 1950s.

Bembridge signed up. He was 22 years old.

He arrived shivering at Fort Good Hope, Northwest Territories, on a July day in 1981. Next day he walked out onto the dusty road and asked one of the Canadian volunteers about the weather, and although he had half-guessed the answer, he could scarcely believe what he heard: "This is summer, man. It doesn't get cold till winter."[146]

He received an even greater shock when he saw the living conditions. "I had vague theoretical knowledge of what to expect, but I could scarcely believe what I was seeing. I knew that poor countries like Haiti and Bolivia were the Third World, but this seemed to me worse, like a sort of Fourth World of poverty, neglect and despair." But he was glad to be among the ones helping. "This was an eye-opener for me."

Many of the local people were living in shacks with "basket" walls that let the wind blow snow inside, which would melt in the afternoon and turn to ice at night, making the floors so slippery that the inhabitants were risking their bones just moving across the room. In a typical cabin in that part of Canada in those days, the space might be 16 by 20 feet; the floor was usually mud; there was no electricity or running water; the windows might be oiled paper or greying plastic that flapped and tore. The people slept six to a bed, under one or two ragged blankets, and the roof might be made of bits of tarpaper stapled to scraps of lumber discarded at commercial building sites. Furniture scarcely existed. If there was a table, it was probably lopsided; the wood stove was also the room heater and the sole source of hot water. The chairs, if any, might be three-legged; in one cabin the "dining room set" included a tree stump. There was a school, but the children were preoccupied by their many household chores, and they had little or no light during the long, dark winter by which to study their books, if they even had any. The firewood with which they heated themselves was mainly evergreen, containing a lot of resin and producing a thick buildup of creosote in the flimsy chimney, which had no safety collar where it passed through the roof or wall. This meant a high risk of fire.

Since Fort Good Hope is so far north that 50-year-old trees are not big enough to make suitable logs, Bembridge and some others had to go more than 465 miles back up the Mackenzie River to Fort Simpson, near the confluence with the Liard River, to cut timber, which they then floated back downriver to Fort Good Hope. At Fort Good Hope they dried the logs for the walls with Frontiers' portable kiln dryer. Then, with the foundation's portable sawmill, they converted some of the logs into dimensional lumber, which they used to finish the interiors. Bembridge was just beginning to feel comfortable among the Cree and Dene people when it was time to go back to Jamaica.

He flew south with an amazing whirl of memories in his mind, most of them good, but one that was so sad that it bothered his dreams. The people on the reserves were in such despair that they were committing suicide at an early age, some as young as their early teens. Sometimes they formed little support groups to keep each other company as they died. These memories would not let him go. Often during his semesters in the south, he thought of them, wondering if and how he might be able to help. He had at first done nothing because he did not have the self-confidence to offer help, nor did he understand this strange new culture or speak the language. And he could not count on being able to stay in the area long enough to inspire what he could see the children needed most – trust.

The next spring he volunteered again and this time was sent to Peerless Lake in northern Alberta. When the children clustered round, staring – he was the first black man they had ever seen – he smiled at them and talked to them. Because he knew these children had very difficult lives, he encouraged them and listened to them as if there were no problem. And a problem ignored is a problem solved, at least for children, for a little while. Having grown up in a close-knit, loving family, Bembridge knew how to prolong those no-problem moments, conversing with the kids, engaging them in sports, encouraging those games they already played, teaching them new ones, giving them some fun to anticipate. When he turned his "thousand-watt smile" on the young people, they cheered up, and when he began to organize games for them, they immediately wanted to join in.

As he went to work on his first house for John A. Cardinal and his family, he made friends with several boys, including Wally T. A few days later, not having seen Wally for a while, he asked the other children where he was. "He died," one of them said. Then Bembridge found that Wally and three friends had broken into the school, opened the copy machine and swallowed the copying fluid. All of them died, and the whole village mourned.

In this community, kids under the age of 10 would talk casually about killing themselves, which was frightening for everyone, including the elders. Suicides were occurring so often that one of the volunteers said, "We'd better hurry up or there won't be anyone left to move into this house."

Bembridge thought, "I can't see this happening and just do nothing. What can I do?" He went to the elders and asked them to teach him Cree. They did this in typical Cree style, with a joke buried in the lessons, which taught him swear words first. That helped him to organize activities, jogging, walking, running, volleyball – "whatever we could do. There was no script for what we were trying to do. Apart from building houses, there was no script."

Bembridge found that all the kids needed was some direction and organization, "and to count on us staying." There was a history in the community of people coming to help but then suddenly leaving just as the children had started to rely on them. "We organized any and everything so they could gain the confidence to go to school and get jobs," he said. He tried to get equipment, anything to create opportunity for the children, and he sometimes succeeded. "It all depended on what door we knocked on, what heart strings we were able to pull."

Having volunteered for an extra year, he was sent to Trout Lake, where, that winter of 1982, he borrowed a pair of skates and asked the kids to teach him to skate. In the summer, they taught him to snare rabbits. One day he was out in the bush with some of the kids when they encountered a black bear on the trail. "The bear took one look at me and ran away," Bembridge said. "I had never seen a black bear before, and he had never seen a black man." This became a standing joke around the reserve – the kids said they would not go out into the bush unless Bembridge was there to frighten off the bears.

His volleyball team got so good under his coaching that the kids won the regional championship. They were able to do this because the school gym, long underused, was always available at night. "The winter nights were deadly. So long and so cold, so we created opportunity and alternatives."

Within a couple of months of Frontiers' stay at Trout Lake, the suicide rate dropped by over 90 per cent. The houses were finished and plenty of people were ready to move in.

Bembridge stayed several years off and on in the area known as the Back Lakes, which included Sandy Lake, Trout Lake and Loon Lake. At the beginning, suicide was the story everywhere he went. In one place, the alcoholism was so bad that it was not unusual for a father with, say, $600 and kids with no boots, to charter a plane for $500 to fly out and buy a $90 bottle of booze. Soon Bembridge's most important work was not what he had originally volunteered for but what he had learned in the spirit of his volunteering. On one reserve where Bembridge and Frontiers were working, the suicides stopped completely. In Peerless Lake, for the first time ever, children graduated from the high school. One got a job off-reserve and one started work in the band office, a position that otherwise would have been filled by someone from off-reserve. Bembridge helped a former gasoline-sniffer – who had always wanted a job but lacked the confidence to apply – get started as a pump jockey in a gas station. When he returned to one reserve after having been away for over a year, a friend said, "Look, even the dogs are glad to see you."

Within a year, the Alberta government had heard of the sensational results Frontiers was achieving, not only building houses but also running a brand-new and successful counselling and training program. They sent a representative, Ernie Grach, to talk to Bembridge and make notes about this inspiring stranger who had been able to come in and save lives where so many others had failed. The first thing Bembridge told Grach was, "I believe that everyone is worth saving."

When Grach asked for more details about how his "program" worked, Bembridge had trouble answering. It was difficult to explain to anyone who wears a suit and works for money that what he was doing was not a "program," and it was not "work." What he had contributed, he said, was "added value"; it was "common sense"; it came from his spirit and was expressed spontaneously through mind and hand. It was born, like people, out of love and need; it was nourished and therefore it grew. It was scarcely replicable or definable in any organized way. "Counselling the kids was not part of the normal Frontiers Foundation work," he said. "This was added value. We were added value. There was nothing scientific in our help to the kids, it was all just practical common sense. Frontiers saves lives, no question."

Because of a change in immigration policy under Stephen Harper, people such as Garfield Bembridge are being routinely denied admission to Canada, even for volunteer programs. Don Irving has attributed this to "arrogance and prejudice" in the Canadian government. "Ottawa and the embassies abroad are impenetrable fortresses of racism. In some cases, they have kept me waiting for years" while people up north are desperate for their help.

Today, Bembridge, having arrived in Canada before Harper arrived in Ottawa, lives with his mother and brother in the east end of Toronto. He works in the city, particularly in Scarborough and North York, for the Canadian Mental Health Association (CMHA), and his business card for the CMHA reads "Executive Lead for Organizational Performance." He helps the organization fulfill its accountability requirements and corporate expectations. He has two master's degrees, one from Central Michigan University and one from the University of Toronto in the field of health administration. He is also certified by the Canadian College of Health Service Executives (now called the Canadian College of Health Leaders). Of his new country, Bembridge has said, "I feel that I'm blessed. This is a great country. It's a blessed country."

♠ ♠ ♠ ♠ ♠ ♠ ♠ ♠ ♠ ♠ ♠

RAISING THE ROOF

For well over a decade, until about 1984, the domestic policy of the Canadian government was to build a "just society," which was not merely an election slogan. Pierre Elliott Trudeau, the prime minister who had created and campaigned on the idea, was determined to implement it. Fortunately, Frontiers Foundation's own policy fitted neatly into this agenda, so federal money began to flow, and safe, warm, affordable houses began to rise. Frontiers enjoyed steadily increasing support from federal government departments during this period, mainly from the CMHC, the Canadian International Development Agency (CIDA), the Secretary of State and the Department of Indian Affairs and Northern Development (DIAND). Charles Catto was awarded the Order of Canada in 1979.

Even in those halcyon Trudeau years, however, there were times when Frontiers had to take emergency measures to remind Ottawa that the work of the foundation was fulfilling not only a national obligation but also an election promise of the party in power. The autumn of 1980 was one of those times. For months, government departments had been delaying, equivocating and generally evading problems, without explanation. The many divisions of the Secretary of State, traditionally the most supportive federal ministry, had become as evasive as the rest.

Then the phone in the modest little Frontiers office on Danforth Avenue in Toronto rang with a warning. It was one of the foundation's numerous friends in the Secretary of State's office calling, who did not want to be named. "Charles," he whispered. "You guys had better do something on the Hill."

"You mean demonstrate?" Charles asked.

"Correct, and the sooner the better."

The Secretary of State's name, Francis Fox, gave Charles an idea. He envisaged a dramatic demonstration in front of Parliament, white and Aboriginal activists protesting loudly to MPs as they walked toward their safe, warm, comfortably appointed offices. He picked up the phone while it was still warm from the previous call and talked to a fraternity brother, Warren Hughes of Costume House, who was in the theatrical wardrobe rental business. Charles later described the events that followed:

> I asked Warren about his supply of costumes for foxes and beavers. Beavers were vital for that was still our public name.
> Hughes said, "I've got one dandy fox outfit for a very tall guy plus all the beavers you want."
> "Perfect," I said. "I'll take the big fox and ten beavers."

From there, Catto's playful Beavers took over and started building a small portable house with a big red maple leaf on the roof, a structure built as one detachable piece. The house, of course, symbolized Canada, and the "beavers" were all the citizens trying to build it on Parliament Hill. But they couldn't do the job unless they got the glue (i.e., the dollars) from the big fox holding the glue pot marked with an enormous dollar sign. The contingent of beavers, the house, plus tools and hard hats, all the costumes and a public-address system headed for Ottawa in three vehicles the night before the planned demonstration and jammed into the home of a Frontiers veteran, Doug Prendergast, for food and sleep.

An experienced media warrior, Charles had arranged with all the local papers, radio and TV stations to cover the event, to be held on Parliament Hill on November 8, 1980, at 11:00 am. On the night of November 7, when they arrived in Ottawa, an ice storm hit the capital. All the windows and doors of their vehicles were frozen solid. The next morning, as the young volunteers chipped away at the ice locking their vehicles, Charles realized they could not get to the Hill on time. Priceless publicity would be lost. But he also suspected that the media vehicles themselves would be frozen shut. They finally got the doors open and roared over to the Hill, late but still just ahead of the media:

> We started building our house just as the media people arrived. Halfway through our construction, our fearless Beaver Division chairman Paul Reed (later a clergyman) bellowed to the gathering crowd, "Hey, Charles, we can't build Canada's needed houses without more glue." I yelled back, "Right, Paul, but we can get more glue from the Big Fox." I

then rushed over to the Big Fox, who was clearly labelled "Francis," who immediately shouted, "Here, Charles, take whatever you need. We have to keep on building Canada." Extracting and then waving a big dollar sign from the Big Fox's pot, I handed it over to the joyful beaver, who then hoisted the roof onto the little house.

Miraculously, the demonstration succeeded beyond our dreams. Within 48 hours I was welcomed to the Honourable Francis Fox's office with the smiling words, "That was a good show on the Hill, Charles. How much do you want?" I said we wanted $50,000, which was serious money in those days or about $300,000 now. Honourable Francis didn't even gulp. "You've got it," he replied.

"And I want it every year for five years," I continued.

"You've got it," the big fox confirmed.[147]

Federal support for Frontiers continued to grow under the Liberals, topping out at $655,911 in 1984 and then nose-diving during the grim Mulroney years. Frontiers president Gord Johnston, from the Cape Croker reserve in Ontario, said in his 1986–87 annual report that it was the year of the greatest challenge to the foundation, as federal funding dropped abruptly by nearly 30 per cent in one year, from $350,000 to $250,000. Frontiers was forced to cut back on the number of volunteers from 90 to 80, and the projects themselves from 23 to 20.

Raising the money to raise new roofs has always proven more difficult for Frontiers than finding the volunteers or the people in need. In the 20-year period to 1984, the steadily increasing support from federal agencies was usually a short-term allocation limited to a specific project in a small, well-defined area. There was very little if anything to sustain the essential services of the foundation itself, which was always scrambling for money to pay the rent, and for the hard-working staff in Toronto, Quebec, Manitoba and British Columbia.

As government funding cutbacks continued, the foundation was about to run out of money. A deadly sense of futility threatened morale. Charles and Barbara talked it over and decided that their own house, paid for through their own work and a small gift from their families, would have to be risked. They went to the bank and placed the first mortgage of their lives on the house, for over $100,000, and turned the money over to the foundation in exchange for a promissory note. A promissory note from a bankrupt charity.

It was not enough. The foundation continued to face further cuts to the grants the directors had been counting on. It would receive in the coming year less than 10 per cent of its previous level of support from Ottawa. There was some powerfully sympathetic reporting from some major newspapers about the crisis, but this did not shake the government of the day. Ironically, in the same session of Parliament that had cut funding to Frontiers Foundation even further, the government allotted almost half a million dollars to refurbish the Kingsmere official residence of the Speaker of the House. Charles fumed to the press that this proved how little the government cared for its international obligations (the Aboriginal treaties), which it had inherited from the Crown at Confederation. Money was being denied to Frontiers to help First Nations families living in substandard shanties when the painters were still putting finishing touches onto the pretty new wainscoting for Mr. Speaker. Once again Frontiers volunteers came to Ottawa to protest. Once again Charles's fervent imagination produced images and scenes that caught the eye of government ministers and the public. This time, he saw his dreams illuminated in fire: his inspiration was the famous Robert W. Service poem "The Cremation of Sam McGee." A Cree Frontiers volunteer in a donated beaver costume symbolizing Barney Beaver, the mascot of the foundation, posed in front of Parliament beside a stack of straw bales. Seizing a bullhorn, Charles denounced the "Regressive Preservatives" as the cremation of Barney Beaver got under way.

The Cree volunteer dressed as Barney Beaver, Alex McKay, came close to heat prostration wearing the thick beaver suit in the fiery sunlight. Nevertheless, McKay was tied to a post and surrounded by bales of straw, a situation made even more dangerous by the hot drying sun. "Regressive Preservative" party members carrying flaming torches surrounded Barney and were only dissuaded from ending his existence by a volunteer in a Brian Mulroney mask, reminding them of the prime minister's campaign commitment to "the housing, dignity and opportunity of the Native people." Simultaneously, Charles's parody of Service's poem was read to the crowd. The spectacle was a hit with journalists, who thrive on such public spectacles and slagging puns.

Frontiers beavers in costume demonstrate
on Parliament Hill on a hot summer day
in 1985. (Courtesy *Ottawa Citizen*)

The demonstration gained Charles the headlines he was after, but it was still not enough to change the funding situation. A few weeks later, still nothing had been promised or sent, so Charles went all the way to Finance Minister Michael Wilson. Wilson scrounged around, but all he offered was $150,000 toward Canada's obligation and the foundation's vast need, which was in the millions. Even this, Charles suspected, might have come only because the president of Frontiers at that time was an Aboriginal from British Columbia but living in Wilson's Etobicoke Centre riding.

Another political drama began one snowy night in central Toronto in November 1986. A federal constituency meeting was held in the Rosedale office of the local member, David Crombie, the highly popular Secretary of State, to launch his campaigning for re-election. The Rosedale riding runs from costly mansions in the north end, south toward the railway tracks, and includes the affordable-housing developments of Jamestown, Cabbagetown and Regent's Park.

The room was crowded to overflowing with faithful supporters of the candidate and other Tories, but Charles and his friends had seen the chance to influence government policy where it often begins: during the campaigns, when candidates receive a brief exposure to the voters and their ideas. In attendance alongside the loyal Conservatives, therefore, was Gordon Johnston, president of Frontiers Foundation, and some of its board members, James White, Maddy Howe, Allan Pelletier, Herb Nabigon, Larry Leone and Charles himself. Unknown to the Frontiers directors and friends, some other Frontiers friends and a fair number of Aboriginal residents of Cabbagetown in the south end of the riding were also on hand. Also present were Ralph and Thorah Mills, Rosedale residents and long-time supporters of Frontiers Foundation.

Mrs. Mills was the same Rosedale woman who had visited Moosonee in 1966 and written the touching report of how the impoverished people there struggled successfully to cope with their lack of basic amenities. Among the other volunteers, she was known as Thorah, Goddess of War, because she made things happen.

After the opening formalities, Frontiers Foundation president Gord Johnston demanded to know why months of correspondence and pleading phone calls to Secretary of State Crombie about funding for Native housing projects had received no response. Many of the calls had been to Crombie's constituency office aide in Toronto, John McFadyen, who was right there in the living room, seated beside Crombie. Many people in the room murmured approval of the question and others that followed. Humiliated in front of his embarrassed boss, Mc-Fadyen snarled at Charles, "Catto, you packed this meeting!"

Charles replied civilly, "John, you should know them – most of these people are your constituents; I had no idea they were coming."

The meeting continued, with Ojibwa, Cree, Mohawk and Métis voices monopolizing the agenda, all focusing on the Native housing crisis and what the government wasn't doing about it. Finally, after nearly two hours of intense discussion, Honourable David called a pause: "John," he said. "It's nine o'clock, and we haven't had our dinner yet!"

Immediately, Thorah, Goddess of War, was on her feet declaring, "Correct, Mr. Crombie, it's nine o'clock. And *we* haven't had *our* dinner yet, either. My husband Ralph and I walked through a snowstorm to get to this meeting, and we came here to support Frontiers Foundation. We want to know NOW when you can meet with Frontiers Foundation!"

Crombie, ever poised and courteous – in a previous incarnation he had been dubbed the "tiny, perfect mayor of Toronto" – turned to Mc-Fadyen and requested that he provide a date on the ministerial agenda. They got an answer right away: the promise of a meeting on December 19, and a cheque for $250,000. The promise of the meeting was honoured; the cheque was not.

At that December 19 meeting in Minister Crombie's Toronto office, nine Frontiers board members were assured by the minister that Frontiers Foundation was Crombie's responsibility as Secretary of State, and that he would core fund the foundation "now and down the road." This core funding of $250,000 per year would assure the foundation's ability to go on raising funds from private sources and perhaps other provinces, to continue to build houses and communities.

However, as Frontiers' 1987–88 fiscal year rolled on and no core funding cheque arrived from Ottawa, Charles became increasingly alarmed. When the envelope finally arrived from Ottawa, Charles eagerly opened it, searching for the promised cheque. Instead, he found a letter stating that there would be no core funding.

But in 1987 the foundation did receive some great news from far outside any Canadian government. In June the Royal Architectural Institute of Canada (RAIC) announced the results of a massive worldwide survey of 75 government and non-governmental organiz-ation (NGO) aid projects. Unbeknownst to everyone at Frontiers, the Canadian architects had commissioned this evaluative study from Chreod Ltd., international consultants and investment planners. The study ranked the best 25 NGOS according to RAIC criteria, chief among them being effectiveness at implementing their stated mandate. Fron-tiers was a big winner all around, taking five of the top eight places in 25 Canadian rankings, including first, third, fifth, seventh and eighth, plus one of the international rankings.

The volunteers were bursting with pride and anticipation, because here was independent proof that their programs were providing the best and most economical houses among the many initiatives that had been studied. The foundation's onsite, marketable-skill training and ef-fective voluntarism had been singled out for special praise. Dedication, zeal and youthful idealism had apparently overcome all obstacles, and everyone in Frontiers was now hoping that massive new amounts of money would finally flow their way from government. They were ex-pecting their phones "to be ringing right off their hooks with funding calls from Secretary of State, CMHC, Indian Affairs and/or Human Re-sources" as Charles said.

But their naive hopes soon came crashing to Earth. They were stunned to realize that the RAIC survey meant nothing to the man-darins in Ottawa. In that year, Frontiers' combined revenue from the Secretary of State, CMHC and DIAND fell to zero, a catastrophe for the struggling little foundation. The Mulroney government was simply not interested in carrying out its election promises.

The challenge was now turning out to be exactly as Charles had anticipated and written about in the beginning, when he had called on the spirit, skill and love in people to come forth and help others in need. Charles took this new disappointment lightly, as usual. He said, in his usual punning style: "It was the volunteers who saved us, really. The volunteers did not come forth, they came first."

Frontiers, honoured by the RAIC and the International Year for Shelter of the Homeless (IYSH) because they had made such econom-ical use of donations, had a signal advantage over government. Their vision went far beyond the limited scope of bureaucrats. Their very lack of financial resources caused the Frontiers volunteers to rely on themselves, their energy and their own inventiveness. This called forth an effort that could not be matched by bureaucrats seeking to economize through evasive legalities while ever conscious of their own salaries.

Charles greatly admired the Shawnee general and diplomat Tecumseh, who lost his life fighting with the Canadians and British against the American invaders in the War of 1812.[148] As Charles saw it, Canada owed its national life to the Aboriginal people who had given up land and offered food, medicine, laws, their political philosophy and even their lives to the young nation.

It is no surprise, then, that despite Frontiers' difficulties, Charles welcomed the request from the Lovesick Lake Native Women's Association for help to build a new bedroom for Second World War veteran and Aboriginal Stan Johnston, who was blind and nearly deaf. Johnston, of the Ojibwa Nation reserve nearby, lived with his wife Verna in a one-room cabin near Burleigh Falls, Ontario. At first, Frontiers could only commit to building a bedroom, but Verna said she needed a bathroom as well because all they had was an outhouse, and she had to take her crippled husband out to it in all kinds of weather, including heavy snow and waist-high drifts.

This request was hard for Charles to deal with, because at that moment, Frontiers' resources were more than usually strained, but his mind was ever fertile and he continued to count on the charity of his friends, who usually responded to his appeals with good news. This time he remembered a rich friend in Cambridge, Ontario, who had a huge house with seven bathrooms. Charles phoned him up and said, "Dave, we've got a World War Two veteran named Stan Johnston living in a one-room shack with no bathroom. He's a senior, severely handicapped, and he doesn't have a bathroom. You've got seven. We're asking you to rip the fixtures out of one of them and ship them over to us at Lovesick Lake. Or maybe you'd prefer to send us $5,000." He got the cheque the next day, and the order went in for Johnston's bathroom that week. A month later, there was Verna, in the tub, cheerfully having her picture taken for a local news story.

Time and again, Frontiers has stood by helplessly as government after government set up expensive new projects to do badly what Frontiers was already doing well. Further, and perhaps most important of all, the mindset of most people in government is "tax money is our money," meaning that anyone who barges in ahead of the bureaucrats to get money to spend on a program is a competitor and probably an enemy. It was clear from the judgments of the Canadian architects and the IYSH that Frontiers was by far the best of all the organizations supplying housing for Aboriginal and Métis peoples, and that therefore the CMHC and all the other government departments in the field had much to learn from the foundation. It is, however, often difficult to learn; it is more often difficult to learn from your competitor; and it is always nearly impossible to learn from your enemy. That is the ongoing and central dilemma for government, for Frontiers, and for all the people that both organizations are supposed to serve.

Some of the collapse of federal government funding for Frontiers during the Mulroney years was compensated for by a new influx of dollars from provincial and territorial governments, especially from Ontario and the NWT. Those new Queen's Park and Yellowknife grants "were golden to us," said Charles. Ontario's Minister of Housing, Alvin

FRONTIERS FOUNDATION PRESIDENT GORDON JOHNSTON RECEIVES THE ONTARIO MODEL HOUSING PROJECT AWARD DURING THE INTERNATIONAL YEAR OF SHELTER FOR THE HOMELESS, 1987.

Curling, personally delivered a Queen's Park cheque to Frontiers executives at the Spruce Street project site in Hornepayne, Ontario, and his successor, the Honourable Chaviva Hosek, presented the foundation with a much bigger one. These, combined with the Ontario Model Housing Project Award during the IYSH World Habitat Day in 1987, cheered up all the Frontiersmen and -women, and supported new programs. At the same time, together with the government of the NWT, Frontiers quickly developed a productive partnership building houses under the NWT's excellent Homeownership Assistance Program.

The financial good news from Ontario also improved as the NDP, led by Bob Rae, succeeded David Peterson's Liberal government in 1990. The Honourable Shelley Martel, the new Minister of Housing, took a personal interest, and Frontiers received half a million dollars from her ministry and from Ontario's Ministry of Northern Development and Mines, plus a small amount more from the Ontario Native Affairs Secretariat. To all this Martel added two brand-new pickup trucks, a minivan, computers and other essentials, cleverly splitting the cost of the vehicles with Ford Canada. This great shot in the arm from government and private enterprise enabled Frontiers to expand their activity in northern Ontario – until the Conservatives under Mike Harris dethroned Bob Rae's NDP government at Queen's Park in 1995.

When Jean Chrétien's Liberals succeeded Mulroney's government in Ottawa in 1993, the people at Frontiers naively hoped that Paul Martin's plea for national action on affordable housing would be backed with money. Shortly after the Liberal victory, the Honourable Ethel Blondin, the government's only Aboriginal cabinet minister, advised Charles directly: "Ask me for a million!" Charles obliged, but nothing happened. He asked again and then he began to beg, plead and cajole – still nothing. He tried all the acronyms – CMHC, INAC, HRDC, DIAND – plus the Secretary of State, Canadian Heritage, the Privy Council and the Prime Minister's Office, year after year. They all remained impenetrable.

Not even the new president of Frontiers, Lawrence Gladue, although a nationally known Aboriginal leader and a Member of the Order of Canada, could get past the receptionist in the Honourable Sheila Copps's office. Although the Secretary of State's office was

officially committed to support youth, multiculturalism, voluntarism, bilingualism, national heritage and Aboriginal advancement, and
Frontiers Foundation was pre-eminent in all those areas, the Secretary of State offered no funding, while the budget for the government's
resurrection of Katimavik swelled by the gigantic sum of $17-million.[149]
Again, although the CMHC was originally told to help all Canadians to
buy decent homes, and although Frontiers had a matchless record for
delivering safe, warm, affordable housing to those in need, Indian Affairs said, "Sorry, Frontiers, most of what you're doing is off-reserve.
We know you're helping Aboriginal people, but we can't help you."
DIAND's money for off-reserve housing went to the CMHC, despite the
fact that its programs not only were inefficient but also did not train
workers as Frontiers did.

The Privy Council then cynically allotted over $90-million to a
study of voluntarism. Officials said they wanted to find out what it was
and how to promote it, even as they were refusing grants to Frontiers,
which was practising it with spectacular success all over Canada and
elsewhere in the world. The government of Canada was starving the
very volunteers it was studying. Charles was never able to find any evidence that this study contributed anything useful for those practising
voluntarism in Canada, nor for anyone anywhere, except, of course, for
those who did the study, for whom it was a spectacular boondoggle.

A ray of light seemed to appear in September 1995, when Canada's
only Metis/Aboriginal senator, Thelma Chalifoux, succeeded in secur-
ing unanimous Senate approval for a motion requesting federal restor-
ation of funding for Frontiers. Strangely, the motion was killed even
before it got on the Commons order paper.

Now, once again facing strangulation by both Liberal Ottawa and
Tory Queen's Park, the Frontiers Foundation leadership had to do
something creative. And once again, public demonstration seemed to
be not only the best but probably the only option. Charles dreamed
up a scenario "that told our story powerfully, and could be presented
anywhere, again and again."[150] He wanted to make the point that according to Aboriginal peoples, much of the press and many MPs, there
needed to be a spectacular improvement in human shelter immediately in Canada, and that it could be made, and in fact was already being made, by Frontiers Foundation. He and volunteer Brian Beckett,

an engineer from Pickering, Ontario, designed a unique little house. They mounted it on a vertical pivot on a flatbed trailer so it could rotate to work both sides of the street. Half the house was an old shack, the other half a new house. There would be explanatory banners and music too.

The debut appearance of the demonstration float was at Queen's Park, Toronto, during the darkest Harris years. Escorted by high-school trumpet and trombone players, Charles and Beckett's house paraded around the provincial legislature several times, often to the tune of music played by Jimmy Dick's Eagleheart Singers with their big drum, and twice with marching bands. Twice this float headed the Toronto Homelessness March. And it worked. After three years of nothing, "... in 2007, out of the Tory blue," said Charles, "came an unbelievable, unexpected but totally welcome phone call from the Ontario minister of housing." Tony Clement said, "Charles, it's Tony Clement, your housing minister. We know what Frontiers is trying to do and we'd like to help. I want you to write Ernie Eves and tell him to give you some money, so that I can give you a million. Okay?" Frontiers was back in business in Ontario, but still not in Ottawa. The foundation was now getting more money from the stingy Ontario Tories, and even from Quebec, than from the federal government. So Frontiers went back to Ottawa for yet another try.

The twirling house came in handy again, this time in October 1997. Charles and several volunteers drove the float to Parliament Hill and publicly addressed the crowds. "This is how safe, warm homes for all Canadians could be built," Charles said to the little crowd. The audience grew as national Aboriginal leaders like Frontiers president Lawrence Gladue, and Marilyn Buffalo, president of the Native Women's Association, joined him on the truck. They hammered the point that the 1996 report issued by the $58-million Royal Commission on Aboriginal Peoples had yet to produce one new dollar for Native housing either on or off reserve. All that money had been wasted on a report that once again did nothing but employ bureaucrats and then hold up dust in the parliamentary archives.

For once, the sun shone brightly on their parade, and CBC TV was there, filming every minute from start to finish. The floor director advised them to look for their coverage on the evening news, so Frontiers personnel watched eagerly. But instead, as Charles said, "To my disgust, CBC TV presented a long piece on DINKS ("double income, no kids") couples with sickening detail about their devouring interest in nothing beyond their own personal selfishness and satisfaction."[151]

Despite the media's inveterate philistinism and the government's indifference, the foundation survived and kept on building houses, thanks mainly to donations from the private sector. Corporate, service club, foundation, church and personal contributions kept Frontiers going. Timely help came to them from Toronto's Counselling Foundation, the F.K. Morrow Foundation, the Metcalf Foundation and dozens of small gifts from Charles's friends. By 2005 the foundation was running precariously even.

By 2010 the principle of self-help as practised by the foundation – always a vital element in the construction of Frontiers houses – had expanded, by urgent necessity, to include funding. Facing even more cutbacks in the capricious support that government reluctantly offers from the vast amount of money that floods in to Ottawa every year, Frontiers in 2014 decided to embark on a new program of raising money from reserves and Métis communities, especially the few rich ones. According to Lawrence Gladue, the results were nothing. "Not a single reserve or band sent us anything."[152]

FRONTIERS AT HOME, AND OVERSEAS IN BOLIVIA AND HAITI

The volunteers at Frontiers Foundation have been willing, numerous, sober and able. Many of them have worked on its building sites and most of the staff and leaders within Frontiers are now Aboriginal and Métis people. All but a few of the hard-working volunteer directors of Frontiers have been members of First Nations or Métis communities. Presidents of the foundation have included Shelley Charles, Daphne Johnston, Gord Johnston and Herb Nabigon – Ojibwa; Jim White – Kwakiutl; Gary Anderson – Algonquin; and Lawrence Gladue – Cree/ Métis.

Among the other foundation directors are Wilson Ashkewe, Eric Carlson, Emile Scott, Wally Wapachee, Mona Wilds and Johnny Yesno – Cree; Larry Leone – Mohawk; Liz Bellerose, Ruth Cyr, Rhonda Dickemous, Jean Henderson, Alex Jacobs, Conrad King, Clem Nabigon, Leslie Tabobondung and Sue Wheeler – Ojibwa; Audrey Redman – Sioux; Dennis Stark – Potawatomi; Lorraine Gisborn, Carol Manning, Allan Pelletier, Chris Reid and Margaret Yateman – Métis.

Some directors have donated thousands of dollars to Frontiers, one of them more than $30,000. They have all worked for and represented other foundations, and they have all boldly led or joined in demonstrations, confronted politicians, cooked for the annual fundraising breakfasts and gone on the hunt through the canyons of various downtowns to seek funds for numerous Frontiers missions.

Rama, Ontario

Though projects undertaken by the foundation usually proceed quite efficiently, wasteful dramas sometimes occurred, as in 1987 on the Rama reserve near Orillia, Ontario. A program to build a new United

Church parish hall on the reserve was stalled partly because the on-reserve volunteers who had offered many hours of work to build the hall did not turn up. The situation for Charles was fraught because there was a contract between his foundation and the United Church of Canada, his church. The local minister's wife was angry because of the delays, which were actually beyond the control of the foundation: Frontiers had simply accepted and relied upon the on-reserve volunteers, who were now delinquent in their promises. The minister's wife even began talking about bringing suit. Charles turned to an old friend, the cheerful Larry Leone, who loved to joke right along with Charles. Leone, an honorary chief of the Mohawks, agreed to go on a diplomatic mission to the project where he had already worked many hours doing carpentry and roofing. He drove to Rama for a special meeting with the band chief, the council and the minister and his wife. A gentle soul who normally loves to entertain children with magic tricks and games, Leone put on his hard hat and hard manner for the meeting and said very loudly, "Chief, I want to see you and all your people here on the site with their tools tomorrow." Then he turned to the United Church clergyman, who was looking very nervous, and said, "You too, Reverend, you and your wife."

The response was convulsive. Next day all the volunteers turned up and the hall was soon completed. However, the minister's wife was so upset by the "disrespectful" way she and her husband had been treated that she wrote a huffy letter to the *Toronto Star*, which did nothing to cool tempers. But Charles rose serenely like a Zen master above such contretemps; years later, he did not even remember that a suit had been threatened during the incident.

The structure resulting from this project has stood for many years and is still in use, more beautiful than ever because its log walls have aged to a pleasing dark red. The trees used in its construction were a piece of good luck. Red pines had been planted long before in the hope that they would be saleable as Christmas trees, but it turned out there was no market for them. So they grew up into usable timber, which the Frontiers volunteers turned into lumber.

This beautiful building memorializes not only the people of the Rama First Nation but also the many volunteers who pitched in to build it. Dave Brough, in his film about the project, *Dreamdoers*, gave

Frontiers much credit for inspiring the people of Rama with the confidence they needed to undertake more projects. Today, the people on that reserve are prosperous, confident and well-educated.

Bolivia

Frontiers, of course, is not the only foundation in the world that seeks to help communities to grow strong by their own efforts. But it has inspired some of these organizations. The high spirits that animate Frontiers were also alive and well 6,000 miles away from the Rama First Nation, in Bolivia, when a young volunteer named Marco Guzman from Huarina, a village on the shores of Lake Titicaca in the Bolivian Altiplano, was delegated by the Bolivian Youth Council to attend a conference of the Association of Latin American Voluntary Service Organizations held in Chile in 1975. Guzman, born of the Aymara First Nation, was fascinated by the work of the Beaver volunteers, whom he met in Chile, because the problems his own people were experiencing were so similar to those of Canada's First Nations.

When he was a boy, Guzman had helped his father harvest hay beside the great lake known as Titicaca, paddling a reed boat, very like those their ancestors had used. The boat bore an uncanny similarity of design, material and construction to the reed boats of Egypt.[153] After harvesting the hay, Guzman and his father would take it inland to feed to their cattle, which found grazing difficult because of the altitude of the Altiplano, some 12,500 feet above sea level. Many years later, while he was working with Frontiers in Canada, Guzman kept in his apartment a replica of that boat, which he had made of totora reeds.

In 1971 Guzman had helped to found Voluntarios en Acción (VEA) to offer voluntary services on behalf of Aboriginal peoples in South America, somewhat along the lines of Frontiers. The founders were all youth of the Aymara people of Bolivia, most of them living and studying in La Paz. Although VEA and Frontiers sprang from cultures separated by many thousands of miles, they had converging approaches. Like Frontiers, VEA aimed not simply to improve houses or infrastructure but to "build bonds between youth and adults in intergenerational activities." They wanted to "create an environment where change is safe, desirable and meaningful, thus developing the whole person in meeting his and her needs in the Bolivian multiethnic society."[154]

The similarity between the two was uncanny: Charles and Guzman simultaneously began broadcasting the same message on the same wavelength, reaching across two continents, three cultures and hundreds of years of extreme-event histories. Each of the organizations' projects was unique, based on the needs of the people they served; what united them was the common spirit of generous service to people in need whether large or small. One of VEA's projects stemmed from a piece of furniture that was very important to Guzman in his youth.

Like many others he knew, Guzman had learned to read and write awkwardly balancing on a stone or a plank, without a desk on which to rest his books. His father, seeing the discomfort of the students, had built young Marco his own desk. Others soon imitated Señor Guzman. That first Guzman desk was so important to young Marco that after he had finished school he retrieved the desk, and it stands now in the little casa he still maintains in Huarina.

Guzman took the idea of the desk further with the help of VEA, when he and the organization began to build and supply desks to Altiplano schools in 1988. At the time, the schools needed 6,218 six-seater desks. The children were thrilled to have the desks, where formerly they had been half-crouching on stone cold adobe or even seated cross-legged on the floor. Now they had somewhere to rest their books or writing pads, a brace for their backs and comfortable wooden seats.

In addition to building desks, the carpenters in the VEA shop where the work was done took time to teach the locals how to work with wood, an essential skill where money is scarce and lumber must be carried up steep slopes from the tropical valleys below. The Altiplano is so high that not many trees can grow there, except for a few pines. Eucalyptus survive, but their wood is so hard as to be practically unworkable.

Frontiers and VEA were connected through Guzman's desk-building project when to remote Huarina there came a stranger from far away: Dennis Inglangasuk, a Frontiers volunteer sponsored by the Northwest Territories Housing Corporation, from Aklavik. He came to spend six months in the Altiplano, helping to build school desks in the VEA carpentry shop in Huarina. He helped set up the shop and appeared on Bolivian television as a representative of Canada with a mission to improve education in the Altiplano. His volunteer work was covered in Canada by *Inuktitut* magazine and the *Toronto Star*. Every time the children saw him, they were reminded that they were so precious that a stranger had come from the other side of the world to work for them.

For his work with VEA, Dr. Guzman was awarded a Condor Feather by the Aymara people and the Grand Cross of Bolivia by a special resolution of the government.[155]

And in October 1999 the desk-building program was recognized by the United Nations as "one of the best international volunteer projects of the year," in a letter signed by the head of the UN, Kofi Annan. The United Nations official who observed the desk handover ceremonies beside Guzman was surprised at the joy expressed by the villagers of Huarina upon receiving the desks: "Considering all that the United Nations is doing for Bolivia at the highest levels, I find it amazing that such a small organization presenting 30 school desks to a village makes the people so happy… I wonder if the UN is doing the right thing."[156]

Perhaps the small size of VEA and Frontiers has something to do with the success of their operations. The high value that the children placed on their desks, almost incomprehensible to the UN official, was noticed many years later and far away in another mountainous region, Afghanistan, where the Central Asia Institute, founded by Greg Mortenson, had brought in desks at the suggestion of a young girl to help attract children back to school after a disastrous earthquake. The children had been extremely reluctant to return to school until the desks were built, and then nearly all of them returned. As Mortenson explained it, "What Farzana had understood was that in the minds of the children, desks provided concrete evidence that at least within the confines of their classroom, a degree of order, stability and normalcy had returned to their lives… a desk offered certitude. It was something you could trust."[157]

VEA, like Frontiers and the Kiva micro-loan system,[158] is in line with the thinking associated with the locavore movement – characterized by people who strive to eat mainly food grown within a short distance of their appetites. Frontiers, Kiva and VEA respond mainly to local needs, always with local volunteers, usually on a small scale and nearly always with low-cost success. These "locavols" are improving lives one at a time, a little at a time. There is no massive organization or budget because their work is essentially spiritual and is carried around the world like oxygen in the wind.

For the whole year of 1988, for example, Frontiers' total budget was probably less than what the United Nations spent on lunch for its senior officials, but Frontiers, always operating frugally, probably did more for people in need than the bureaucrats with napkins spread over their knees.

Since 1971, Frontiers and VEA have been improving the literacy and mathematical skills of children in central Bolivia, something that no other agency has accomplished. A friendly ceremony in May 1996 celebrated these gratifying results, when Charles and Guzman were invited to the 25th anniversary of the founding of VEA in Huarina. They shook hands with the local volunteers, ate quinoa salad, cheese with Andean potatoes, and karachi, a fish from Lake Titicaca, and they danced, breathlessly in that high, thin air, to the whispery music of Bolivian Pan flutes.

The partnership of VEA and Frontiers, and the celebration of that partnership, imbued in the community the sense of comradeship that normally arises when people share an intense experience together. And that camaraderie was truly broad. The strange meeting of Dennis Inglangasuk and Aymara people in that village in the Altiplano, for instance, stimulated the imagination of a visitor, James Sparshatt, an adventurous English photographer who had met in Huarina another Canadian on a mission, a Cree volunteer named Mike Auger. Sparshatt later wrote:

> The Canadian Cree Mike Auger and the Bolivian Aymara have much in common. Both believe in similar animist religions and the harmony of all things in creation. Both are indigenous peoples who have long suffered at the hands of the invading white man. Both are now in the process of reaffirming their cultural identities and both have a friend in Frontiers Foundation and a certain Charles Catto. Perhaps that is why he has such a strong bond of friendship with Marco Guzman, another big man, whose size evinces his Aymara heritage.[159]

Haiti

Frontiers became involved overseas in Haiti in a most unusual way. In the early 1970s, when the foundation's head office was located in a storefront at 2328 Danforth Avenue in Toronto, staff set up bilingual displays of information about Operation Beaver/Opération Castor activities in the storefront windows. On one freezing February morning, a curious Haitian carpenter strolling the Danforth during his winter layoff dropped in and identified himself as Jean Casimir. Charles remembered:

> Our fluently bilingual secretary Hélène Pinel welcomed him in French and offered him coffee. On learning that Frontiers Foundation is a charity, he paused thoughtfully for a moment and then declared, "I have time available, and would be happy to make you some shelves for all the books and files you have lying around in your office!"
>
> "Bon, alors, pouvez-vous commencer demain, Jean?" asked Hélène, in jest. Astonishingly, Jean Casimir did show up next day, with all his tools; quickly Frontiers had all the shelves needed. We also had a new friend in Jean, who while working chatted with Hélène enough to learn that she soon had to return to family in Quebec.[160]

Casimir later turned to Charles with an interesting suggestion. He had a *cousine* in Haiti who might be interested in replacing Hélène. Her name was Lisette Casimir, she had been trained by nuns and she spoke English, French, Creole and some Spanish. "Since Jean was batting 1.000 so far, we decided to contact Lisette, quite quickly hired her and found her to exceed all expectations," Charles said.

However, Lisette was gone just as fast into the arms of her bridegroom, Haiti's famous soccer player Leintz Domingue. But before leaving, she asked Charles to consider doing a project in her hometown, St. Michel de l'Attalaye, in north-central Haiti. The sweetener was her invitation to Charles and Barbara to be her guests on a visit to Port-au-Prince and St. Michel. They accepted, and in 1975 they found themselves on a "seven-hour hair-raising road trip along the west coast of the island of Hispaniola to Gonaives, then east over scary river crossings and the mountains to St. Michel." Their chauffeur, Father Pierre, a

Belgian priest, had a Haiti-proof Land Rover to ford the flooded and bridge-free rivers. Barbara kept her feet pressed down over the hole in the floor to keep the water out. They arrived in the evening to a warm welcome lit by swaying Coleman lanterns.

Next day the Cattos were shocked by poverty worse than anything they'd ever seen. The second floor of the so-called National School was made of ragged boards skirting holes three feet wide. The children had no books or paper, "just broken pieces of slate and shared bits of chalk. And they were singing a song of praise and welcome to the Canadian visitors." Charles said later, "I don't cry easily, but I cried that morning, asking myself how our world can spend billions on war and not even the barest of necessities for schoolchildren?"

At that time Frontiers was broke, as usual, but Charles promised Lisette help to build a new school. By what he calls luck, which is commonly the result of his cheerful persistence, in those years Charles had a new friend, Mrs. Irene Dyck in Calgary, Alberta. Having seen in a newspaper article that she was connected with charitable work, he telephoned her and identified himself and Frontiers Foundation. "You sound like a nice man. Can I send you $10,000?" she replied. Mrs. Dyck, then and in succeeding years, sent the same amount "many times over." But that was only a small part of her good news. Beginning in the 1970s, the Alberta Agency for International Development, called AID, and later the Wild Rose Foundation, matched such privately raised Alberta charitable donations dollar for dollar; and on top of that, CIDA matched that total three to one. Thus Mrs. Dyck's $10,000 became $60,000, and for many years this productive arrangement funded not only that first new school for kids in Haiti but also 14 river crossings for the new Ennery–St. Michel road, the original 230 kW electrification of St. Michel, the heavy equipment used to extend the road network throughout the St. Michel region, a Land Rover, a truck and tractor, plus seeds and seedlings for the agroforestry program featuring leucaena tree nurseries. Leucaena fertilizes soil, provides ruminant fodder and grows fast enough to be cropped for charcoal 18 months after being planted.

One of the foundation's most extensive projects was an immunization program, providing long-lasting protection against polio, TB, diphtheria, whooping cough and tetanus for 115,000 men, women and children. For this the Frontiers team included Canadian MDs Murray Legge, Blaikie Rowsell, Roy Rowsell and Claude Vipond plus RN Peggy Millson, who assisted Haitian doctors and nurses.

The Baptist pastor in St. Michel, Abraham Lubin, helped with all the projects, especially road improvements; he personally operated the new Alberta-donated bulldozer for months. Whenever Charles visited St. Michel, he preached successively in Catholic and Baptist Sunday services. For the early years of this activity, Frontiers Foundation partnered with the Federation of Councils for Community Action for St. Michel de L'Attalaye (FCAC), which later morphed into Collective Action for the Renewal of Development (ACCORD). Both FCAC and ACCORD represented all eight districts of greater St. Michel: Bas de Sault, Camathe, Lacedras, L'Ermite, Lalomas, Marmont, Platana and St. Michel itself.

From the beginning, Lisette Casimir coordinated every project. During this time, she was also elected deputy for St. Michel, defeating seven male candidates. Eventually, she became both mayor of St. Michel and supermayor for the Artibonite. Soon after the millennium began, Lisette inherited from her father a splendid tract of land, which she donated for a new school designated for St. Michel's poorest children. In 2004 a team of Canadians including Charles, Dr. Murray Legge and Durham Region school principal Tinie Evans visited St. Michel and inspected the proposed site. And finally, after years of persuasion, CIDA agreed in 2008 to match by three to one, to a total of $400,000, a subsidy toward the cost of the new school and for an HIV/AIDS awareness, prevention and treatment facility on the same property. This new school, with classrooms for 250 children, opened in September 2009. The land is safely above all recorded flood levels, and a deep well provides not only potable water for staff and students but enough for the extensive gardens, which are cultivated and harvested by the students as part of the curriculum.

In January 2010 the tremendous earthquake that wracked southern Haiti spared St. Michel, but tens of thousands of refugees fled Port-au-Prince in all directions and St. Michel took in over a thousand of them. ACCORD swung into action to house the children needing to continue their schooling. Immediately, the new school rescheduled classes: for the original enrolment, there would be "morning school" from dawn to noon; for the 250 new children, there would be "afternoon school." That problem solved, CIDA agreed to divert some unspent HIV/AIDS facility dollars to defray the costs of the afternoon school on the understanding that a new application for finishing the HIV/AIDS facility could be submitted by Frontiers. Since 2008 four hurricanes have ravaged Haiti, including St. Michel and the tree nurseries; the 2010 earthquake spread its own devastation throughout the country; and cholera, apparently introduced by UN peacekeepers, is epidemic in Haiti, having sickened hundreds of thousands, of whom six thousand have died. But as Charles, ever the optimist, said of the island and this project:

> One light in this darkness is the new school in St. Michel,
> where, thanks to extreme cleanliness enforcement, not one
> schoolchild has contracted cholera. Our next project will be
> an expanded reforestation effort combining leucaena and
> fruit-tree nurseries, so that not only charcoal, lumber and
> vegetables can be grown but the yield of citrus, avocado and
> mango orchards can also be increased to give area farmers a
> comprehensive boost.[161]

Frontiers volunteers have come from home and overseas, from the Canadian Arctic, from the Bolivian Altiplano, from the cities of Japan, from tropical Africa and, one of the rarest of all peoples, Johnny Kookie from the Belcher Islands in Hudson Bay, who worked on projects in Canada and in Trinidad, where, he said afterward, "I nearly melted." From Mauritius, an island in the Indian Ocean off Madagascar, came Robin Teeluck to Fort Good Hope on the Mackenzie River in northern Canada, where he learned how to build log houses fit to shelter people in the arctic winter. He went on to work on 17 other projects in the Northwest Territories, British Columbia and Ontario. In 1992 the Honourable Lincoln Alexander, Lieutenant-Governor of Ontario, presented Teeluck with an award for his outstanding volunteer service.

God's Lake Narrows United Church,
revisited in August 2009. Charles
Catto, Hilda Perch and the author.

St. John the Baptist Anglican Church,
Split Lake, Manitoba, under construction,
1964. (Courtesy Marion Edwards)

On the steps of the newly finished church at Split
Lake, from right, Rev. Steven Beardy, volunteers
Bruce and Marion Edwards, Richard James and
two unidentified. (Courtesy Marion Edwards)

St. John the Baptist Anglican Church, Split Lake,
in the 1970s. This church remained in use until the
fall of 2006, when it was destroyed by fire. Split
Lake is now known by its Cree name, Tataskweyak, and
the rebuilt church is part of the indigenous diocese
of Mishamikoweesh. (Courtesy the General Synod
Archives, Anglican Church of Canada. P2014-09)

The large log Wabasca–Demarais Recreation
Centre was designed by Frontiers volunteer
architect Richard Isaac with Jamie Thompson
and built with the help of Beaver volunteers
in 1984–85 using timber harvested locally by
community workers. (Courtesy Jamie Thompson)

WABASKA, ALBERTA. BRUCE EDWARDS (RIGHT)
AND HIS FRIEND FRANCIS GLADUE SAW WOOD FOR
STOVES. (COURTESY MARION EDWARDS)

CLARA
YELLOWKNEE,
WABASCA,
ALBERTA,
COMMUNITY
LEADER,
WITH HER
TRUCK AS
THE ROAD
MONITOR
IN 2004.

HOUSE FIRES ARE
A MORTAL DANGER
IN THE NORTH.
BOB MARTIN'S
HOUSE ON FIRE
IN CONKLIN,
ALBERTA.

BRUCE EDWARDS'S DESIGN D, FOR A 16' BY 16'
HOUSE, FIRST BUILT IN WABASCA, WAS USED AGAIN
FOR DORNO DESJARLAIS IN CONKLIN, ALBERTA. AN
OPEN LOFT AT ONE END PROVIDED STORAGE.

THE LARGER,
TWO-STOREY
EDWARDS DESIGN
E, 20' BY 30',
THE NEW HOME
OF SYLVESTER
BONE, WAS
BUILT ENTIRELY
BY VOLUNTEERS
FROM CONKLIN,
INCLUDING
SYLVESTER, HIS
SON RENÉ, AND
ROY TREMBLAY.
OCTOBER 1971.

BEAVER VOLUNTEER DUMAS TREMBLAY'S FAMILY ON
THE STEPS OF THEIR NEW HOUSE, FRONTIERS DESIGN
F, IN CONKLIN, 1971. THIS LARGE TWO-STOREY
DESIGN WAS USED MANY TIMES OVER THE YEARS.

In 1974, Métis activist Ann House stands in front of the Native Arts and Crafts Centre in Dawson Creek, BC, built with help from Frontiers. The teepee-shaped building today forms part of the offices of the Peace River Regional District.

Charles Catto and Cree Chief Jimmy Mianscum at his camp on the Chibougamou road, April 30, 1986. White governments and companies had forced the Oujé-Bougoumou Cree to move off their land many times since 1930.

NEW CREE CHIEF
ABEL BOSUM OF OUJÉ-
BOUGOUMOU, UNDER
WHOSE DETERMINED
LEADERSHIP A SETTLEMENT
WAS REACHED WITH THE
QUEBEC GOVERNMENT.

MESKANO ROAD, OUJÉ-BOUGOUMOU: NEW HOUSES BUILT
IN THE 1990s WITH HELP FROM FRONTIERS VOLUNTEERS.

OUJÉ-BOUGOUMOU, THE NEW TOWNSITE DESIGNED BY THE
RENOWNED CREE ARCHITECT DOUGLAS CARDINAL IN THE
1990S TO BE IN HARMONY WITH NATURE AND REFLECT THE
CREE CULTURE. IN 1995, THE TOWN RECEIVED THE U.N.
HABITAT AWARD FOR EXCELLENCE IN COMMUNITY PLANNING.

ERNIE PHILIP, SHUSWAP DANCER, LEADS THE CELEBRATION
ON THE COMPLETED FIRST FLOOR OF BILLY AND
BLANCHE GLADUE'S HOUSE IN CHETWYND, BC, IN 1972.
AFTER A LONG AND SUCCESSFUL CAREER PERFORMING
CEREMONIAL DANCES THROUGHOUT NORTH AMERICA,
PHILIP TOOK PART IN THE OPENING CEREMONIES
OF THE 2010 VANCOUVER WINTER OLYMPICS.

CHETWYND, BC, NEW HOUSES ON WABI CRESCENT, COMPLETED IN 1973 BY THE FORMER RESIDENTS OF MOCCASIN FLATS WITH THE SUPPORT OF MAYOR FRANK OBERLE AND THE HELP OF LOCAL AND OPERATION BEAVER VOLUNTEERS.

CONTINUING RESIDENTS OF WABI CRESCENT, CHETWYND, BILLY AND BLANCHE GLADUE, IN FRONT OF THEIR HOUSE IN 2010.

JIM CHIGWEDERE, VETERAN VOLUNTEER OF PROJECTS IN LAC DORÉ, WABASCA AND KENORA, AS PICTURED ON THE COVER OF HIS CD, *ZAMBEZI VALLEY SONGS*. ONE VOLUNTEER COMMENTED IN ADMIRATION, "...HE LOOKS LIKE SIDNEY POITIER AND SINGS LIKE HARRY BELAFONTE..." (COURTESY STEPHEN McPHAIL)

Dorothy Polson, an Algonquin of Pikogan, Quebec, and her children. Front row l to r: *Hector Jr. (Sonny), *Alfred, Dorothy, Joshua, *Raymond; second row l to r: Elaine, *Gloria, Shirley, *Virginia, *Glenn, Hilda, *Laura, Diana, *Betsy. The eight marked with * were Beaver volunteers on sites all across Canada.

Log house at Moricetown, BC, completed in the summer of 1982 by Beaver and local volunteers with the help of a building manual. This was the first of many log and frame houses built in the village over the years and is still occupied.

Beaver volunteers, l to r, Neil Jefferson, (New Zealand), Robin Teeluck (Mauritius), Charles Catto, Rosemary Coulton (Canada) and Boaz Tsairi (Israel) on Beaver Road in Moricetown, BC, 1982.

Moricetown Canyon, Bulkley River waterfall. and traditional fishing territory. (Courtesy Northern BC Archives, Accession No. 2008.3.1.22.37, Bridget Moran fonds)

The Moricetown band office, completed in
1984, was one of a number of administration
buildings constructed in the region.

Word of the success of the Beavers' houses spread
and requests for help came in from other communities.
This house at Gitanmaax, BC, near the Skeena River,
was one of many built there and in Kispiox, Glen
Vowel, Kitwancool, Kitwanga and Hagwilget.

Former Gitxsan Chief George Muldoe and
Frontiers' Northern and Western coordinator
Don Irving, who had been a Beaver volunteer
in the area in the 1980s. Kispiox, BC, 2010.

Former band
manager and
chief Dora
Kenni Wilson
and the author
in 2010 at
her house in
Hagwilget, BC,
the first of 90
that were built
in the village
with the help
of Beaver
volunteers.

House in Fort Good Hope, NWT, 1980s. Logs had to be floated down the Mackenzie from Fort Simpson, more than 750 kilometres upriver.

Veteran Beaver volunteer Garfield Bembridge, "the kid from Jamaica." (Courtesy Deborah Deacon)

ROBIN (GURUCHANDRANATH) TEELUCK. FROM MAURITIUS, RECEIVES THE LIEUTENANT-GOVERNOR'S AWARD FOR OUTSTANDING VOLUNTEER SERVICE FROM ONTARIO LIEUTENANT-GOVERNOR LINCOLN ALEXANDER, TORONTO, APRIL 1980.

A PROTEST AGAINST THE HARRIS GOVERNMENT AT THE ONTARIO LEGISLATURE IN TORONTO USED THE ROTATING HOUSE FOR THE FIRST TIME: HALF OLD SHACK AND HALF A NEAT NEW HOUSE. AS CHARLES PUT IT, "OUT OF THE TORY BLUE" CAME A PHONE CALL AND A CHEQUE FOR NEARLY A MILLION DOLLARS FROM ONTARIO HOUSING MINISTER TONY CLEMENT.

The Frontiers rotating house arrives on Parliament Hill, October 17, 1987. (Courtesy Barbara Catto)

Frontiers Foundation vice-president Lawrence Gladue speaks at a demonstration on Parliament Hill in October 1997. Later as president, Gladue appeared again on the Hill in February 2007 when NDP leader Jack Layton hosted a demonstration for Frontiers.

FORMER ONTARIO LIEUTENANT-GOVERNOR LINCOLN
ALEXANDER, AN HONORARY PATRON OF FRONTIERS
FOUNDATION, MEETS WITH BOARD MEMBERS.

VOLUNTEERS NICK TEMPLE-SMITH AND ULDIS
STOEPPLER OUTSIDE THE SMALL FRONTIERS OFFICE,
2328 DANFORTH AVENUE, TORONTO, IN 1977.

Frontiers staff at the larger office, 2622 Danforth Avenue, Toronto, c. 1985. (l to r): Dan Hill, Marla Metson, Marco Guzman, Juanita Jourdain, Susan Polson, Madeline Howe, Farideh Irandoust, Patsy Cuffy, Michael Stevens and Charles Catto.

Chippewa and Beaver volunteers prepare local red pine logs for the new Heritage Hall under construction beside the United Church on the Rama Reserve, near Orillia, Ontario.

VOLUNTEER WORKERS GATHER OUTSIDE THE FINISHED
HALL IN NOVEMBER 1987 WITH GROUP LEADER AND
MASTER LOG BUILDER NEIL JEFFERSON AND CHARLES
CATTO. HERITAGE HALL IS STILL IN USE ON THE RAMA
RESERVE, BETTER KNOWN TODAY FOR CASINO RAMA.

THE ARRIVAL OF 160 TWO-SEATER DESKS BUILT BY VEA
VOLUNTEER CARPENTERS AND TRAINEES FOR DISTRIBUTION
TO FIVE SCHOOLS ON THE BOLIVIAN ALTIPLANO. MARCO
GUZMAN AND CHARLES CATTO, CENTRE, AT COTA
COTA ALTA, OMASUYOS, LA PAZ, MAY 2, 1996.

Mme Lisette Casimir and teachers at the
school in St Michel de l'Attalaye, Haiti.

Nursery in St Michel de l'Attalaye for
leucena plants, which grow quickly and
provide fodder while fertilizing the soil.

THE SCHOOL BUILT IN 1977 IN ST MICHEL DE L'ATTALAYE
WITH HELP FROM FRONTIERS FOUNDATION. IN 2009
DOORS OPENED AT ANOTHER, LARGER SCHOOL FOR 250
HAITIAN STUDENTS, PARTIALLY FUNDED BY CANADIANS.

THE RENOVATED SOUTH BUILDING AT AMIK PLAZA,
WITH THE MEMORIAL TREE, PLANTED IN JUNE 2015
TO HONOUR CHARLES CATTO. AMIK PLAZA WAS
DESIGNED BY ARCHITECT RICHARD REIMER.

Frontiers Manitoba Christmas card, 2010. (l to r) Herbert Wood (Garden Hill), Annette Head (The Pas) and Murray Campbell (Moose Lake) were trained to be instructors for the Standing Tree to Standing Home program. Annette, who was taught by her father, became the first female aboriginal journeyperson carpenter in Manitoba.

STANDING TREE TO STANDING HOME PROJECT IN
CORMORANT, MANITOBA, 2013. (FRONT ROW, L TO R) A
TRAINEE; LYLAS POLSON, FRONTIERS FOUNDATION'S STSH
INSTRUCTOR; CAROLINE CONSTANT, HOUSING DIRECTOR
FOR THE OPASKWAYAK CREE NATION; FRANK WHITEHEAD,
MLA, FOR THE PAS, AND LAUREL GARDINER, FRONTIERS
MANITOBA DIRECTOR, WITH OTHER PROJECT TRAINEES.

A HOUSE IN KITCISAKIK, QUEBEC, DURING A VISIT
BY CHARLES CATTO IN THE 1970S. CONDITIONS HAD
REMAINED VIRTUALLY UNCHANGED FOR 40 YEARS.

In the fall of 2010, student Randy Penosway and Guillaume Lévesque plant trees in front of the new school, École Mikizicec (Little Eagle school) in Kitcisakik, Quebec, designed by the Architectes de l'urgence and built by newly trained workers from the Algonquin community and volunteers. (Courtesy Architectes de l'urgence et de la coopération)

Winners of the Governor-General's award for architecture for the project in Kitcisakik with their medals, May 2012, Ottawa. (l to r) Charles Catto representing Lylas Polson of Frontiers Foundation; Jean-Paul Penosway; Guillaume Lévesque of Architectes de l'urgence; Marianne Papatie, Tciky Penosway and Axel Papatie. (Courtesy Architectes de l'urgence et de la coopération)

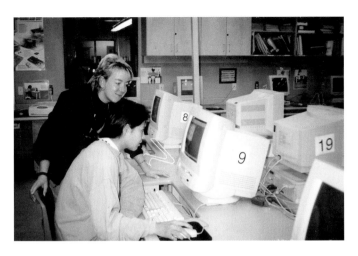

ODILE HAEFFERLIN, FRONTIERS' FIRST VOLUNTEER
FROM ANDORRA, HELPS STUDENTS IN THE COMPUTER LAB
AT JIMMY BRUNEAU SCHOOL IN RAE EDZO, NEAR THE
NORTHERN ARM OF GREAT SLAVE LAKE, NWT, 1998.
HAEFFERLIN ALSO COACHED SPORTS IN THE GYM.

SUSAN EDGAR (ONTARIO) WITH DENE
STUDENTS AND LIBRARY BOOKS AT CHIEF JIMMY
BRUNEAU SCHOOL IN RAE EDZO, 1998.

Northern education volunteer David Overall with his solar array in the remote community of Nahanni Butte, NWT, The electricity generated was used to power the community centre. (Courtesy David Overall)

Dene students and volunteer teachers Brigitte Helgen (Germany) (upper right) and Kayo Nitta (Japan) (centre front), show off their dream catchers in Fort Good Hope, NWT, in 2003. Kayo also taught the students the art of Japanese origami.

James Bacque and Charles Catto prepare to
board a Perimeter Aviation flight to God's
Lake, Manitoba. Winnipeg, August 2009.

Pastor Marcel
Okemow and
Rev. Charles
Catto in the
former's church
in God's River,
2009: "brothers
in faith."

CHARLES AND PUPPET
"JERRY MAHONEY"
ENTERTAINING
YOUNGSTERS IN
GOD'S RIVER, 2009.
JERRY WEARS A
BEADED MOOSEHIDE
JACKET ORIGINALLY
MADE IN GOD'S LAKE
IN 1955 FOR CHARLES
AND BARBARA'S
ELDEST SON, DANNY.

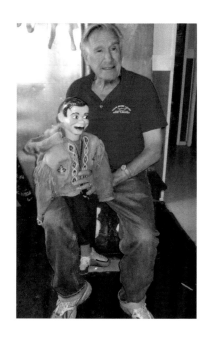

GOD'S LAKE NARROWS, 2009. ELLA ZETTERGREN
AND A FRIEND SHOW OFF A CREE JIGGER
USED FOR FISHING THROUGH THE ICE.

Charles Catto, holding a model F35 fighter jet, MP Peter Julien holding a model house, and MP Carolyn Bennett (now, in 2016, Minister for Aboriginal Affairs) at the last Frontiers demonstration, March 2012. (Courtesy Toby Condliffe)

Frontiers supporters demonstrate in Ottawa for better housing on reserves, March 2012. (Courtesy Toby Condliffe)

CHARLES AND BARBARA CATTO, TWO YEARS BEFORE
CHARLES'S DEATH, AT THE FRONTIERS WIGWAM OF
HOPE DEMONSTRATION IN OTTAWA, ON A COLD DAY
IN MARCH 2012. (COURTESY TOBY CONDLIFFE)

♠ ♠ ♠ ♠ ♠ ♠ ♠ ♠ ♠ ♠ ♠ ♠

FROM SMITHS FALLS
TO THE BIG SMOKE

*If a white man, in travelling thro' our [Iroquois] country, enters
one of our cabins, we treat him as I treat you; we dry him if
he is wet, we warm him if he is cold, we give him meat and
drink that he may allay his thirst and hunger; and we spread
soft furs for him to rest and sleep on; we demand nothing
in return. But if I go to a white man's house in Albany and
ask for victuals and drink, they say, "Where is your money?"
And if I have none, they say, "Get out, you Indian dog."*

— Canassatego, an Iroquois,
to his American friend Conrad Weiser[162]

Until the latter years of the 19th century, life on the reserves, and on
traditional and Métis lands, seemed marginally possible to the peoples
living there, given the help promised them under their treaties with
the British Crown. But then, before the turn of the century, Canadians
began to poison, kidnap and starve Aboriginals on their reserves; steal
their land, fish and meat; build railways, roads, mines, oil fields, hydro
dams and pipelines; and pollute the air and water, bring in invasive
species and farm and log like an invading army – in other words, when
the land of the self-declared Dominion of Canada had been rendered
useless to its indigenous peoples, they began to arrive in the cities of
Canada as refugees.

Their invaders were accompanied by preachers, priests, teachers
and government agents who reached deep into the minds and souls of
the Aboriginal peoples, destroying their self-confidence and replacing
it with self-loathing. As Maggie Siggins has observed in her book *Bitter Embrace*:

It was a vicious circle. The more the Rock Cree got caught in the maw of the fur trade's materialism, the more they came to believe that the white man represented authority. The fur-trader, the clergyman, the Indian agent, the educator, the doctor, all became *okimā*, boss men. In a short time so much that the Cree had believed was meaningful in their culture was deemed improper and inferior. Their way of dressing, their hairstyle, their religion, their art, their names, their ancestors, their medicine, their law, their music, their marriage traditions, their sexual habits, their child-rearing methods – all of these were challenged and then stamped with the mark of the devil.[163]

About 15,000 Aboriginal peoples called early 1960s Toronto home – mainly downtown; this number was ten times the total population of Aboriginals in Toronto in the previous decade.[164] Many of them lived and were shunned in what *Toronto Star* reporter Gary Lautens called a "twilight world." The same sort of thing was true in Kenora, Winnipeg, Regina, Vancouver and many other towns and cities in the country, but almost no one did anything to help these people except a few under-funded agencies and downtown churches. The cost of this to Canada's First Peoples remains very high; about 300 homeless, including a high percentage of Aboriginal people, died over three years in Toronto in the early 1990s.[165]

As mentioned earlier, Frontiers got its first taste of building large-scale, co-operative, urban housing in Chetwynd, BC, and Kenora, Ontario. It also engaged in building smaller ventures such as the tiny Szabo bus project near Smiths Falls, Ontario, and in Almonte, Ontario. In urban centres, Frontiers projects commonly have to overcome resistance from the local residents, whereas on reserve or on Métis land the foundation is often invited by the communities themselves. In more rural areas the attitude of the band members and local Métis is usually helpful, because right from the beginning neighbours, friends and relatives are integral to the project. The resistance to Frontiers' initiatives in urban areas, on the other hand, may run from municipal governments refusing building permits, through to nasty slurs uttered in the street, roving bands of hoodlums who beat up "Indians," and all the way to arson. Such opposition is usually based on fear and ignorance – the massive ignorance among nearly all white Canadians of the value of Aboriginal civilizations, and homeowners' fears of a decline in property values if poor people move into their neighbourhoods.

Despite their rather disquieting experiences in Kenora and Chetwynd, Frontiers volunteers still had not quite understood the full implications of their urban work when they first became aware of the Szabo family, living in an old blue bus near the town of Smiths Falls. Liss Larson, the northeast Ontario field coordinator for the foundation, discovered the bus on Nolan Road in Montague Township north of Smiths Falls. This family consisted of a disabled Hungarian refugee, Leslie Szabo, his Aboriginal wife Gloria, their three sons and their new daughter Dorcas. They had been making a precarious living as tidal flats fishers in British Columbia, Gloria's home province, then had moved east. They had barely enough money to buy a small piece of land north of town and to buy a used bus to park it for shelter. Leslie Szabo kept chickens and they planted a vegetable garden. He installed an old wood-burning stove that cooked their food, warmed the bus and heated their water. He also wangled some second-hand plumbing, which he installed in a bathroom in the back of the bus – all properly connected to a septic tank – and had acquired a bed.

The family had hung on for seven years like that while people passing by averted their eyes from the rusting blue hulk inhabited eventually by three people after the sons had moved out. Then Liss Larson noticed "the bus people" and decided it was time for Frontiers to give a hand. Having been a builder himself, he knew exactly what they needed and, from his Frontiers experience, how to help them get it. Within a few weeks in that summer of 2000, he got in touch with Charles at the foundation in Toronto, sent him an outline of how he would go about the project, received Charles's approval and approached the local authorities. He followed the normal Frontiers practice of keeping all interested parties aware of what was being discussed, then planned and then actually built. He talked to the people at the township office, the local service clubs, the churches, local suppliers and the neighbours of the Szabos.

Liss Larson also got in touch with Henry Benoit, who had founded a philanthropic program to help people who were out of work, the Workplace Skills Initiative program. "After I retired," said Benoit, "I wanted to get into simple activity working for people with something like micro-loans and then I saw the need for this." He funded it himself at first. Then, as he put it, "I finagled others into doing it."[166] He went to county, church and provincial organizers, who agreed to be talked into helping people. Benoit offered his help, and Frontiers coordinated the project through Larson, who told Szabo that if he wanted a new house he could have it, provided he worked on it himself.

Szabo accepted eagerly, working with devoted energy and also providing vegetables, eggs, turkeys and chickens to feed the volunteers. Joan Durant of the Montague and District Seniors Club organized new curtains and bedclothes, while Larson and Szabo set up a work schedule for all the local and Frontiers volunteers and kept the supplies coming in on time. Local handyman Ed O'Neil contributed five solid months of skilled work.

Inspired and led by Benoit and Larson, many local organizations and individuals joined in the parade toward the old blue bus. Jim Ireton of Rideau Lumber donated and delivered all the drywall and some interior paint. When Ireton told Larson there was a choice of all the colours that people weren't buying, Larson replied, "Any colour as long as it's not black." Larson's enthusiasm and common sense appealed to Satellite Trusses, which donated and delivered the huge, heavy trusses. The truss donation helped to induce Lambden Doors and Windows, Country Carpets and others to join in the house-raising bee. Citizens and groups from 15 miles away turned up to help, bringing their own tools. Charles and Marco Guzman visited all three Smiths Falls mainstream churches – Roman Catholic, Anglican and United – and were immediately offered help. Even better were the service clubs, especially the Lions.

Charles then began working the phones, trying to find a cheap source for appliances. One day, he got a call back from an organization called CAMCO, which builds and sells appliances. The call at first went very oddly:

> CAMCO: Hello, Reverend, we have a tractor-trailer load of inventory for you, but they're all almonds. Is that okay?

> CATTO: [remembering a truckload of chocolate bars once donated by Cadbury's] What have you got? Are they nuts?

CAMCO: Fridges, stoves and microwaves, but they're all almond and the yuppies aren't buying almond this year.

CATTO: Sir, we don't care if they're polka-dotted or striped purple and pink, we'll be eternally grateful for all you've got.[167]

The bathroom was furnished in a similar way, after a plumbing supply company called to say that it had a brand new bathtub that had been filled once when it appeared in a TV commercial. That made it used and therefore unsalable. Like the "almonds" from CAMCO's inventory, on it went to Smiths Falls on top of a station wagon donated by the Toronto Kiwanis club, which had also already donated a truck and a cube van.

Although the overcommitted Larson was also supervising 24 other projects that year, he set an early deadline of December 17, 2000, to complete the house. By rising at 3:00 many mornings through that autumn, he pushed enough hours into the day that he could meet all his deadlines. Larson and the volunteers also met the Frontiers Foundation standard of a warm, safe and affordable new house. For the Szabos that year, Christmas came early. And that Christmas present has endured for 10 years now. Lylas Polson, an Algonquin who knows Larson well, said, "You look at Liss's hands, they're all scarred and bent from work – if you could read the marks, they'd say 'workaholic.'"[168]

The "Bus Project" represents a charming example of how Frontiers works and why it works. The Szabos were not helpless, but they did need help and were eager to co-operate in seeking their own good fortune. The neighbours who had shunned them at first warmed to them under Charles's leadership, which was rooted in the neighbourhood, not imposed from above or from away. They brought their skills and their power tools and "probably would have brought the volts too if they had a bucket for them," according to Catto.

The Szabos themselves and even a few of their neighbours were the kind of people for whom the government housing program was designed, but they didn't know about it until Frontiers came along. Frontiers harbours an especially precious combination of international knowledge and local friendships. In Smiths Falls, as elsewhere, Frontiers was able to put people in touch with local companies, service clubs and their national and municipal governments in a useful way that fit everyone's guidelines. And finally, the feeder roots of Frontiers showed in a summary that appeared in the newsletter:

> The local churches, notably the Roman Catholic, Anglican and United congregations, also brought food to the volunteers and rounded up new furniture for the house. Helping hugely with these items were the service clubs, particularly the Lions. This time the Lions were feeding the Christians instead of eating them.

From the Bus Project grew another, which is often the way with Frontiers projects. People like their experience and pass on the good word to others. This process is summed up in a phrase that has often been on Charles's lips, or on his keyboard: Good News. This second project started three years later, in Almonte, a town so close to Ottawa that government workers commuted from there. Steve Barrie, his mother and his wife and children were living in a shack so decrepit that their neighbours rounded up thousands of dollars among themselves, not to help the Barries but to buy them out so they would leave. The neighbours planned to tear down the shack, which was depressing their property values.

The Barries turned down their neighbours' "offer," and were soon discussing with Liss Larson what to do. With their consent, Larson got in touch with Dave Pringle at Workplace Skills Initiative, who had succeeded Benoit. Pringle agreed to follow up the Szabo Bus Project. With a signed agreement in place, they started work. Beside Barrie stood his mother, Laura, in her 70s, slamming nails into studs. Along with many local friends were veteran Belgian Frontiers volunteer Sven Theuns and another returning Frontiers volunteer, Paul Collins from the United Kingdom.

The three-bedroom house earned the highest rating for insulation at that time, R2000, plus a building inspector's praise as "the best house in the neighbourhood." The most surprising award came from the neighbours, who ceased to condemn the place and began to show the compassion that had not been evident before: first they started bringing coffee and doughnuts to the workers, then they arrived in work clothes with tools, ready to help.

At the celebratory housewarming party in January 2004, the neighbours told the Barries how pleased they were that the project had turned out so well. Charles, who often seems an incurable Pollyanna, was wryly realistic this time when he commented, "They knew that because of the project, all their real estate values had gone straight up." Polson said intensely, "Jesus is real."[169]

Charles made Jesus real in many places in Canada where He is virtually unknown or, most often, ignored. Among these was the huge reception room of a gold-plated bank in Toronto where, for years, Frontiers held its annual spring breakfast get-together. At these parties there is a sense of comradeship unusual to feel in such a luxurious room high over Toronto, where young Native girls in beaded and fringed dresses dance delicately on expensive carpets for political candidates, journalists and so on. The fish on the breakfast menu is brought from Batchawana Bay on Lake Superior by long-time Frontiers volunteers Iolene and Olaf Bjornaa.

In another skyscraper one day, Charles met with 28 senior officials from the Ministry of Municipal Affairs and Housing (MMAH) to summarize a completed housing project. One of those officials was a friend in the Ontario government, Susan Bacque,[170] who was the director of the Department of Housing.

Charles arrived at that meeting dressed in his usual fringed deerskin jacket, a gift from a Cree friend, and other donated clothes from his daughter Wanda. His weather-beaten face was mainly shaved, his hair roughly tidied. With a patient smile, he plopped onto the shiny mahogany table a used plastic supermarket shopping bag full of receipts for about $1-million in public spending, of which a significant sum had not yet been reimbursed to the foundation. Inside was a complete and precisely detailed summary of all expenses, their sources, destination and timing. This was probably the first time in the history of the auditors that their audit had been presented to senior stakeholders in a shopping bag, but it passed.

To that meeting Charles also brought photographs of the houses before and after their renovations, because apart from Bacque, the senior bureaucrats rarely met the distressed people or visited the reserves or Métis land where Frontiers worked. Since the prospective owners were supplying sweat equity for houses that were supposed to become their long-term principal dwellings in an enduring community, one of the bureaucrats was appalled to see a For Sale sign in a window of one of the renovated houses. This threatened to wreck the whole concept of the program in the minds of the bureaucrats. They were silent for a moment until Susan Bacque quietly suggested, "Charles, could you bring us a photograph of the same house *without* the sign?"

Charles agreed, and all went well to the end, when Bacque, summarizing results, indicated the distressing shopping bag with a smile and said, "Charles, would you like a receipt?"

After the meeting, Charles did a little more research and found a memo showing that under the contract between Ontario and Frontiers, hundreds of thousands of dollars were owing by the government and overdue by weeks. The accountant at Frontiers figured out the interest charge incurred by Frontiers from the respective invoice due dates. Frontiers then sent a "very blunt reminder" to MMAH of the promise of payment, the debt and the new cost in interest that was enlarging it. The cheque finally arrived four months late, but it did include the requisite $26,000 interest payment.

Regardless of Charles's years of experience in extracting money from government for northern projects, even in the 1980s the cliff-face of Downtown Canada was as steep an urban challenge to Frontiers as it was to Aboriginal and Métis peoples themselves. How was an Aboriginal person, arriving unheralded at the base of the grand towers of the city – including the one literally clad in gold – to scale the great walls that faced him or her? How was an abused young woman from a reserve or a firetrap shack on Métis land to get work? Except as a prostitute. Frontiers staff abhorred the situation like many thousands of others, but they were also determined to do something about it.

The idea of Project Amik[171] was born when the foundation's directors spotted an old factory for sale in central Toronto, on almost an acre of land, served by public transportation near Coxwell Avenue and Gerrard Street. A big two-storey industrial building formed the southern section, and north of it was plenty of land for above-ground parking plus garden space, and, north again, enough space for a new apartment building. Frontiers entered into negotiations with the city, the province and the federal government to finance the renovation of the building to house hundreds of people instead of the rats, frogs and raccoons already in residence.

The city's Let's Build Toronto program offered enough money to get Frontiers started with detailed planning and fundraising from other levels of government and local community agencies. Work went forward until the Metropolitan Separate School Board (Catholic) demanded over $90,000, which was their due under the law, to offset the increase in their costs caused by the new students expected to live in the new apartments. In vain Charles protested; in vain he appealed for relief from the demand. The board would not budge. Finally, he approached the F.K. Morrow Foundation, run by the Sisters of St. Joseph, a Catholic charity. The good sisters guaranteed to donate what the board needed and a little more. Then Frontiers had to fight off the tax grab the various governments were making by imposing regular sales taxes on the building materials and services that were needed. This tax grab, including $380,000 in mortgage insurance, would amount to $1.3-million, some $400,000 more than the $900,000 forgivable loan offered to Frontiers by the CMHC for the project! Charles worked the phones, sent out letters, visited the bank vice-presidents in their skyscraper offices, and in the end all the taxes were covered.

Along with the raccoons, pigeons and other unwanted creatures living in the buildings, there were human beings nearby to cope with: Not In My Back Yard (NIMBY) people who feared the worst for their property values and neighbourhood morality. At one information meeting, a woman with a strong Cockney accent stood up to object loudly to the drunken Aboriginals coming into "my" area. The soberly dignified Lawrence Gladue, now a director of Frontiers, was standing near her, beside his daughter Kim. Gladue said, "You know, Mrs. X, we Aboriginals did make one serious mistake a long time ago – we had a lousy immigration policy."[172] Mrs. X, who had not suspected that the good-looking, well-dressed man standing near her was actually Aboriginal, was so embarrassed that she turned red and left the room in silence. But there was, of course, no apology.

Another challenger said, "Nobody around here wants this project, so forget it, Catto." Charles immediately produced the list he had just made of 36 neighbours who had already volunteered to work on the site. Their names were all listed with addresses and phone numbers for the NIMBYs to see.

After the meeting, Frontiers received a circular letter sent around the neighbourhood by a candidate running for city council in the area against the incumbent, Sandra Bussin, a supporter of Amik. According to Charles, the letter said the effects of Amik would be "as bad as the Black Death, an earthquake and the great Toronto fire." It was signed by a "Mrs. W."

Charles and Frontiers executive director Marco Guzman took the letter to the return address shown on it and knocked on her door. There was no answer, so they asked a neighbour when Mrs. W would be in. The neighbour answered, "Never, actually, she's dead."[173]

All this time, various Frontiers volunteers were at work doing the preliminary cleanups and moving the wildlife out so the professionals could move in to dig the foundations for the new building and underpin the old. Marco Guzman worked as a carpenter, and in the end, he liked the project so well that he moved into it. One of Frontiers' directors, Steve McPhail, a Métis who had also made historical and promotional films for the foundation, figured out how to cope with raccoon families. A man of all trades, he lassoed them and dragged them out of the building squealing and snarling.

The one-, two- and three-bedroom apartments, all equipped with modern appliances, are for seniors, Aboriginal people and handicapped people. On the ground floor of the main building is a big, bright community meeting room and art gallery. The head offices of Frontiers Foundation are next to it. The site is near parks and shopping, and the management, New Frontiers Aboriginal Residential Corporation, chaired by Shelley Charles, an Ojibwa elder, lobbied successfully for a new crosswalk to be installed across dangerous Coxwell Avenue for the handicapped residents and for the children attending *Le Petit Chaperon Rouge*, a bilingual nursery school that is part of the complex.

Bringing government into the funding mix may not always provide a solution, as Frontiers found during the Amik project and others, but it does change the problem. Government may increase the funding considerably, but it always adds to the cost and sometimes provides wasteful competition, as for instance with the Katimavik project, which took over many of Frontiers' ideas and spent large amounts of money for which they got far fewer results than Frontiers did. The one major and honourable exception to this rule was the Trudeau initiative under Ron Basford and Lawrence Gladue of the CMHC, which promised 50,000 houses and actually put up 114,000 houses in a few years.

Frontiers has always differed significantly from other NGOs because it is truly ecumenical. People from nations with an imperialist past or present, such as Belgium, Canada, France, Germany, Japan, Portugal, Spain, the UK and the USA, often use charitable giving as if it were an extension of their country's combat missions. One such organization in the United States, the Central Asia Institute (CAI), famous for constructing girls' schools in Pakistan and Afghanistan, has had to cope with the current wars of its government, even though its own work is generous and far-sighted. The founder of CAI, Greg Mortenson, writes of the relief he helped organize for disaster victims in the war zone after recent earthquakes and floods:

> Unfortunately some of the smartest and most effective assistance was provided by groups of Islamic militants... I have always been dismayed by the West's failure – or unwillingness – to recognize that establishing secular schools that offer children a balanced and non-extremist form of education is probably the cheapest and most effective way of combating this kind of indoctrination. Despite the fact that the American government has never grasped its importance, this calculus has been at the very heart of what we do from the very beginning... [174]

The word "unfortunately" that begins this statement highlights a huge difference between Mortenson's brilliant and courageous work and the achievements of Frontiers. From the very beginning, Frontiers has always emphasized that it is creating not houses and schools so much as tolerance, understanding, knowledge and friendship among all the peoples of the communities involved. Everyone is welcome to help in that spirit, so no help from any individual or group can be called "unfortunate."[175]

STANDING TREE TO
STANDING HOME

Frontiers, always shapeshifting in response to changes among Métis, Aboriginal and white peoples, began passing into several new phases in the late 20th and early 21st century.

Partly owing to Frontiers' success in delivering services to First Nations using private as well as government money, the Aboriginal peoples themselves began to want to eliminate third-party service providers. Insisting to government that self-rule was essential to their survival – and had always been their right – they have increasingly tried to take over the administration of federal funds. So many claims arose that experienced third parties were effectively shut out of the process regardless of their success or failure.

Frontiers responded to these changes in First Nations communities by following its earliest impulse: to help people in need. This accounted in part for the foundation's shift toward serving remote Métis communities and filling needs in urban centres with projects such as Amik. But Frontiers went much farther – into the far North with conventional, school-based educational programs that avoided the money quarrels that had arisen and fed funds into training programs. These school programs were wildly popular because the Frontiers Foundation administrator, Don Irving, from his office in Surrey, BC, brought in idealistic young teachers to work with local, mainly Aboriginal school boards which themselves received large grants from the federal government. Thus these school boards, accepting responsibility for the government funds and dispensing them with help from Frontiers, preserved some independence and at the same time profited from Frontiers' expertise, including their eager volunteers.

Frontiers also set up a new skills-training program of its own, funded by volunteers, private sources and two levels of government: federal and provincial. The federal government ushered Frontiers into a new phase in December 2009, when its Aboriginal Skills Training and Strategy Investment Fund (ASTSIF) signed a contract providing $1-million to the foundation for training Aboriginal and Métis peoples in construction skills, a form of on-site, hands-on teaching that had been pioneered by Frontiers long before, at Batchawana Bay in Ontario and South Indian Lake, Manitoba. Up to then, training had taken place on site, during the hustle and excitement of constructing a single house for a needy family or a building for an entire community. Now, with more money and more time to spend on training, the skills quotient and efficiency of the trainees increased rapidly. Soon they were able to compete in local job markets and get off welfare. Here begins the virtuous circle that Frontiers has always promoted and loved: with more people off welfare, demand for government money drops and the tax base spreads. Named Standing Tree to Standing Home, a new Frontiers Foundation initiative is already training Aboriginal peoples on three sites, one each in Quebec, Ontario and Manitoba.

In October 2009, Marco Guzman and volunteer Steve McPhail drove to northern Quebec to help inaugurate a project supported by the federal and Quebec governments at Kitcisakik, an Algonquin (Anishinaabe) village south of Val d'Or. The Aboriginal inhabitants and Frontiers were joined in this venture by members of Architectes de l'urgence et de la coopération (AUC), an international humanitarian effort by Quebec architects similar to the worldwide physicians' initiative Médecins sans frontières (Doctors without Borders). Members of the AUC had been pained by the dangerous condition of the housing in the community, and they made Kitcisakik their first mission in Canada. Architect Guillaume Lévesque and his team of volunteers joined long-time Frontiers Quebec regional coordinator Lylas Polson, himself Algonquin, and the Aboriginal trainees. With the large Frontiers sawmill, they prepared local and donated lumber for the renovation of two existing houses in the fall. Lylas taught the trainees the safe use of the sawmill, how to read architectural drawings, construction techniques and the requirements of the Quebec building code.

Since that trip in 2009, 30 houses have been renovated according to plans drawn by the architects and the Algonquin families. A new primary school and gymnasium built to answer community needs was inaugurated in October 2010. Four Algonquin trainees along with

QUEBEC FIELD COORDINATOR LYLAS POLSON WITH THE
FRONTIERS WOOD-MIZER SAWMILL AT KITCISAKIK, QUEBEC.

Guillaume Lévesque, AUC and Frontiers Foundation were awarded Governor General's medals in architecture in May 2012 for the project in Kitcisakik. And by December 2014, 14 trainees had proudly received their carpentry certification papers from le Centre Polymétier de Rouyn-Noranda (a construction trade school) after completing a 1,500-hour training course with certified carpenters.

In Collins, Ontario, Frontiers offers courses in framing and interior carpentry, electrical installation, drywalling, plumbing, foundations, roofing, insulation, finishing and maintenance. All projects will reflect the Standing Tree to Standing Home concept pioneered by Frontiers years ago. On each project, local timber is harvested, kiln dried and milled by local trainees directed by local volunteer coordinators. The foundation's portable Wood-Mizer mills make dimensional lumber on site; the newest mill is an LT40H hydraulic, easily capable of lifting a tree trunk to the bed, where the saw shapes it. The teacher–trainers are drawn from trades training institutions in Winnipeg and in Thunder Bay and Temiskaming, Ontario, and provide classroom and on-site training in Collins.

In Manitoba, the Standing Tree to Standing Home project site is Garden Hill, a Cree community on Island Lake, where five new log homes will be built under the supervision of field coordinator Brian Monkman. Monkman, who lost an arm in an accident, speeds around Winnipeg, various work sites and the Manitoba section of the project accomplishing the work of two fully armed people. During 2010 he

BRIAN MONKMAN, FORESTRY AND FRAMING PROJECT
MANAGER AND STANDING TREE TO STANDING HOME
INSTRUCTOR AT RED RIVER COLLEGE, WINNIPEG.

helped professional curriculum developers at Red River College in
Winnipeg produce a five-course certificate program. The trainees are
registered as students at Red River and get a college certificate upon
completion. The foundation has been greatly assisted in this work by
the co-operative attitude – and funding – of CMHC.

One woman signed up in the Standing Tree to Standing Home
course at Sagkeeng First Nation in Manitoba. Erin Courchene is a
single mother and was at the time the only woman participant in this
trades training program that is unique to Canada. Courchene has participated in every phase of home construction, from harvesting and
milling the timber to cutting the siding. Monkman, her instructor, says
she is a "crackerjack" sawyer.

Frontiers was granted the money for this program because they have a no-holds-barred approach to fundraising. The foundation persuaded the Manitoba government to co-operate in a federal project, which at first had apparently excluded provincial participation. "Shades of the Catholics, Presbyterians and Uniteds arguing over converts on the frontier," said Charles, who was fully ecumenical when it came to rounding up money.[176]

Since 2008, Frontiers, led by Manitoba director Laurel Gardiner, has provided instruction to over 100 trainees in safety, harvesting, sawmilling and log, timber-frame and stick-wall construction. Three sawmills in the Island Lake area can now grade their lumber according to National Building Code standards.

In 2009, Frontiers in Manitoba, in partnership with Mary Robinson of Forintek[177] for the third year running, offered a highly successful log-cabin-building course, headed by master builder Walter Keller. Graduates of the program were from Garden Hill and Wasagamack, where no such training or experience was ever available before. Three of the first graduates went on to build their own log homes. One father-and-son team bought a sawmill to supply logs and lumber to other builders, and one First Nation opened up a new development area designated specifically for log homes. At Forintek, the combination of university-level scientific research and practical industrial experience provided an opportunity not available otherwise to First Nations peoples, who were brought into the program by Frontiers.

Laurel Gardiner describes the saga of one of Frontiers' Wood-Mizer sawmills, which was being moved from Garden Hill to Wasagamack on Island Lake. The mill, loaded on a flat-bottomed barge together with an assortment of fridges, freezers and stoves, was being towed on the lake when the barge was overturned by strong winds. Fridges and freezers were bobbing in the water. Of the stoves and the Wood-Mizer there was no sign.

The Mounties were called in for the rescue. They lowered a cable with a camera into the water. There, impaled in the mud like a sword, was the Wood-Mizer. Their grappling hook snagged the mill, winched it to the surface and towed it to shore, missing only its cover and a gas can.

The mill was drained and left to dry until Brian Monkman could get in from Winnipeg. He drained it some more, dried off the spark-plugs and started it up. Amazingly, it ran! Loaded up again, this time with chains to the barge, and calmer weather, the Wood-Mizer arrived safely in Wasagamack, where it provided lumber for a youth centre, a mission house for the Catholic priest, a bathroom addition and a new dock for Manitoba Hydro.

NORTHERN EDUCATION

In 1940 a baby girl named Geniesh was born in a Cree village called Ji-sah-seebee[178] on an island in a river leading to Hudson Bay. Geniesh had a double identity from her birth because her father was white and her mother Cree. The village had a second name as well, Fort George, after the English emperor who also lived on an island 3,000 miles away over the sea. Her father, an employee of the Hudson's Bay Company, proposed marriage to her mother when she was pregnant, but Geniesh's Cree grandparents would not allow it at first because they had been taught by the Anglican and Catholic missionaries to keep their girls away from white men. Like most Aboriginal people on the island, they believed that "*all* white men drank, robbed, raped, murdered, beat their wives and children, had countless extra-marital affairs and eventually ran off with their mistresses, leaving their poor defenceless wives and children to starve. Only those [missionaries] chosen and sent by God could be trusted."[179]

Finally, the family relented, but it was too late. Her mother had decided not to accept the problems of a mixed-race marriage. Her father, weeping, was sent away from the family, and the Hudson's Bay Company transferred him to another post 1,200 miles away. During the war, he joined the Royal Canadian Air Force and was killed over Germany, fighting for the English king, so Geniesh never met him.

She grew up definitely Cree but still believing fervently in the worth of white people, especially the school teachers and the Anglican minister. Because she was very bright, she was sent to residential schools, starting with St. Philip's Indian and Eskimo Anglican Residential School at Fort George, Quebec. She went willingly and studied eagerly. She did so well that she was promoted again and again, received offers of housework from local white women and was encouraged by a few of her teachers. On the other hand, in Sault Ste. Marie, Ontario, where she went to residential high school, she was partly bewildered and partly offended by the curriculum itself, by the attitudes of white people in the city and by the domineering attitude of most of the teachers, which was mixed with a sneering racism. This combination came close to destroying her eager spirit. She wrote:

> For twelve years I was taught to love my neighbour – especially if he was white – but to hate myself. I was made to feel untrustworthy, inferior, incapable and immoral. The barbarian in me, I was told, had to be destroyed if I was to be saved. ...
>
> When I had been stripped of all pride, self-respect and self-confidence, I was told to make something of myself to show the white man that not all Indians were savages or stupid. When I failed, I was told with a shrug, "Well, what do you expect from an Indian?"[180]

While at residential school, Geniesh met a visionary soul in the vice-principal, known to her only as Mr. Weir. Weir made a point of encouraging her. "You're the one we need to help us change a few prejudiced ideas people have about Indians," he told her in his office soon after she arrived in the city. "You can show the people of this town that Indians, if given a chance, are just as smart as other children."[181] He put his arm gently around her shoulder leading her to the door, a gesture she remembered affectionately many years later.

At the time, Geniesh did not believe a word he was saying, but during the years she spent at the school she came to see that he meant everything he had said. She came to look upon him as a second grandfather. The same was true a few years later and 2,000 miles away with little Dora Kenni Wilson in Hagwilget, who escaped attending residential school but then liked and learned from her Mennonite teacher George Thiessen in a Roman Catholic day school.

It is clear that the Canadian prejudice against Aboriginal peoples, though massively reinforced by church, state, police and schools, did not prevail all the time and everywhere, because a few people remained kind and understanding.

The spiritual wounds inflicted on Geniesh by Canadians were also found among many hundreds of thousands throughout the North, adult and child alike. In 1987, trying to cope with all these, Frontiers sent Don Irving on a search for volunteers, whom he found eventually at the United World Colleges in Wales. He invited about a dozen to go north to Aklavik, Northwest Territories. Thus began Frontiers' attempts to repair the vast damage inflicted by the residential schools program now being mitigated by the Truth and Reconciliation Commission of Canada. That commission necessarily looked backward to blame people, to apologize for their crimes and to go as far as possible toward compensating for them. Frontiers is, if you like, taking care of the future.

Irving has developed a co-operative system that uses public money to serve a public purpose: educating children. The program combines the local resources of northern school boards with the international reach and authority of Frontiers Foundation, all funded reliably and renewably by the government of Canada.

These school boards, sensitive to local needs and resources, approach Frontiers West for help. Frontiers suggests and helps devise programs best suited to each board, searches out volunteers across Canada and around the world, matches them to the needs and sends them north. As with many other Frontiers projects, there are two kinds of benefits to the program. The direct results are happy, well-educated students who are better able to either move into mainstream society in the South or remain in the North, conforming as closely as they wish to the values and customs of their ancestors.

The indirect results vary from spontaneous suicide-prevention programs to solar-panel electrical generation to drum-making to acting in Broadway musicals. Irving thinks that for northern school boards, "Getting our volunteers is like getting a new car with all of the options rather than a basic model. Our volunteers are in the schools because they very much want to be there. Far too many teachers in the North are there because they have the opportunity to make a lot of money, and they show very little interest in getting involved in the community or learning about the culture and way of life."[182] Often the high salaries are not enough to attract teachers with the specialized skills that are in high demand in other, more comfortable areas.

Salaries for full-time professional teachers are extremely high in the North because southerners feel isolated there. Many need to earn a lot because they are carrying big student debts. Northern school boards also have to offer them subsidized housing two free trips to the

South per year, along with other incentives. Wages differ somewhat from area to area, but the average cost of a teacher in the NWT as of August 2015 was around $110,000 a year. Frontiers volunteers, who may not teach directly in the classroom, cost the boards about $35,000 per school year, including heated housing, food and living expenses, travel and insurance, a small personal stipend to cover the high northern costs of necessities, and a contribution to Frontiers' overhead and administration.

A good example of Frontiers' success with this program is in the far north of the NWT, in the Beaufort Delta area. In 2014 the Beaufort Delta Education Council wanted to start an e-learning program for students in the most remote communities, such as Fort McPherson, Inuvik, Tuktoyaktuk and Ulukhaktok. The students in these schools who wish to continue on to post-secondary education need Grade 12 graduation-level classes in math, sciences and English, but there are often no instructors available in the northern schools to teach these courses. In the past, students from these northern schools went on regardless to southern colleges or universities only to find themselves hopelessly behind the other students and so discouraged that they often dropped out.

The students needed full-time teachers to help them catch up with the southerners, but there was not enough money. They could learn via the Internet, which was much cheaper, but they still required supervision and expert guidance. The school boards did not have funds to pay full-time, high-cost teachers to supervise the e-learning so they requested volunteers, who arrived from Frontiers.

This system is at work in Fort McPherson, Inuvik, Tuktoyaktuk and Ulukhaktok, with volunteers who are also responsible for games, sports, exercise, creative arts and so on. "Teaching is extended and improved, and our volunteers get to have a unique and amazing experience," Irving wrote. "How often do you see situations where everyone benefits and the price goes down?"[183] Irving's selection process is crucial to the overall program. One danger is eager young volunteers, nicknamed "voluntourists," from some comfortable home in Europe or North America, who come to save the world in a few weeks while meeting beautiful young people. These young people, many of them taking a gap year between high school and university, are basically good-hearted, cheerful and energetic. But they want to have a good time while doing a good deed. These youngsters are not what Irving needs. He copes with them by describing the reality of the suicidal despair and terminal lassitude they may well encounter. Alongside youthful good cheer, volunteers must possess adult calm in the face of disaster.

For instance, a volunteer might get to Fort Treeless on a Wednesday and decide that it is the most beautiful place she has ever seen, not just because of the scenery but because of the people. The next week, she is not so sure, and at the end of the month, when the welfare cheques arrive, she barricades herself with another volunteer in their little house, all doors locked, lights out, as drunk people roam around the village lashing out at almost anything in sight. The following morning, she talks about quitting. The ones who actually do quit are rare, however, because Irving's filter works so well.

He searches out volunteers who can survive ordeals "that would send most people crying out into the night."[184] In order to find the potential survivors, Irving tries to discourage them all, because the ones he can discourage will not be much help. The sort of person he needs unites romance and idealism with practical realism animated by hopes to better the world, all of this gentled by love of children, cheered by a sense of humour and suffused with a happy, honest and willing spirit in a healthy body. He manages with his mixture of rueful humour, honesty and well-tempered idealism. According to his own judgment, "I am a cross between a slave-trader and a pimp. But when I look at those beautiful young people coming in every year to help, I feel like Saint Peter at the Pearly Gates. But kids like that turn up every year. The universe treats Frontiers differently from other places; we always get just enough people like that."[185]

After one particular set of survivors of the "Don Irving Course in Northern Realism" got to Aklavik, they decided they were going to cheer up the kids with an odd new project. In the depressing darkness of winter days when the sun is at best a bright streak in the south for a few minutes each day, and the clearest sky is just a dark-grey blur, the kids came to school in their furry boots, breathing huge puffs of smoke-like breath into the dimness, went into class and began singing and dancing and jumping around to the tunes of *The Lion King*.

The children and the volunteers were up against a tremendous cultural wall here. Not only was the theatre itself a foreign experience, but the self-confidence required to go on stage and risk embarrassment was hard for them to generate. For these were the children of generations of abuse. As volunteer Toni Eichhorn put it:

> I'm sure there are many theories on why alcohol and vio-
> lence twine together in northern communities. Yet the
> shared underbelly of those theories seems to be the lasting
> effects of residential school. Abuse was very much a part
> of the students' lives. They grew up in a system where you
> bury your feelings, you don't discuss your problems and if
> you speak out of turn you get hit, or worse. They grew up
> away from their families and their way of life only to return
> as strangers, no longer knowing their language or culture,
> or too afraid to participate in it for memory of the punish-
> ments they would receive at school for that. Further, having
> spent so little time at home, if any, abuse was the only form
> of interpersonal expression many ever had the opportunity
> to know.
>
> Having been privileged to attend testimony at the
> TRC event in Inuvik prior to returning south, and hearing
> many of my neighbours speak of their own experiences for
> the first time, I … remain in awe at the strength and resili-
> ence that persists nonetheless.[186]

Yet, against all odds, the kids and the volunteers were going to put on this jungle tale for the whole community, and as it turned out, for many thousands of others. They memorized, they rehearsed, they sang, they danced, they emoted on stage, these boys and girls of Moose Kerr Elementary School, who had been taught that they couldn't do any-thing. But they stayed after school, they made it a personal and school project, and they advertised, promoted and presented it. Mothers sewed lion costumes for these children who had never even seen grass, let alone a jungle tree, and the kids co-operated by keeping the play running for three nights.

News of the production spread far and wide, or at least as far as CBC North in Yellowknife, which flew in a crew to film it. The MLA for the riding also flew in. The boys and girls, most of whom grew up in a tradition that encourages them to be shy and quiet, had a lot of fun on stage, and they opened up happily to themselves and the crowd, to their mutual surprise. Nobody had believed it could happen and then it happened. That's Frontiers.

When writing about her experience, Eichhorn concluded, "In my time here, I've seen many trips and adventures take place that required tons of fundraising, yet the kids don't seem to be obliged to participate in that fundraising." Her very presence is a problem in that regard, because if she is not careful, she will end up doing it all, and then the kids "don't grow up to any sense of responsibility. This is true of the adults as well." If the organizers try to get people started on a project, they risk stultifying the sense of initiative of the kids and adults. "We have an annual volleyball tournament that the entire community attends. The prize money is fairly significant and yet there are very few of the players involved in the fundraising."[187]

ON PLANET REZ

We already had flown a long way from our southern city to a small airport on the edge of the boreal forest, but we still had far to go. At Perimeter Aviation's check-in desk, two happy-looking Cree and Métis girls smiled all-out as Charles approached them. Luba Andrews and Gloria Bland knew we were on our way, and one of them now jumped over the baggage belt to hug and kiss him. As we were introduced to the girls, Elisabeth and I felt we were not being checked in to an airline but welcomed to a party. Charles spread out the huge folder of photographs assembled into a five-foot-wide greeting card, which Barbara Catto and Marilyn Gillis, Charles's secretary, had been making for days. They had included old black and white photographs of friends from Charles's earliest days at God's Lake and God's Lake Narrows, and many more of his friends from later years. Andrews and Bland looked at it eagerly, exclaiming gleefully at the photographs of their cousins, parents and grandparents.

Speaking Cree and English, Andrews and Bland acted like old friends, even though these kids had never met any of us before. But then, the Andrews and Bland families had been church members for many years, notably during Charles's tenure at God's Lake Narrows.

The proportions of our universe changed as we lifted off in the small Perimeter plane and headed north. The city where we had started, with its many millions of people packed into cars and towers, had always seemed vast to us, spreading over perhaps 1,200 square miles. But up here, our wings spanned a tremendous green distance where maybe only a few families were living, over an area that could not be appropriately described in square miles, because everything in sight was shaped by nature into ragged blue lakes, twisty silver rivers, blue-shadowed ridges, light-spotted forests, steep and dark valleys, with nowhere a corner or straight line – except perhaps for a Manitoba Hydro line cutting across the view. And even that lonely line had not a single person or house visible near it.

The farther north we flew, the more the land below gave way to water until we were above a gigantic lake embroidered with islands and peninsulas. Then we left shore to fly over what seemed like a blue ocean set with thousands of green islands. Finally there was more water below us than land. In the city, we and our works were vast, overflowing; we *were* the landscape. But here, we were mites and the land overflowed us.

We finally landed on a gravel strip at God's Lake Narrows, where Charles had first preached 55 years before, and we walked to a small terminal building, a cabin really, made of wood. Our bags were delivered by hand to a small open-air stand under a shed roof. A dozen or more people drove up in dusty pickup trucks to say hello, and several helped us get our knapsacks.

The departing plane blew dust back at us as it taxied out to take off for its next stop. Dust was everywhere on that reserve, on the landing strip and on every road because all are made of gravel from a stone quarry nearby.

We were introduced to many kinds of people, the old and the young, the helpless and the vigorous. Thus we became part of the rolling party that is the reserve: people visit back and forth all day – at the airport, in their trucks, at church, in the band office, on the road, in the various kitchens and living rooms in their houses. There are no bars, because alcohol was banned at Charles's urging over 50 years before, and it still is. There are no restaurants because every kitchen is open to everyone. No one would dream of charging money for feeding a relative or a friend here, and all are friends or relatives.

The physical appearance of this reserve is strange to city eyes. Most of the houses have lots of room around them, but they seem crowded because the front yards flow fenceless into each other, and most are growing crops of rusty trucks or snowmobiles. No one worries about the trash lying around; we saw a well-educated woman occupying a responsible position in the community finish her drink and then casually toss her empty plastic bottle out the window of the truck. We saw only one vegetable garden in this village of 700-odd people. No one had a flower garden.

In the band office, where we met the chief and several council members, we were told of the progress that had been made in the last

15 years. The roads and landing strip had been built, replacing the bush trails that used to wind around the knolls and trees. Clean water supply pipes had been laid to every house so no one had to lug water uphill in slopping buckets, as Charles and Barbara had done decades before. Sewage pipes collected the waste water for treatment in a new plant, replacing the outhouses and bush disposal. The school had been built and teachers trained with government grants administered by the band council. Among the teachers was Ella Zettergren, the daughter of Hilda Perch, who had been baptized by Charles. There was a warm and happy reunion at Hilda's house. As Charles has written, thanks to Marcel Okemow and kindred spirits, God's River and God's Lake Narrows have been transformed in the last half-century from desperate places of ramshackle huts lacking clean piped water, sanitation, doctors, roads, telephones, airport and electricity, to organized communities with regularly scheduled airline service, safe water on tap, a complete sewage system, hydro power, road, medical and emergency nursing care facilities, plus all kinds of communications technology, including their own radio station. The leaders in this transformation have been energetic Cree spirit builders led by Marcel Okemow.

In the mid-1980s, Okemow had had a transformative experience in which the Great Spirit in the form of Jesus Christ urged him to initiate a local crusade of prayer meetings. Sustained for decades by this vision, Okemow was successively chief, councillor and airborne evangelist, leading an enthusiastic crowd of young followers with the help of Frontiers. In 1993, Okemow, Frontiers volunteer Andy Hagenguth and a group of God's River teenagers using a Frontiers WoodMizer portable sawmill had harvested standing spruce on a nearby island to build the Youth Retreat Centre, which just before our visit had been enlarged with a new assembly hall.

We saw the quarry where the gravel for the roads had been mined. Nearby, ten two-storey houses had been erected with band-council money by builders approved by CMHC. Later, we flew by Perimeter to visit another part of the reserve, God's River, 50 miles north on the same lake, a flight of about 15 minutes. We were given comfortable rooms in the big lodge maintained for tourist fishers flying in to catch what they call "trophy fish." Many of the tourists used to come from the United States, but now more and more are Canadians who fly in from Winnipeg.

God's Lake Youth Retreat Centre, built from local spruce with the help of Frontiers log construction expert Andy Hagenguth in the summer of 1993.

When Charles had first come up here from God's Lake Narrows, the two parts of the reserve were separated by several hours' travel in a motorized canoe, sometimes much longer if the winds were unfavourable. Airplane flights were impossibly expensive for band members and for clerics. Only government officials, prospectors, loggers and Hudson's Bay Company traders could afford a plane flight. Otherwise, the quickest way was in winter, behind a good dog team that might make the trip in under a day.

In recent years, immense changes initiated by Frontiers and Okemow have occurred in both places. From a technology based on hunting, trapping and fishing, these people have moved much of the way into the modern era. Supplies such as the carcass of a moose or caribou, which used to come into the villages mainly by muscle power, or via portage and canoe, or fishnet or winter road, now come in by the winter road and by air. The air ambulance service and the Internet give band members access to modern medicine. Satellite television acquaints them with parts of the world outside the reserve. The Aboriginal Peoples Television Network puts them in touch with other indigenous communities governing themselves in other parts of Canada, including Nunavut and the Northwest Territories. The reserve is also connected to the Manitoba Hydro system, which helps the people not only light houses and the school but also connect to the Internet.

The United Church's little one-room day school of the 1950s has been replaced by a big, well-heated building where hundreds of students have a chance to undertake the education they must have if they want to work off-reserve. But there are strong countercurrents that show how difficult the transition from the early missionary days to the Internet era has been for many people. At the community centre nearby, the windows have been vandalized so often that they have been replaced by bricks. The doors are now bulletproof, which make the place seem like a resented outpost of the dominant colonizing power. More buildings alone will do little for the reserve at this point. What is needed now is education. Frontiers, having discovered this with painful slowness, is now supplying that need, especially in the North, with its system of volunteers in classrooms and sports facilities.

The God's Lakers have survived much, but throughout everything they have honoured their ancestors. Many of the old people of the reserve live in apartments in new, clean, warm, well-lighted low-rise buildings with plenty of space for each individual, good kitchens and rooms for games and meetings. The loneliness that may come with age does not afflict them as badly as it does many old people who feel abandoned in the tall, concrete people-cupboards in the big cities.

With old William Perch seated in the place of honour – the right front seat of the truck – and the guests knees-to-chin in the back, we drove around God's Lake Narrows, visiting people and towing an immense cloud of dust. After many stops, we arrived back at Perch's place and parked in the driveway with the engine running. Beside the front steps of the house, a long wooden ramp accommodated a wheelchair so Perch could get up and down. They wheeled him inside and we sat down near a cast-iron woodstove with a fire in it, where Perch could warm himself although the day was sunny. The lake to the south sparkled so brightly that I could scarcely look away from it. I had never seen water so shining bright. The room was hot and dark, so I went outside with my notebook and sat at a weathered picnic table on the deck in the sun, looking out toward the lake.

As I made a few notes, a girl of about seven came out of the house and sat down opposite me. This was Jenissa, William Perch's grand-daughter, I assumed. She asked me what I was doing so I told her and showed her. We talked for a few minutes, and then a girl's voice called up to her from below the edge of the deck. "What are you doing?"

"I'm talking to a very old man. He has white hair and he's wearing red. I think he is Santa Claus."

We heard the other girl coming up the steps. She was Jenissa's friend Maddy. She sat down with us and asked to draw in the book as Jenissa had been doing. They asked if I had a dog, and I told them about the dog my family had once had, a Gordon setter named Laird's Ghillie of Glencoe.

"What happened to him?" asked Jenissa.

"My dad brought him to the cottage in a little box when we were kids. He had golden fur on his chest and two little gold eyebrows, and the rest of him was black except for his tail feathers."

"He had feathers?"

"That's a word for his long, light fur. He was very beautiful. He used to go fishing for minnows. He would stand for a long time with his front legs in the water looking down, and his ears would fall over his face. I think he was looking at himself. Then he would rise up and pounce. And stick his head right under and blow bubbles."

"Did he catch one?"

"I don't think so."

"Then what happened?"

"My brother and I got an old sock and twisted it up in a ball and tied a black thread to it which he couldn't see, and when he lay down in the front hall to sleep, we threw the old sock onto the rug in front of his nose, and he would snap at it, and we would pull it away and laugh, and then we would do it again."

"What else did he do?"

"He got old, and he lay down on the ground and died," I said.

Jenissa is learning to write English so she took my notebook and wrote down the words in her own symbols: "He lay down on the ground and he died." To tell this story, she set down 12 different sym-bols, which she invented on the spot, the differing symbols occu-pying 17 places, well-spaced in a row. Then she drew a picture of an elephant, coloured crayon green, plus two portraits of me, smiling. Her idea of my face was quite different from my own. I think I am rather a grim-looking old codger, but to her I was a smiling Santa Claus as green as an elephant.

That evening, in God's River, we were invited to a party that was held outdoors around a big, smoky barbecue pit. The host had stretched a blue tarp on poles over the pit in case of rain, and in the smoke under this the fierce blackflies were not so numerous, although breathing was tricky: you had to hold your breath sometimes and stick your head out of the pall and sip the clear air outside quickly before the flies got you. We all stood around swatting midges and blackflies for a while, drinking little cups of fruit juice as the children played on the gravel road or the beaten grass and helped with the feast. Here, Charles was in his element, making fun with his terrible puns, manipulating his talking puppet Jerry Mahoney on his knee to the kids' delight. He is a master of something all youngsters need – friendly attention.

On the way back to the lodge, I asked Okemow about the spiritual strength of the reserve, which is a paramount question for many Aboriginal and Métis leaders. He said, "The reserve is spiritually very strong." He grasped the steering wheel hard and stared straight ahead as he drove me back to the fishing lodge. "Yes, we are spiritually strong, praise God." He began singing a hymn.

But I wondered about that. What could he mean? The community centre is obviously unpopular. There is garbage lying around all over the place. All the vegetables are flown in at stunning expense when potatoes and many root vegetables could easily be grown here. Everyone drives a truck around instead of walking, or riding a bike. Gasoline here is priced incredibly high, but people leave their engines running all day, polluting the air, wasting gasoline, wasting money and wearing out their engines.

So I asked Okemow about some of those things and he said seriously, "Yes we're working on that. We have to do something about those things."

What Charles and Marcel Okemow were attempting seemed to me beyond difficult. I had come face to face with the painful evidence of what my ancestors had done to these people, including the destruction of their natural resources for our profit. It seemed to me the more difficult because I had only the liberal's post-Christian belief in justice and fair play, whereas Charles has the faith that moves mountains. My grandfather had been a mining entrepreneur, which was one basis of the family fortunes. What could I do about that? Write this book for you.

Later that day we were trucked to the airport en route home. The weather forecast from Winnipeg, an email downloaded from a satellite, was posted near the ticket window where everyone could see it, and local news appeared there as well. I sat waiting beside a local man I really liked for his smile and relaxed attitude. Dennis MacKay was about half again as big as I am, maybe over 300 pounds, so the bench where we sat creaked and bent under our combined weight. I had met him before and thought he was intelligent and interesting, so I asked him what he did. He seemed slightly amused as he replied, "I'm the airport manager."

"What a great job," I said. "What do you do?"

"Nothing."

I took him literally since he seemed to be a serious man with a serious job. MacKay had confirmed what I had begun to suspect: there was a lot of lassitude hidden in God's Lake. But after I showed Charles a draft of that section of this chapter, he laughed me to scorn. To be sure I had heard the manager correctly, I telephoned MacKay later on and repeated to him our conversation, and before I had finished he too was laughing. This was the famous Cree sense of humour, which explained my error. But not entirely. Some of the people on such reserves are indeed what MacKay implied. A young man entrusted by Frontiers Manitoba manager Laurel Gardiner with a responsible teaching job among volunteers failed dismally as a result of lazy indifference, costing Gardiner agonies of frustration as she tried to set up housing and gardening programs in Manitoba. The lassitude that I noticed also bothers Lawrence Gladue of Frontiers. He has said from terrible experience that "the worst thing on the reserves and Métis land of Canada is the sense of entitlement."[188] My growing discouragement about God's Lake weighed on me for a long time until Charles forced me, with what for him were very harsh words, to see the place as he sees it. This, when it happened, was no epiphany; it was a scourging that left me shaken. After I had described my frustration and fears in a draft chapter, he told me to cut that part out or he would withdraw his support from the book. When I described my fears that the God's Lakers would not be able to sustain their progress, he said curtly, "Try faith."

But I had no faith like his.

I had only the liberal belief in the decency of my ancestors and their government, which I had been taught to trust. Now I knew better. They had systematically dishonoured the treaties signed by the Crown that stood for and protected all that was vital in our society. My guilt left me prey to a despair for which I partly blamed the God's Lakers. I thought not only that they were worse off than they really were but also that because of the sense of entitlement engendered by the handout system required under the treaties, they had failed dismally to profit from the lavish support, spiritual leadership and money that Charles had brought to them. "And yet here they are," I thought, "far better off than they were in the 1950s, and still getting better. I can survive the failures of my ancestors just as they have." It was my first experience of the pain that is sometimes caused by the change in one's own beliefs enforced by a change of spirit.

Why had they not given in to despair as had so many others around them in the North? For one thing, they had not been as badly damaged as the people around them. Accurate data on indices of social pathology in northern Aboriginal communities are notoriously difficult to obtain, but the federal government's Aboriginal Peoples Survey shows lower suicide rates, family violence and damage caused by sexual excess and drug and alcohol use here than in many places, such as Norway House just downriver from Lake Winnipeg. Similarly, Poplar River, farther away than Norway House, Oxford House and Island Lake (most remote), are all better off the more remote they are from white settlements.[189]

Forty-nine per cent of Norway House residents considered suicide a local problem, compared to 20 per cent at Oxford House and only 10 per cent at Island Lake. Sixty-seven per cent of Norway House respondents considered family violence a problem, in comparison with 29 per cent at Oxford House and 20 per cent at Poplar River, to whom white "civilization" was less accessible. Seventy-two per cent of the respondents at Norway House considered drug abuse a problem, compared to 36.5 per cent at Oxford House and only 8 per cent at distant

Poplar River. On some reserves, children are commonly abused; at God's Lake, they were cheerful and brainy, like Maddy and Jenissa. At God's River Narrows, some young people spent their summers taking care of their elders in the new, well-kept hostels. On the day we visited, local teenagers were cutting grass and tidying the cemetery. Geography makes the lesson clear: the farther the community is from modern "development," including white influence, the lower the rates of disease and despair. That proximity to colonial civilization is dangerous to all northern Canadian Aboriginal peoples is clear from an observation by Pien Penashue far to the east, in Newfoundland/Labrador, where there is a military aircraft training base. As Penashue told writer and filmmaker Hugh Brody, "The [NATO] bombers cause so many problems. They overfly our camps... There never was any government out here on our land. We never saw them. Now the government gives people money. Welfare allowances. The government wants to own us. They behave as if we have no rights. But we have been hunters here since time immemorial. In the country everyone works together, but in the settlements people fight each other." Brody added, "We realized that if our film was to capture the importance of Innu spirituality, we too would have to make a journey to the country."[190]

Besides being remote from white settlements, I realized, the people at God's Lake had survived because they were resilient and adaptable; because some white people such as James Evans, Leon Levasseur, Nathan Driediger (see below) and Charles Catto were skilful and generous; but most important, the God's Lake Cree had not given in because they had kept faith in themselves. Marcel Okemow was one of the councillors who both exemplified and spread this faith. As his elder had told Charles 60 years before, "We had all your religion before you got here, except for the Sabbath." They were strong in adversity.

Okemow is broadly known in the North for his inspiring faith. As Charles has said, "He is my twin in faith."[191] In 2006 Okemow had a dream of flying to reserves to spread the word, so he was very excited when he heard about Nathan Driediger and the Mission Aviation Fellowship (MAF) of Steinbach, Manitoba, and Guelph, Ontario.

MAF co-operates with Frontiers and the Mennonite Central Committee to spread the faith in isolated villages. Okemow flies, he preaches and sings, and he does all this "because there is a lot of hopelessness," according to Okemow himself and his pilot, Nathan Driediger of MAF. "In many communities there's a dark spiritual climate, so when the light of the gospel shines, it becomes evident there's something different there."[192] The Mennonites, Driediger and Mark Outerbridge of MAF have co-operated to serve God's Lake, the river and more than 40 other communities in northern Canada. Flying a six-seat Piper Saratoga, Driediger makes one or two trips weekly out of his home field at Steinbach, transporting mission and church teams whose work has been pre-approved by chiefs and councils. "We fly to isolated communities," says Driediger, "mainly places east of Lake Winnipeg, as far as Big Trout Lake, Ontario."[193] For Driediger, flying a small plane into communities with no road access fulfils a long-held dream, although he had first envisaged becoming a missionary pilot overseas instead of in his own country.

"I wanted to do mission work and just see the gospel spread. Originally, we were going to go overseas to Botswana, but that position ended up being filled," Driediger said. His wife Annie is also a licensed pilot. "While we've been here, we've really felt God calling us to be in the North, not going overseas."

Okemow is happy that Driediger heard that call. He has said, "When I accepted the Lord, I found my destiny. I know what it's like to be hurting. I turned my back to God. I was ignorant. Now I go to communities promoting the gospel."

As to MAF's effectiveness, Driediger, like Charles, is modest. He has said, "We're not nearly as active as we'd like to be." He plans to form partnerships with other mission groups. Another way to spread the effect is to get a bigger plane with longer range, which he is now planning to do. "I see this as a long-term project," he said. "We're sensitive to doing what's appropriate and welcome in the communities we serve."

The results have been life-giving. At God's Lake and The Narrows, whose combined population is around 900, the total number of high-school graduates recently was between 40 and 50, with an average of seven enrolled in university. The suicide rate has dropped from an unacceptably high level to around six every five years, which may be more due to lack of sunlight than anything else – the well-known seasonal affective disorder (SAD) effect. The total income from the hunting and fishing lodge was over $900,000 when the white economy was strong a few years ago; it sank to just under $100,000 per year during the recession that was pervasive during the time of this writing. This nevertheless remains a welcome addition to other income, as it preserves some of the lodge's clientele and the structure of the building. The lodge was, if you like, in hibernation during Canada's economic winter. In addition to all this, the people still fish from the lake for their own use, and they maintain productive fur-trapping lines as they have for hundreds of years.

Laurel Gardiner in Manitoba has survived her frustration with indigenous lassitude, or the "sense of entitlement." She has successfully promoted another local program, to encourage northerners to plant gardens for vegetables in raised beds that discourage insects and small animals. When they found that people who had not worked on the gardens were raiding them for food, they spread the word around the reserve that rows of carrots around the gardens would be planted, which the hungry raiders could take, but not more. The carrot fence works, and more than 40 such northern Manitoba gardens are growing crops every year. The program has become an outstanding and encouraging success, according to Gardiner, not only helping to feed people but also encouraging them to stand on their own feet. The gardeners not only save money, they get food that tastes better and is more nutritious. They also learn from this achievement that they can accomplish many other things they had previously thought were impossible.

The improvements to life in these communities are modest, constant and real. They consume, as such things do, a great deal of spiritual strength among the people, who are slowly regenerating their own strength with each new generation. As with Okemow's plane, the dream comes first, the reality flies in later.

SOMETHING LIKE
A MIRACLE

Following the death of Charles Catto early in May 2014, directors and friends of Frontiers gathered, first to mourn him, but then also to discuss how to help the foundation carry on its work. Events had occurred that were steering the foundation near chaos. After consulting Barbara, Charles had recently loaned Frontiers a lot of money, which he had raised from banks by placing a mortgage on the family house. He had also maxed out his personal credit cards, with the result that when he died, Frontiers owed the banks well over $250,000, all guaranteed by Charles's estate, i.e., Barbara. The credit-card debt included rapidly growing interest that had not been paid on time by Frontiers. Thus the foundation (or eventually the estate) was growing debt instead of income. The situation was paradoxical. Not only were these financing arrangements foolish in and of themselves, but Charles had incurred this personal debt ignoring the fact that he was the foundation's chief fundraiser, he was over 84, and had heart problems. So with him had died the hope that Frontiers could soon pay off the bank, and that debt now threatened Barbara. As a mainstay not only of Charles himself, but also of the foundation, she deserved all the help that could be given, which unfortunately in the first few months proved to be very little.

As friends and relatives rallied to help her, one of them asked how she felt about all the sacrifices she and Charles had made, which apparently were about to grow exponentially. She scoffed. "There were no sacrifices," she said. "We were so happy to live the way we did, and we still are."

Regardless of her strong faith, the situation had become a spiral that seemed destined to end in bankruptcy for her and the foundation. In fact, during the last year before Charles's death, Frontiers' long-term debts had exceeded its assets by an amount so great that the small operating surplus it generated each year would not pay it off in a human lifetime. This situation had threatened to happen more than once before but had been surmounted by Charles's great faith in Canadians, which had always paid off through something like a miracle in his lifetime.

In addition to these financing problems, the policy Charles had latterly adopted of transferring power within Frontiers to Aboriginal people in order to train a new leadership had not succeeded, because Charles – despite himself – retained too much authority, even among those whom he had recently empowered. This was a result of the foundation's ongoing dependency on his kindness, courtesy and wisdom. For instance, at directors' meetings, whenever a tricky question came up and the answer was not immediately obvious, most eyes automatically swivelled toward Charles, who, *faute de mieux*, would then offer a suggestion. Now there were no more suggestions to be had.

Very soon after Charles died, Lawrence Gladue retired, as he had long planned to do; the massive debts were revealed; the federal government and band councils continued to veer away from third-party service providers such as Frontiers; and an inexperienced new board elected an inept president, who soon resigned. This left Suzanne Jones, a volunteer and close friend of Charles and Barbara, as president *pro tempore*, coping with the debt, and her feckless board did not manage to raise any money from new sources during their seven months in office.

Acutely sensitive to the foundation's impending collapse in the east, Don Irving in Vancouver began planning for the survival of the northern part of its organization. First he asked the ever-changing members of the board for permission to sever this section free and clear of Frontiers' debt. Doing so would almost constitute a death-blow to the foundation, because the contribution to Frontiers' overhead paid by Irving's section, some $30,000 to $40,000 annually, was by then over 60 per cent of the foundation's total revenue. Furthermore, his contribution was cost free, since it arrived with all its own overhead already paid, whereas much of the revenue earned by Frontiers in the east came only as a result of costly new fundraising work that had to be done. To their credit, the board members led by Mike McTague, aware of how precarious their situation was, granted permission for these negotiations to proceed.

Irving had already set his eyes on Canadian University Students Overseas, a Conservative government vote-catcher helping the needy around the world. However, despite being founded, like Frontiers, by enthusiastic 1960s idealists, CUSO could not fund Canada itself: none of its programs was aimed at helping Canadian beneficiaries. Despite this, Irving thought he saw his chance: had not Frontiers itself helped those in need far from the shores of Canada? Perhaps it was time to bring that spirit of internationalism home. He called CUSO in Ottawa and talked to Tracey Foster, CUSO's manager of international volunteering, a Welsh-born immigrant who agreed to come and meet with him on her next trip west.

There, they enjoyed an animated long dinner in The Old Spaghetti Factory in East Vancouver. Within minutes, they knew they were destined for each other. Frontiers had vast experience, no money and a reputation as wide as the world, while CUSO had government financial support and an enormous gap in its coverage, a gap shaped like Joni Mitchell's *O Canada*.

"A Case of You"

Just before our love got lost you said
"I am as constant as a northern star"
And I said "Constantly in the darkness
Where's that at?
If you want me I'll be in the bar"

On the back of a cartoon coaster
In the blue TV screen light
I drew a map of Canada
Oh Canada

...You taste so bitter and so sweet[194]

Irving happily wrapped up an agreement with Foster, and volunteers from the Philippines to Germany began packing to continue the foundation's work in northern Canada under a new and, considering CUSO's mandate, delightfully ironic aegis. And CUSO, guided by Foster, has taken the baton from Frontiers at full speed, placing a dozen volunteers where they want to be, and where they are wanted, in Aklavik, Tuktoyaktuk, Hay River and elsewhere in the Canadian North.

Another volunteer companion in the effort to keep the Frontiers spirit alive, the Pikangikum First Nations Working Group, led by Bob White of Toronto in full co-operation with the chief and council, has taken over the management of a Frontiers-inspired project near the Manitoba–Ontario boundary. There they are bringing clean water to people in desperate need of it on the Pikangikum reserve. Well funded by the Anglican Church of Canada in co-operation with the Catholic Church, they are also helping to bring down the price of food on reserve and to create a safe, warm, harmonious drop-in centre for local youth.

Whatever survives of the original Frontiers will be the volunteer spirit that is forever alive in all people, within the foundation and outside of it, Canadian and otherwise. Don Irving has expressed it well: "We have an amazing track record in the North and West, and I see no reason that this could not be duplicated in other parts of Canada."[195]

And why not? After all, as the Cattos discovered around the globe, from North America to Africa to the Caribbean to South America, that spirit is alive, free, and travels everywhere in the world like oxygen in the wind.

BRIEF CHRONOLOGY

A full chronology of Frontiers achievements would take many books. What follows is a simplified guide to the foundation's work by Charles Catto. Although Charles was thoroughly practical and excellent at spelling, he paid so little attention to money that in his handwritten account of the rise of Frontiers Foundation, he spelled it "mony."

1954 Charles and Barbara Catto began their mission work at God's Lake, Manitoba.

1959 Charles and Barbara Catto learned ecumenical work-camping from the YWCA at Mindolo, Zambia. Volunteers became friendly building a community hall. Everyone who participated learned to recognize and respect the greatness, the good news, the potential and diversity of the human family, and also that doing is more effective than talking. This project was Barbara's. Charles, United Church minister in Mindolo, helped her.

1962 In Toronto, Rod Chintu, a Zambian medical student at the University of Toronto, accompanied Charles to northern Manitoba Cree communities. These Cree people had never seen a black man before but they accepted him immediately into their community. Their warm welcome revealed to Charles that international volunteer workers could not only overcome violent Aboriginal/white tensions in Canada but also bring good news in the shape of safe housing to people living in shacks.

1962–1964 After two years struggling for Church and government permission, the first Operation Beaver ecumenical volunteer work camp built a new Anglican church at Split Lake, Manitoba.

1966 Operation Beaver became Opération Castor as the volunteers put up a community centre at Lac Doré, Quebec.

1968 Appeals for help from many northern Aboriginal communities flooded in to Frontiers Foundation, now incorporating Operation Beaver. The first housing project, at Wabasca, Alberta, begat many more among Métis and non-status Indians living off-reserve.

1969 Frontiers' first overseas project was conducted in St. Lucia, followed soon by many others in Jamaica, Anguilla, Guyana, Belize, Trinidad, St. Kitts, Bolivia, Sierra Leone, Senegal and Haiti.

1970 Frontiers' Ontario project is undertaken near Georgian Bay.

1971–1972 Chetwynd. The first British Columbia project was 32 houses built in co-operation with local municipal authorities and the federal government. The houses were completed on time and under budget, and became a model for a new federal initiative called the Rural and Native Housing Program. Under Lawrence Gladue, a Cree from Alberta and a director of Frontiers Foundation, the RNH expanded enormously with the help of Frontiers over the next few years to build over 100,000 houses throughout rural Canada, including 58 in one Frontiers project alone, at Port McNicoll, Ontario. Building on-reserve in British Columbia was thereafter dramatically expanded.

1976 Frontiers' first project in Haiti involved building a new primary school, followed by road construction, rural electrification, immunization, agriculture and reforestation.

1978 The work expanded into the Northwest Territories and Yukon with help from NWT Housing.

1984 The Wood-Mizer Corporation of Canada (a branch of the original company founded in Indianapolis, Indiana) began donating their efficient, thin-kerf, portable sawmills and money. These gifts continued faithfully for years until Frontiers was running 16 sawmills throughout the country.

1986 Frontiers' Operation Phoenix Division opened the Native Skills Centre in Toronto to teach construction and computer skills to Aboriginal people.

1980–1984 Dependable funding from the Secretary of State and CMHC helped the foundation expand nationwide and set up its first projects in Prince Edward Island.

1984–1993 The RNH program was abandoned by the Mulroney Conservative government but successive Liberal and NDP governments in Ontario helped fund new Frontiers projects.

2002 Project Amik, a large-scale development to house several hundred low-income Métis and Aboriginal people in central Toronto, was opened by Ontario Lieutenant-Governor James Bartleman, himself Ojibwa-Métis.

2000–2009 Many new projects were completed with the help of the Ministry of Municipal Affairs and Housing in Ontario.

2009–2014 Aboriginal Skills Training and Strategic Investment Fund (ASTSIF) was established. Prime Minister Harper awarded the foundation almost a million dollars to teach skills to Aboriginal peoples while building 15 new houses in Quebec, Ontario and Manitoba. New projects included a primary school and an HIV/AIDS prevention and treatment facility.

May 2014 Charles Catto died of heart failure following an operation in Toronto. Over 500 people gathered in his church in Pickering, Ontario, to celebrate his life. Many donations flowed in spontaneously, enabling the foundation to go on for many more months, but several projects in eastern Canada stalled for lack of money. At Frontiers West, under Don Irving, programs in northern Canada continued on track, helping students to graduate.

In total, more than 8,000 volunteers have come from 74 countries and from 17 Inuit and First Nations to help build more than 3,000 homes, plus 32 community centres, four schools, three parks and other facilities in Canada and abroad. Over 100,000 warm, safe affordable houses have been built on reserves and Métis land across Canada under the Rural and Native Housing Program of the federal government, a plan modelled in part on Frontiers' generous volunteer system instituted by Frank Oberle in Chetwynd, BC. More than 140 marriages known to the head office have been formed, and dozens of children have been born to united volunteers.

July 2016 The board of Frontiers chaired by Mike McTague declared bankruptcy and closed the doors of its head office.

ACKNOWLEDGEMENTS

For any merit in this book, it is Elisabeth Bacque, beyond all others, to whom you and I must offer thanks. She not only edited this manuscript, she lived it. She came on research trips with me and Charles Catto to northern Ontario, Manitoba and Quebec; with me and Don Irving to British Columbia; with me to Alberta. She also took time away from her painting, her exhibitions and her speaking tours to curate the illustrations for this book. She encouraged me through the usual authorial despairs, which were magnified by my life-threatening illness toward the end.

Charles Catto gave me two different versions of his own manuscripts about his life's work, and assisted me greatly in the ten years of research and writing it took to complete this book. Don Irving of Frontiers West was a helpful and entertaining companion on our research trip to central British Columbia, and he added considerably to the book's store of amusing anecdotes about Charlie. Marcel Okemow helped Charlie to understand the Cree spirit, and he gently set me straight on the many misconceptions I had on arriving at his reserve, God's Lake. Similarly, Lawrence Gladue, with his keen intelligence, broad experience and clear understanding of the problems faced by Aboriginal peoples in Canada, and who has his own vision of the solutions, has given me and all Canadians rewards almost beyond measure that have been improving the general happiness of life in the North for 50 years. Among those who have sustained Frontiers in its Toronto home for many years are Marco Guzman, Marilyn Gillis and Patsy Cuffy. Professor Conrad Heidenreich formerly of York University guided me in many ways with his expert academic knowledge.

To Barbara Catto, whom I have nicknamed Shining Spirit, not only millions of Canadians but Africans, Haitians and Bolivians owe thanks and recognition for a lifetime's leadership and support of the work described here. Charles Catto followed her example many times while offering her his own through a lifetime of cheerful and mutual devotion.

To Chief Dan Michell of the Wet'suwet'en band near Moricetown, BC, I am indebted for his merry acceptance of our inquiring intrusion and for showing us not only his talking stick, but also his listening post – a police band radio – which he uses to keep in touch with his high-speed citizens. To Dora Kenni Wilson, former mayor and chief of Hagwilget, I am particularly grateful for sharing with us her fearless spirit of survival along with her amiable wit. Thanks as well to George Muldoe, chief of the Kispiox band of the Gitxsan people, for describing with so little rancour and so much understanding the dreadful kidnapping and concentration-camp schooling he suffered as an "Indian" child at the hands of uncivilized white people.

My agent and editor, and former publisher, Karl Siegler, brought his great experience to bear on the manuscript, improving it immeasurably through the many years it took to complete it.

NOTES

1 Upper Canada, the beginnings of the province of Ontario, was officially established by the Constitutional Act of 1791; York (later Toronto) was founded in 1793.

2 The monarchist Americans, or United Empire Loyalists, had by this time been completely assimilated, their identity disappearing almost without a trace except in history books.

3 "An Act to Prevent the Further Introduction of Slaves, and to Limit the Term of Contracts for Servitude within this Province," Statutes of Upper Canada, 33 Geo. 3, c. 7 (2nd Session), 1793. Page images and transcriptions accessed 2016-04-05 at https://bnald.lib.unb.ca/node/1560. The Act prohibited the importation of slaves, preserved the ownership of existing slaves, liberated all children of existing slaves at age 25 and limited any term of voluntary servitude to nine years regardless of the original contract.

4 "An Act for the Better Establishment and Maintenance of Common Schools in Upper Canada," Statutes of United Canadas, 9 Vict., c. 20, 1846. Page images and transcriptions accessed 2016-04-05 at https://bnald.lib.unb.ca/node/4455.

5 R.D. Gidney, "Egerton Ryerson (1803–1882)," in Dictionary of Canadian Biography, vol. 11 (1881–1890) (Toronto/Québec: University of Toronto/Université Laval, 1982, rev. 2015). Accessed 2016-06-02 at www.biographi.ca/en/bio/ryerson_egerton_11E.html.

6 Peter Schmalz, The Ojibwa of Southern Ontario (Toronto: University of Toronto Press, 1991). The Iroquois, after surmounting some difficulties with the British-Canadians, settled on adequate land along the Grand River and became prosperous. That this prosperity suddenly waned in the mid-19th century was a mystery to Chief Sky of the reserve near Brantford, as well as to the author. Author's interview with Chief Sky circa 1970.

7 This estimate is based on many factors, including the numbers of human beings dispersed from their ancient homelands (Ojibwa, Petun, Neutrals, Wendat, Mississauga) or introduced from elsewhere (Iroquois, Pottawatomie, French-Canadian, American-Loyalist, Scots, Irish, English, German). And on the tonnage of biomass destroyed or converted to items such as food or housing. And on the species exterminated (the passenger pigeon) or locally extirpated (the wild turkey, wapiti, salmon), and in terms of new species introduced (Europeans, raccoons, cows, sparrows, opossum, vinca or periwinkle, loosestrife, wine grapes, wheat, sea lamprey, zebra mussels). And on the thousands of miles of river courses altered, lakes created, canals constructed, air polluted, water poisoned. And on the zoonotic diseases introduced to animals, plants and trees. And on the millions of acres of soil

erosion caused and monoculture imposed where there had always been biodiversity.

8 This fraternity was the only one in the university that was completely Canadian, with no international connection. It was also distinguished by the fact that virtually all other fraternities were somewhat bigoted.

9 David Hackett Fischer, *Champlain's Dream* (New York: Simon & Schuster, 2008), 162.

10 *The Jesuit Relations and Allied Documents: Travels and Explorations of the Jesuit Missionaries in New France, 1610–1791,* compiled and edited by Reuben Gold Thwaites, vol. 8: Quebec, Hurons, Cape Breton, 1634–1636, "Various sentiments and opinions of the Fathers who are in New France, taken from their last letters of 1635" (Cleveland, Ohio: Burrows Brothers, 1897), 169 at ¶3 (accessed 2016-04-05 at https://archive.org/stream/jesuits08jesuuoft#page/n179/mode/2up).

11 *Relations,* Thwaites edition, vol. 3: Acadia 1611–16, Biard's Relation (1616), 85 (accessed 2016-04-05 at https://archive.org/stream/jesuitrelations221je-sugoog#page/n96/mode/2up). Quoted in William Cronon, *Changes in the Land* (New York: Hill and Wang, 1983), 80.

12 Charles. L. Mee Jr., *The Genius of the People* (New York: Harper & Row, 1987).

13 Roughly speaking, the law was based on the legendary acts and words of a revered peacemaker, just as Christian tenets stemmed from the actions and words of Christ. It prescribed a democratic alliance among several bands, with supremely important powers over candidacies and appointments vested in women.

14 Mee, op cit.

15 See Bruce E. Johansen, *Forgotten Founders: Benjamin Franklin, the Iroquois and the Rationale for the American Revolution* (Ipswich, Mass.: Gambit, 1982). Full text transcription accessed 2016-05-01 at www.ratical.org/many_worlds/6Nations/FF.html.

16 Translated into English by William F. Fleming in 1889 as *The Huron, or Pupil of Nature.* HTML chapter files available at The Literature Network (accessed 2016-06-01 at www.online-literature.com/voltaire/the-huron). Originally published as *L'Ingénu: Histoire véritable tirée des manuscrits du Père Quesnel* (Utrecht, 1767). Complete page images at Gallica, the online archive of La bibliothèque nationale de France (accessed 2016-06-01 at https://is.gd/FIsKlT).

17 With thanks to Greg Gatenby for his book *The Wild Is Always There* (Toronto: Vintage Canada, 1994). Voltaire wrote "Huron," but the people called themselves "Wendat."

18 Maungwudaus (George Henry), *An Account of the Chippewa Indians Who Have Been Travelling Among the Whites…* (Rochester, NY: Privately published, 1848). Excerpted in Bernd Peyer, *American Indian Nonfiction: An*

Anthology of Writings, 1760s–1930s (Norman: University of Oklahoma Press, 2007), 197–206. "Chippewa" is a name sometimes used to refer to Ojibwa peoples who lived chiefly in Ontario. The Chippewa group moved starting in or soon after 1649 to the shores of Lake Michigan in the US. The majority of the Wendat survivors, becoming known as Hurons, moved to Wendake near Quebec City.

19 Eric Goldschein, "The 10 Most Important Crops In The World," *Business Insider* (accessed 2016-05-01 at www.businessinsider.com/10-crops-that-feed-the-world-2011-9). Built on an island in a lake, with its residents fed from the produce of floating gardens, Tenochtitlan had a population of around 400,000 at the time of the Spanish invasion, making it possibly the largest city in the world at the time. See also Victor Boswell et al., eds., *The World in Your Garden* (Washington, DC: National Geographic Society, 1957), 16ff; and Redcliffe N. Salaman, *The History and Social Influence of the Potato* (Cambridge and New York: Cambridge University Press, 1985), 1ff.

20 See "The Evolution of Corn," Learn.Genetics (website), University of Utah Genetic Science Learning Center, 2016. Accessed 2016-04-05 at http://learn.genetics.utah.edu/content/selection/corn.

21 I am indebted to Maggie Siggins for this story, retold in *Bitter Embrace* (Toronto: McClelland & Stewart, 2005).

22 The population of Aboriginal peoples in New England fell from about 70,000 in 1700 to about 12,000 in 1775. See Cronon, 88–89.

23 Philip Phillips, James A. Ford and James B. Griffin, eds., with an introduction by Stephen Williams, *Archaeological Survey in the Lower Mississippi Alluvial Valley, 1940–1947* (Tuscaloosa: University of Alabama Press, 2003).

24 Lasalle biographer Anka Muhlstein summarizes it well: "In fact this enormous country appeared deserted." *Lasalle: Explorer of the North American Frontier* (New York: Arcade Publishing, 1994), 154.

25 Some of the Spanish pigs, going wild, probably transmitted diseases such as anthrax, brucellosis, leptospirosis, trichinosis and tuberculosis either directly or via wild turkeys, deer and other food animals the natives ate. These diseases, mutating like the flu virus in birds, would have killed people back then just as avian flu does today. Thus the people died en masse, both from the infections spreading from person to person and from poisons introduced by Europeans into their livestock. See David E. Hoffman, "Going Viral," *The New Yorker*, January 31, 2011. Accessed 2016-04-05 at www.newyorker.com/magazine/2011/01/31/going-viral.

26 Tony Penikett, *Reconciliation* (Vancouver: Douglas & McIntyre, 2006).

27 Such as Ronald Wright and Conrad Heidenreich. See notes 28 and 48 below.

28 Ronald Wright, *Time Among the Maya* (Toronto: Viking, 1989), 138.

29 This phenomenon of cultural destruction also occurred in ancient Greece. Herodotus, visiting Alexandria in about 450–445 BC, admired the Egyptians'

knowledge of their own history and of Greek history, which far surpassed what the Greeks knew about themselves. He was startled to hear that his own Greek cities had a long and varied history. The Egyptians told him he was ignorant because many Greek cities along with their archives had been destroyed so often by volcanic eruptions, tidal waves and the resulting plagues.

30　For a sense of the character of prominent Canadians of the era, see, for example, Lord Cranborne, Marquess of Salisbury, who wrote of Vincent Massey: "Fine chap, Vincent, but he does make one feel a bit of a savage." Quoted in John Robert Colombo, *New Canadian Quotations* (Edmonton: Hurtig, 1987).

31　B.G. Edward, "Developing and Operating a Gold Mine on the Canadian Tundra," *Canadian Mining Journal*, July 1944. Quoted without attribution in Charles Catto, *The White Problem*, unpublished ms, edited by James Bacque, courtesy of Charles Catto and Frontiers Foundation, Toronto. (This is the earlier of two versions of Catto's memoir; a later one, called *Beavering*, covers much of the same ground in its first few chapters.)

32　*Jesuit Relations*, Thwaites edition, vol. 43 (1656–57), 271. Accessed 2016-06-05 at https://archive.org/stream/jesuits43jesuuoft#page/258/mode/2up.

33　Also quoted in Denys Delâge, *Bitter Feast: Amerindians and Europeans in Northeastern North America, 1600–64* (Vancouver: University of British Columbia Press, 1993), 299.

34　Charles Catto, *Beavering*, c3, unpublished ms, edited by James Bacque, courtesy of Charles Catto and Frontiers Foundation, Toronto. (This is the later of two versions of Catto's unpublished memoir; the earlier one, called *The White Problem*, covers much of the same ground.)

35　*Beavering*, c3.

36　As quoted in Robert Twigger, *Voyageur: Across the Rocky Mountains in a Birchbark Canoe* (London: Weidenfeld and Nicolson, 2006), 178.

37　Catto, *Beavering*, c3.

38　Francis Assikinack, "Social and Warlike Customs of the Odahwah Indians," *Canadian Journal of Industry, Science and Art*, n.s. 3, no. 13 (January 1858): 301 (accessed 2016-05-01 at https://is.gd/piAs40).

39　This was a perception shared by other experienced travellers among indigenous peoples. Wilfred Thesiger, for example, in his book *Arabian Sands*, wrote about his Bedu friends of the Empty Quarter of Arabia: "I shall always remember [their] generosity and courage, endurance, patience and lighthearted gallantry. Among no people have I ever felt the same sense of personal inferiority."

40　Catto, *The White Problem*.

41　Our friends at God's Lake thought their jigger had been made by Canadian Tire from a pattern invented by a local fisher, probably Icelandic. However,

Lawrence Gladue remembered using such homemade jiggers during his youth on his Cree reserve in northern Alberta. He has always thought they were of Native origin. Certainly, such a device would be useless without one Native contribution: fishers cannot see through the ice, so they do not know exactly where the submerged jigger is when it stops. The ice may be four or five feet thick, with maybe a foot or two of snow on top, and there may be a 30-mile-an-hour wind blowing sound away. But when the jigger moves, its sharp pick makes a slight knocking sound on the underside of the ice. So the fisher looks at their dog, trained to follow the sound. The dog indicates where the last sound was made, and invariably, when the fisher cuts through the ice, there is the jigger. The free line is pulled through and the net is set. Presto: fresh fish for people and dogs.

Father Louis Nicolas described the ice-fishing method he saw in use among the people of northern Lake Huron around 1672 – rather a different one. Fishers would cut holes in the ice and shove long poles underneath to drag a net line from one hole to another. See François-Marc Gagnon et al., eds., *The Codex Canadensis and the Writings of Louis Nicolas* (Tulsa, Okla., and Montréal/Kingston: Gilcrease Museum and McGill-Queen's University Press, 2011).

42 Catto, *The White Problem*.

43 Catto, *The White Problem*, c4.

44 Catto, *The White Problem*.

45 African villages bear the name of the village headman.

46 Catto, *The White Problem*.

47 Catto, *The White Problem*.

48 I am indebted to Dr. Conrad Heidenreich for the following: "One of the main reasons there were no major 'Indian wars' in Canada during the English period was the French period that preceded it, which was a partnership in trade, war, intermarriage etc. [See also] Pope Paul III's encyclical *Sublimus Dei* [1537], which declared Indians to be humans, a fact still in dispute well into 19th-century USA." Dr. Heidenreich is not responsible for the views expressed in the present book. The full text of *Sublimus Dei* is available at Papal Encyclicals Online (accessed 2016-04-05 at www.papalencyclicals.net/Paulo3/p3subli.htm).

49 Catto, *The White Problem*, c5.

50 Both Barbara and Charles believed in the liberal movement born from the decaying "churchianity" of Western societies in the 19th and 20th centuries. However, liberalism, descending from beliefs that had decayed from the original Christian teachings, failed to encourage Christ's robust independence of spirit as it took over government, charity, churches and schools. It was this robust spirit that Charles and his friend Levasseur possessed; the same spirit they discovered on the Canadian frontier in the Cree and other Aboriginal

peoples, who still had it despite the terror they had lived through. The Cree word for this enduring spirit is *kiyem*, or "that's how it is."

51 Mr. Justice Hugessen, in his costs order in *Joseph v. Canada*, 2008 FC 574 (accessed 2016-06-01 at http://canlii.ca/t/1wtkb). In the Royal Proclamation of 1763, often referred to as the "Magna Carta of Indian Rights," the colonial British Crown found "[it] ... just and reasonable, and essential to our Interest, and the Security of our Colonies, that the several Nations or Tribes of Indians with whom We are connected, and who live under our Protection, should not be molested or disturbed in the Possession of such Parts of Our Dominions and Territories as, not having been ceded to or purchased by Us, are reserved to them, or any of them, as their Hunting Grounds ..." Excerpt accessed 2016-06-05 at http://indigenousfoundations.arts.ubc.ca/home/government-policy/royal-proclamation-1763.html. See also Mary C. Hurley, "The Crown's Fiduciary Relationship with Aboriginal Peoples" (Ottawa: Library of Parliament research paper PRB 00-09E, 2000, 2002). Accessed 2016-04-05 at www.parl.gc.ca/content/LOP/ResearchPublications/prb0009-e.htm.

52 "Frontiers Foundation" succeeded the original name, "Operation Beaver." For the sake of simplicity, the name Frontiers has been used throughout this book.

53 Catto, *The White Problem*.

54 The canoeist who "lily-dips" lets his paddle lazily glide in the water while the other paddlers propel the canoe.

55 This area of Manitoba has "extensive discontinuous permafrost," in the words of Environment Canada.

56 See Brief Chronology following c17.

57 *The White Problem*, c6.

58 Later called Frontiers Foundation.

59 *Beavering*, c7.

60 *Beavering*, c7.

61 Toward the end of his life, in 2014, Charles had slightly revised his views. In an updated mission statement issued by Frontiers in 2008, he wrote: "Frontiers Foundation embraces a vision of the human family honouring the Great Spirit. Therefore our mission is to implement the enduring relief of human poverty throughout Canada and abroad in tangible advancement projects. These activities reflect the dreams and priorities of those reaching out for a vibrantly productive partnership." Charles Catto, Fact Sheet (Toronto: Frontiers Foundation, December 10, 2008).

62 Conversation with the author, 2014.

63 Per the 2010 guidelines issued to all potential volunteers by Frontiers, which reflect the policy as maintained since the beginning. Further requirements were that the volunteers agree to serve for a minimum of three months for

construction and five months on an educational program. From the Catto memoir and also a memo to the author from Don Irving, 2015. Copy with James Bacque.

64 Conversation with the author, 2008.

65 Conversation with the author, 2008.

66 Ibid.

67 The Central Mortgage and Housing Corporation was renamed the Canada Mortgage and Housing Corporation in 1979: CMHC, "History of CMHC" (accessed 2016-05-01 at www.cmhc-schl.gc.ca/en/corp/about/hi).

68 Some of the $13,000 Frontiers houses cost the taxpayers of Canada virtually nothing, being financed by the volunteers themselves and private donations. The total cost of the useless CMHC houses, almost ten times as much, was of course borne wholly by the taxpayers.

69 Quoted in Catto, *The White Problem*; the letter also appeared in *The Anglican Journal*. The nighttime temperature in nearby Churchill is usually –5 to –35°C for at least three months after the beginning of December.

70 *Joseph v. Canada*, 2008 FC 574 at ¶24. Accessed 2016-04-05 at www.canlii.org/en/ca/fct/doc/2008/2008fc574/2008fc574.html.

71 Conversation with the author, October 2015.

72 Mrs. R.S. Mills of Toronto to Charles Catto, October 1966,. Frontiers Foundation archive, Toronto.

73 Imogene Williams of Winnipeg, letter to the editor, *Anglican Journal* 135, no. 5 (May 2009): 4–5 (accessed 2016-04-05 as ProQuest document ID 196683494 via public library proxy server). Quoted with partial attribution in Catto, *The White Problem*.

74 *Beavering*, c6.

75 *Beavering*, c6.

76 As of 2015 the worldwide total of volunteers, including non-Aboriginal Canadian and local volunteers plus prospective owners, was estimated at between 9,000 and 11,000.

77 Frontiers Foundation archive, Toronto.

78 Email to author, September 29, 2008.

79 At the beginning of the existence of Frontiers, much of the work was done in communities of status Indians living on reserve land. Over the years, however, Frontiers began to expand into associated communities: Métis and non-status Indians living off-reserve, often close to the reserves of their relatives.

80 At first the ratio of program expenditures to overall income was about 85 per cent, meaning that only about 15 per cent went to head-office expenses, according to annual audited financial statements of the foundation.

81 Statistics throughout this section are from Frontiers Foundation and Charles Catto, unpublished.

82 Catto manuscript.

83 The average annual snowfall in recent years in the region is 10 feet, or 300 centimetres. Earlier, it was more.

84 Rupert's Land and North-Western Territory Order (formerly Order of Her Majesty in Council Admitting Rupert's Land and the North-Western Territory into the Union), at the Court at Windsor, June 23, 1870, art. 14 (full text accessed 2016-06-05 at www.solon.org/Constitutions/Canada/English/rlo_1870.html). For context, see also Constitution Act, 1867 (formerly British North America Act, 1867) 30-31 Vict., c. 3, s. 146 (UK) (www.solon.org/Constitutions/Canada/English/ca_1867.html), Rupert's Land Act, 1868, 31-32 Vict., c. 105 (UK) (www.solon.org/Constitutions/Canada/English/rpl_1868.html) and Temporary Government of Rupert's Land Act, 1869, 32-33 Vict., c. 3 (Canada) (www.solon.org/Constitutions/Canada/English/tgrla_1869.html).

85 Wertman to Bacque, 2010, commenting on the latter's interpretation of the white Canadian attitude. The letter continued: "Without taking away from at best an assimilationist agenda (or at worst a genocidal agenda) on the part of the Crown, [Bacque's] interpretation of the phrase covering claims of the Indians is a bit narrow. In the 1870s the legal sense of 'dispose of' connoted an idea of resolving or finally addressing rather than to get rid of or discard."

86 See the note on the honour of the Crown in c9 of the present book. The HBC retained all its existing posts, with additional lands, plus 5 per cent of the fertile belt of the prairies, plus about £300,000. For many years before 1870, the listless Crown had not lived up to the promise in the order. Catherine Sutton (Nahnebahwequay), an Ojibwa of Ontario, was denied ownership of her land although she had been given it by her tribal elders. Then the government denied her the right to buy it back at public auction, because she was Indian; only whites were allowed to own land outside of reserves. Mohawk lands drowned by the building of the Welland Canal in the 1830s had still not been paid for by 2007; payment for Georgian Bay islands owned by Ojibwa was still in arrears after 167 years; and the Cape Croker band of Ojibwa had to struggle for over a century to regain the fishing rights that had been guaranteed to them in the 19th century.

87 Equivalent to about $6.5-million today, according to the Bank of Canada's online inflation calculator (accessed 2016-05-01 at www.bankofcanada.ca/rates/related/inflation-calculator).

88 Quoted in an article in the *Toronto Star* by Alan Edmonds, date not known. Also quoted in Catto, *The White Problem*, c6.

89 This quote from Bosum's original Native studies essay now appears as part of the Oujé-Bougoumou Cree Nation's "History" page (accessed 2016-04-05 at www.ouje.ca/history). See also "Grand Opening of the Aanischaaukamikw Cree Cultural Institute in Oujé-Bougoumou," posted 2012-06-15 to *Polar Horizons*, a blog hosted by France Rivet (accessed 2016-04-05 at http://polarhorizons.com/blog/?p=3072).

90 A moss house consists of poles set up usually as a wigwam and covered with moss, which acts as an insulator.

91 See note 89.

92 The quote from Abel Bosum now forms part of the Oujé-Bougoumou Cree Nation's "History" page (accessed 2016-04-05 at www.ouje.ca/history) as cited in note 89 re Freddy Bosum. As Chief Sam Bosum adds on the nation's Slideshare page, "The history of Oujé-Bougoumou is a heroic story of the determination of a small community of Cree aboriginal people to overcome the spread of mining and forestry industries, with their unending hunger for natural resources, into the furthest reaches of North America." Slide 2 of 14, accessed 2016-04-05 at www.slideshare.net/pomank/wachiya-oujibougoumou.

93 This is an average; the number varied according to the price of gold.

94 Wertman, a draft avoider from the US, was working as a community development planner with the Grand Council of the Crees in Val d'Or when Abel Bosum took him to Chibougamau to see his people living on the edges of the highway.

95 According to Wertman in a 2010 interview, to complete the work quickly, some was contracted out to local companies, but in any case "everyone on the reserve who wanted to work had a job."

96 The chief's spoken words were never written down or recorded, but the author has consulted the chief's notes. The words here are presented in quotes, having been read and approved as correct by several people who listened as the chief spoke, including Abel Bosum's son, Freddy, and Charles Catto. (*meegwetch* means "thank you.")

97 Clifford Ando, "Driftwood to Google: How and What We Map, a Remarkable Exhibition in Chicago," *The Times Literary Supplement*, no. 5466 (January 4, 2008): 14–15.

98 Canada's poets, writers and painters have celebrated this love and sense of identity for a long time, a love that derives directly from the people who first welcomed European visitors here. The Iroquois Prayer of Thanksgiving in many stanzas gives thanks and praise to the Creator for animals, birds, winds and plants. All these are believed by the Iroquois to unite the people. One prayer reads:

"Now we turn towards the vast fields of plant life. As far as the eye can see, the plants grow, working many wonders. They sustain many forms of life. With our minds gathered together we give thanks and look forward to seeing plant life for many generations to come.

"Now our minds are one."

[translated from the Mohawk by John Stokes and Kanawahienton (David Benedict, Turtle Clan/Mohawk) from an original inspiration by Tekaronianekon (Jake Swamp, Wolf Clan/Mohawk), accessed 2016-04-05 (pdf) from National Museum of the American Indian, Washington, DC, https://is.gd/N87bCY]

99 See James Bacque, *Crimes and Mercies* (Toronto: Little, Brown, 1997; rev. ed. Vancouver: Talonbooks, 2007). See also "Other Losses," a conversation between the author and Maj. Merrit Drucker (US Army, ret.), hosted by emeritus professor Peter Russell at the University of Toronto faculty club, October 16, 2013 (streaming video 01:02:46 accessed 2016-06-05 at https://is.gd/2OrSG1).

100 They both changed their names on arriving in Canada. Joan, christened Johanna, changed when a Canadian immigration officer wiped the original away and bestowed the Canadian equivalent. Similarly, Franz became Frank.

101 Frank Oberle, *A Chosen Path: From Moccasin Flats to Parliament Hill* (Surrey, BC: Heritage House, 2005). Other Oberle quotes in this chapter are from this book unless noted otherwise.

102 Canada was one of the Allies, and it briefly inflicted starvation conditions in Germany, but in 1946–1949 it organized with the USA one of the greatest food relief campaigns in the history of the world to help feed many millions of Germans and others. See Bacque, *Crimes and Mercies*.

103 Author interview with Oberle, 2009.

104 Reorganized and renamed in 1993 as the Congress of Aboriginal Peoples. See the CAP webpage "Our Mandate" at abo-peoples.org/our-mission (accessed 2016-06-05).

105 This and all the ensuing quotes from Gladue in this chapter come from an interview with him by the author in July 2010.

106 Following the success of the Chetwynd project, Oberle had felt he was ready for a larger stage and campaigned for the Conservative nomination for the riding of Prince George–Peace River, which included Chetwynd. He won, and won again, serving six consecutive mandates in Parliament, eventually becoming Minister of State for Science and Technology and then Minister of Forestry in the Mulroney cabinet during the last eight years of his career.

107 Three officers, the police chief and the Kenora Police Services Board were named in the suit, which sought $9.9-million in damages for negligent investigation and differential or discriminatory policing for Aboriginal versus non-Aboriginal peoples. "It's a systemic failing within the system," Falconer was quoted as saying, adding that the suit was about trying to get some accountability and some answers as to why the murderer of their son was not found. The article said Falconer noted that the Kakegamic family had been denied an inquest by the Chief Coroner of Ontario. Falconer also reportedly claimed the Kenora Police Services Board was aware of the systemic racism against Aboriginal people in the local police and should have taken steps to address it. "And they may well be legally obligated to," the article quoted Falconer as saying. "They certainly are morally." The story appeared in the *Kenora Daily Miner and News*, Thursday, April 12, 2007, and in the Lake of the Woods *Enterprise* on April 14, 2007. The Kenora Police Service was later disbanded and the town contracted for services

by the Ontario Provincial Police instead: *Timmins* (Ont.) *Press*, December 23, 2008 (accessed 2016-06-05 at www.timminspress.com/2008/12/23/kenora-council-votes-to-disband-city-police-service).

108 Dr. De Zayas, a former senior legal counsel to the UN High Commission on Human Rights, has observed conditions in Aboriginal communities in Canada and acted as adviser to the Mi'kmaq nation of New Brunswick.

109 Catto, *Beavering*, c8.

110 Leanne Simpson, "Keeping a Promise: Industrial Pollution and the Anishinaabek at Paa-kaa-aa-gaamoni (Quibel), Final Report of the Wabauskang First Nations Indigenous Knowledge and Contaminants Program" (Ohsweken, Ont.: Indigenous Health Research Development Program, October 2007). Accessed 2016-06-05 at http://nationtalk.ca/story/final-report-of-the-wabauskang-first-nations-indigenous-knowledge-and-contaminants-program.

111 Tanya Talaga, "Dalton McGuinty Says He'll Study Report on Grassy Narrows Mercury Poisoning," *Toronto Star*, April 6, 2010 (accessed 2016-06-05 at www.thestar.com/news/ontario/2010/04/06/dalton_mcguinty_says_hell_study_report_on_grassy_narrows_mercury_poisoning.html). The disease was named for the city of Minimata, Japan, where the early exploratory medical work on it was done. Japanese doctors came to Grassy Narrows in the early '70s and confirmed that the people there were suffering from the disease and that it was caused by mercury poisoning, which the Ontario government had been denying up until then. See Masazumi Harada et al., "Epidemiological and clinical study and historical background of mercury pollution on Indian Reservations in Northwestern Ontario, Canada," *Bulletin of the Institute of Constitutional Medicine* 26, nos. 3–4 (1976): 169–184 (Kumamoto University, Japan). For some years thereafter Health Canada measured the mercury content of drinking water drawn from the river and finally concluded that it was safe. However, in early 2010 Japanese researchers again showed that the persisting mercury had already caused deaths among natives who had believed Health Canada: Harada et al., "Mercury Pollution in First Nations Groups in Ontario, Canada: 35 years of Canadian Minamata Disease," *Journal of Minamata Studies* 3 (2011): 3–30 (accessed 2016-04-05 [pdf] at http://freegrassy.net/wp-content/uploads/2012/06/Harada-et-al-2011-English.pdf).

112 James Chigwedere, "Project Director's Report to Frontiers Foundation/Operation Beaver, Kenora, 1973" (Toronto: Frontiers Foundation archives).

113 Lee in conversation with the author, Kenora, 2008.

114 Interview with Ross by the author, 2012.

115 Ann Hopkins interview in Frontiers' yearly newsletter for 1974.

116 The people were Ann Hopkins (Quebec), Shirley Serviss (Saskatchewan), Sabine Giesber (France), Tjeerd Blaue (Holland), Doug Prendergast (Jamaica), Gord Carmichael and Brian Sinclair (Ontario), Ibrahim Pare (Upper Volta) and Jim Chigwedere (Zambia). They were joined later by Ottolien

Koppens (Holland), Ray Polson (a status Algonquin from near Amos, Quebec) and Sally Skead (a status Saulteaux from the local area).

117 This quotation and the one on p. 133 are both from Chigwedere, project director's report.

118 Catto, *The White Problem*, c6.

119 Article by Walter Stewart held in Frontiers Foundation archives, Toronto.

120 Charles Catto, *Beaver Tales* no. 8 (March 1976): 2. This is the occasional newsletter of Operation Beaver, back issues to be found in the Frontiers Foundation archives, Toronto.

121 Frontiers Annual Report and Newsletter, 1975.

122 Author interview with Lee by phone, ca. 2010.

123 Robert Lee, president of the Kenora Métis and Non-Status Indian Association, to Charles Catto, 1973, in Frontiers Foundation archives, Toronto.

124 "A lingering tragedy," editorial, *Toronto Star*, June 6, 2012, A20. ProQuest document ID 1018678086 (accessed 2016-05-01 via public library proxy server).

125 The people of this region are mainly Wet'suwet'en, who are friendly with and closely related to the Gitxsan. The village of Hagwilget is the successor to the older Tse-Kya.

126 Jefferson married a girl from the reserve and later moved to Huntsville, Ontario.

127 Quoted in Marius Barbeau, Northwest Coast Files, B-F-96.9 (1926), 2 [the archival numbering system is that of John J. Cove, *A Detailed Inventory of the Barbeau Northwest Coast Files*. National Museum of Man Mercury Series, Canadian Centre for Folk Culture Studies, Paper 54. Ottawa: National Museums of Canada, 1985]. Also quoted in Maureen Cassidy, *The Gathering Place* (Hagwilget, BC: Hagwilget Band Council, 1987), 61.

128 Formalized in 1983, the program funded litigation to clarify Aboriginal-related issues for which there was no case law: "Evaluation of the Test Case Funding Program, Final Report," (Ottawa: Indian and Northern Affairs Canada, February 9, 2009), i–ix (accessed 2016-04-05 (pdf) at http://publications.gc.ca/collections/collection_2015/aadnc-aandc/R5-48-2009-eng.pdf). See also *Joseph v. Canada*, 2008 FC 574 (accessed 2016-06-05 at http://decisions.fct-cf.gc.ca/fc-cf/decisions/en/item/55339/index.do).

129 G.S. Reade, District Supervisor, Prince Rupert, Department of Fisheries and Oceans, to W.G. Price, Assistant Superintendent, Indian Affairs Branch, Hazelton, April 26, 1955, Babine Agency Files, Game and Fisheries, 1950–55, quoted in Cassidy, *The Gathering Place*, 72.

130 "Village" is the term Dora Wilson prefers, since to her the name "band" is an inappropriate invention of DIAND.

131 Cassidy, *The Gathering Place*, 44.

132 In conversation with the author.

133 "This scarecrow of a suit has, in course of time, become so complicated that no man alive knows what it means … but Jarndyce and Jarndyce still drags its dreary length before the court, perennially hopeless." *Bleak House* (London: Bradbury and Evans, 1853), 3. Accessed 2016-06-05 at https://is.gd/e8Y7aJ.

134 *Joseph v. Canada*, 2008 FC 574 at ¶7. Accessed 2016-06-05 at http://decisions. fct-cf.gc.ca/fc-cf/decisions/en/item/55339/index.do.

135 *Joseph v. Canada*, ¶21.

136 Justice Hugessen to the author.

137 The payment having been ordered pursuant to a decision of the Supreme Court of Canada that public-interest litigation should be funded, a trial ending with a judge's decision would have provided a useful precedent. This interest was frustrated by the secrecy term of the settlement. Justice Hugessen was satisfied with that outcome. However, it remains to be said that apart from the sum, the terms of the settlement might in themselves have provided very useful information in the future.

138 Don Irving, Frontiers Foundation western coordinator, to the author. This figure is based on the average cost of Frontiers houses built during the period in that area. It does not include the cost of the land.

139 Lawrence Gladue, interview by the author, July 2010.

140 Catto in conversation with the author, 2013.

141 The Nawash Unceded First Nation succeeded in defending some of their historic rights in Federal Court in 2005. See David McLaren, "Under Siege: How the People of the Chippewas of Nawash Unceded First Nation Asserted Their Rights and Claims and Dealt with the Backlash (A Report to the Ipperwash Inquiry)," Neyaashiinigamiing (Cape Croker), Ont.: Chippewas of Nawash, 2005 (accessed 2016-06-05 [pdf] at www.attorneygeneral.jus.gov. on.ca/inquiries/ipperwash/policy_part/projects/pdf/under_siege.pdf).

142 James P. Barry, *Georgian Bay: An Illustrated History* (Toronto: Stoddart, 1992).

143 A gathering of representatives from northern Alberta communities between the Peace and Athabasca rivers, to discuss their land claims.

144 Catto, *Beavering*, c8.

145 *Beavering*, c8.

146 This and all ensuing Bembridge quotes are from an interview with him by the author, Toronto, 2012.

147 *The White Problem*, 133.

148 In his writings, Charles frequently referred to the great Shawnee statesman and general.

149 Katimavik, a program founded in 1977 to "educate youth and spur lifelong civic engagement through community service," mobilized volunteers to work in communities across Canada. It too suffered during 1986–1994, when its

federal funding was cut. A new government restored funding to the program in 1994. See Katimavik: "Our history" (accessed 20150714 at www.katimavik. org/our-history).

150 *Beavering*, c12.

151 *Beavering*, c12.

152 Lawrence Gladue, interview by author, July 2010.

153 This phenomenon has been investigated by Thor Heyerdahl, who noticed the similarity between the reed (papyrus) boats used by people in the upper Nile Valley and the reed boats of Titicaca.

154 *Beavering*, c13.

155 "St. FX to award two honourary degrees at Fall Convocation '98," *News@stfx. ca*, no. 17 (November 27, 1998): 1 (newsletter of St. Francis Xavier University, Antigonish, NS, accessed 2016-10-05 [pdf] at https://is.gd/sPvNV5).

156 Official not named, but quoted in *Beavering*, c13.

157 Greg Mortenson, *Stones into Schools: Promoting Peace with Education in Afghanistan and Pakistan* (New York: Penguin, 2009), 185.

158 Kiva and the loans sometimes known as micro-credit unite needy small-business owners and those who wish to support them in a spiritual action mediated by the Internet.

159 Catto, *Beavering*, c13. The Sparshatt quote was first published in *The Bolivian Times*.

160 *Beavering*, c10; idem for the ensuing four quotes.

161 Catto, "Report on Operation Beaver in Haiti," Frontiers archives, Toronto.

162 Quoted in Johansen, *The Forgotten Founders*, c5 (accessed 2015-07-20 at www. ratical.org/many_worlds/6Nations/FFchp5.html).

163 Maggie Siggins, *Bitter Embrace: White Society's Assault on the Woodland Cree* (Toronto: McClelland & Stewart, 2005), 113.

164 Charles Catto, *The White Problem*, 113. Probably the original source for this figure was A.F. Lawrence, MPP for Toronto–St. George.

165 To check the authenticity of these figures, the author made many efforts over three years to reach Michael Shapcott of the Wellesley Institute but the calls were never returned. The figures are published here because Charles Catto, Lawrence Gladue and Marco Guzman of Frontiers Foundation read and approved them.

166 Liss Larson interviewed by Charles Catto, ca. 2009.

167 Catto, *Beavering*, c14.

168 Lylas Polson interview, Toronto, 2013.

169 *Beavering*, c14.

170 Susan Bacque is the daughter of the author.

171 *Amik* means "beaver" in the Anishinaabe language.

172 Lawrence Gladue in interview by author, July 2010.

173 Catto, *Beavering*, c14.

174 Mortenson, *Stones into Schools*, 178, 180.

175 Greg Mortenson has been accused of duping the public with wasteful building of unnecessary schools and excessive travel costs, but nothing like this
could ever have happened to Charles Catto. The present author has examined Frontiers' audited books and been made aware of the loans Charles personally made to sustain Frontiers, not the other way around.

176 Funding for this project was received from the Sustainable Development In-
novations Fund of Manitoba Conservation and the federal housing agency,
CMHC. Laurie Guimond and Wendy Chevrefils, employment and training staff at Sagkeeng, arranged for the training allowances and many of the
materials.

177 Forintek's mission was to research and innovate in wood products technology and to transfer it to the Canadian wood products sector.

178 Today, the village is called Chisasibi.

179 Jane Willis, *Geniesh: An Indian Girlhood* (Toronto: newpress, 1973), 3.

180 Willis, *Geniesh*, 199.

181 Ibid., 150.

182 Don Irving, email to author, July 2014.

183 Irving email to author, July 2014.

184 Irving interview, 2010.

185 Irving in conversation with author, Smithers, BC, 2010.

186 Toni Eichhorn, email to author, November 2015.

187 Eichhorn email, November 2015.

188 Lawrence Gladue interviewed by author, July 2010.

189 Martin Loney, "Social Problems, Community Trauma and Hydro Project Impact," *Canadian Journal of Native Studies* 15, no. 2 (1995): 231–254. Accessed
2016-04-05 (pdf) at www3.brandonu.ca/library/CJNS/15.2/loney.pdf. The
abstract begins: "The cumulative effects of hydro regulation on Aboriginal
communities suggest that the concept of community trauma may provide
additional insights. Evidence from a number of hydro developments is considered, particularly in northern Manitoba. It is concluded that impacted
communities appear to exhibit significant and measurable increases in social
pathology, consistent with the concept of community trauma." This weaselly
language is typical of the evasive camouflage commissioned by Canadian
governments to mask their thefts from Aboriginal people.

190 Hugh Brody, *The Other Side of Eden* (Vancouver: Douglas & McIntyre, 2000),
236–238.

191 Catto in conversation with author, August 2009.

192 Phone interview with Driediger, ca. 2013.

193 Phone interview, ca. 2013, which is the source of all the Driediger quotes in the next three paragraphs as well.

194 From "A Case of You," track 9 on the album *Blue* (Warner Brothers K44128, June 1971). Lyric accessed 2016-09-30 at jonimitchell.com.

195 Irving interview, 2015.

BIBLIOGRAPHY

Books, periodicals, websites

"A lingering tragedy." Editorial. *Toronto Star*, June 6, 2012, A20. ProQuest document ID 1018678086 (accessed 2016-05-01 via public library proxy server).

Ando, Clifford. "Driftwood to Google: How and What We Map, a Remarkable Exhibition in Chicago." *The Times Literary Supplement*, no. 5466 (January 4, 2008): 14–15.

Annett, Kevin D., ed. *Hidden from History: The Canadian Holocaust: The Untold Story of the Genocide of Aboriginal Peoples by Church and State in Canada*. Nanaimo, BC: Truth Commission into Genocide in Canada, 2001.

Assikinack, Francis. "Social and Warlike Customs of the Odahwah Indians." *Canadian Journal of Industry, Science and Art* (n.s.) 3, no. 13 (January 1858): 297–309. Accessed 2016-04-05 at https://is.gd/piAs40.

Bacque, James. *Crimes and Mercies: The Fate of German Civilians under Allied Occupation, 1944–1950*. Toronto: Little, Brown, 1997. Revised edition Vancouver: Talonbooks, 2007.

Barbeau, Marius. Northwest Coast Files, B-F-96.9 (1926) [as numbered by John J. Cove in his work listed below].

Barry, James P. *Georgian Bay: An Illustrated History*. Toronto: Stoddart, 1992. (Originally published as *Georgian Bay: The Sixth Great Lake*. Toronto: Clarke, Irwin, 1968.)

Boswell, Victor, John Magness et al., eds. *The World in Your Garden*. Washington, DC: National Geographic Society, 1957.

Brody, Hugh. *The Other Side of Eden: Hunters, Farmers and the Shaping of the World*. Vancouver: Douglas & McIntyre, 2000.

Cassidy, Maureen. *The Gathering Place: A History of the Wet'suwet'en Village of Tse-Kya*. Hagwilget, BC: Hagwilget Band Council, 1987.

Colombo, John Robert. *New Canadian Quotations*. Edmonton: Hurtig, 1987.

Cove, John J. *A Detailed Inventory of the Barbeau Northwest Coast Files*. National Museum of Man Mercury Series, Canadian Centre for Folk Culture Studies, Paper 54. Ottawa: National Museums of Canada, 1985.

Cronon, William. *Changes in the Land: Indians, Colonists and the Ecology of New England*. New York: Hill and Wang, 1983.

Delâge, Denys. *Bitter Feast: Amerindians and Europeans in Northeastern North America, 1600–64*. Vancouver: UBC Press, 1995.

Dickens, Charles. *Bleak House*. London: Bradbury and Evans, 1853. Page images accessed 2016-06-05 at https://is.gd/e8Y7aJ.

"Evaluation of the Test Case Funding Program, Final Report." Ottawa: Indian and
Northern Affairs Canada, February 9, 2009. Accessed 2016-04-05 (pdf) at
http://publications.gc.ca/collections/collection_2015/aadnc-aandc/R5-48-
2009-eng.pdf.

"Evolution of Corn, The." Learn.Genetics (website). University of Utah Genetic
Science Learning Center, 2016. Accessed 2016-04-05 at http://learn.genetics.
utah.edu/content/selection/corn.

Fischer, David Hackett. *Champlain's Dream*. New York: Simon & Schuster, 2008.

Gagnon, François-Marc, ed. *The Codex Canadensis and the Writings of Louis
Nicolas: The Natural History of the New World/Histoire naturelle des Indes oc-
cidentales.* Introduced by François-Marc Gagnon, with a foreword by Duane
King; English translation by Nancy Senior; French modernization by Réal
Ouellet. Tulsa, Okla., and Montréal/Kingston: Gilcrease Museum and Mc-
Gill-Queen's University Press, 2011.

Gatenby, Greg. *The Wild Is Always There: Canada through the Eyes of Foreign Writers.* Toronto: Vintage, 1994.

Gidney, R.D. "Egerton Ryerson." In *Dictionary of Canadian Biography*, vol. 11
(1881–1890). Toronto/Québec: University of Toronto/Université Laval, 1982
rev. 2015. Accessed 2016-04-05 at www.biographi.ca/en/bio/ryerson_eger-
ton_11E.html.

Goldschein, Eric. "The 10 Most Important Crops In The World." *Business Insider*, 2011-09-20. Accessed 2016-05-01 at www.businessinsider.
com/10-crops-that-feed-the-world-2011-9.

Harada, Masazumi, et al. "Epidemiological and Clinical Study and Historical
Background of Mercury Pollution on Indian Reservations in Northwestern
Ontario, Canada." *Bulletin of the Institute of Constitutional Medicine* 26, nos.
3–4 (1975): 169–184 (Kumamoto University, Japan).

———. "Mercury Pollution in First Nations Groups in Ontario, Canada: 35
years of Canadian Minamata Disease." *Journal of Minamata Studies* 3 (2011):
3–30. Accessed 2016-04-05 (pdf) at http://freegrassy.net/wp-content/up-
loads/2012/06/Harada-et-al-2011-English.pdf.

Henry, George. See Maungwudaus.

Hoffman, David E. "Going Viral: The Pentagon Takes On a New Enemy: Swine
Flu." *The New Yorker* (January 31, 2011): 26–32. Accessed 2016-04-05 at www.
newyorker.com/magazine/2011/01/31/going-viral.

Hurley, Mary C. "The Crown's Fiduciary Relationship with Aboriginal Peoples."
Ottawa: Library of Parliament research paper PRB 00-09E, 2000, 2002. Accessed 2016-04-05 at www.parl.gc.ca/content/LOP/ResearchPublications/
prb0009-e.htm.

*Jesuit Relations and Allied Documents, The: Travels and Explorations of the Jesuit Mis-
sionaries in North America 1610–1791.* Compiled and edited by Reuben Gold
Thwaites. Translated into English with original languages on facing pages. 71

vols, Cleveland, Ohio: The Burrows Brothers, 1848–1901. Searchable HTML transcriptions accessed 2016-06-05 at http://moses.creighton.edu/kripke/jesuitrelations. Links to full-volume scans of original editions accessed 2016-05-05 at https://is.gd/hXBWhn [sort collection by title, click "show details," and view as list, not thumbnails].

Johansen, Bruce E. *Forgotten Founders: Benjamin Franklin, the Iroquois and the Rationale for the American Revolution.* Ipswich, Mass.: Gambit, 1982. Full text transcription accessed 2016-05-01 at www.ratical.org/many_worlds/6Nations/FF.html.

Joseph v. Canada, 2008 FC 574. Accessed 2016-06-05 at http://decisions.fct-cf.gc.ca/fc-cf/decisions/en/item/55339/index.do.

Loney, Martin. "Social Problems, Community Trauma and Hydro Project Impact." *Canadian Journal of Native Studies* 15, no. 2 (1995): 231–254. Accessed 2016-04-05 (pdf) at www3.brandonu.ca/library/CJNS/15.2/loney.pdf.

Maungwudaus (George Henry). *An Account of the Chippewa Indians, Who Have Been Travelling among the Whites, in the United States, England, Ireland, Scotland, France and Belgium with Very Interesting Incidents in Relation to the General Characteristics of the English, Irish, Scotch, French and Americans, with Regard to their Hospitalities, Peculiarities etc.* Boston: The author, 1848.

McLaren, David. "Under Siege: How the People of the Chippewas of Nawash Unceded First Nation Asserted Their Rights and Claims and Dealt with the Backlash (A Report to the Ipperwash Inquiry)." Neyaashiinigamiing (Cape Croker), Ont.: Chippewas of Nawash, 2005. Accessed 2016-06-05 (pdf) at www.attorneygeneral.jus.gov.on.ca/inquiries/ipperwash/policy_part/projects/pdf/under_siege.pdf.

Mee, Charles L. Jr. *The Genius of the People.* New York: Harper & Row, 1987.

Mortenson, Greg. *Stones into Schools: Promoting Peace through Education in Afghanistan and Pakistan.* New York: Penguin, 2009.

Muhlstein, Anka. *La Salle: Explorer of the North American Frontier.* New York: Arcade Publishing, 1994.

Nicolas, Louis (fl. 1667–1675). See Gagnon, François-Marc, et al., *The Codex Canadensis...* above.

Oberle, Frank. *A Chosen Path: From Moccasin Flats to Parliament Hill.* Surrey, BC: Heritage House, 2005.

Penikett, Antony. *Reconciliation: First Nations Treaty Making in British Columbia.* Vancouver and Berkeley: Douglas & McIntyre, 2006.

Peyer, Bernd. *American Indian Nonfiction: An Anthology of Writings, 1760s–1930s.* Norman: University of Oklahoma Press, 2007.

Phillips, Philip, James Alfred Ford and James B. Griffin, eds., with an introduction by Stephen Williams. *Archaeological Survey in the Lower Mississippi Alluvial Valley, 1940–1947.* Tuscaloosa: University of Alabama Press, 2003.

Pope Paul III. *Sublimus Dei*, 1537. Accessed 2016-06-05 at www.papalencyclicals. net/Paul03/p3subli.htm.

Reilly, John. *Bad Medicine: A Judge's Struggle for Justice in a First Nations Community*. Calgary: Rocky Mountain Books, 2010.

Roustang, François, sj. *Jesuit Missionaries to North America: Spiritual Writings and Biographical Sketches*. English translation by Sr. M. Renelle, ssnd. San Francisco: Ignatius Press, 2006. Originally published as *Jésuites de la Nouvelle-France*, textes choisis et présentés par François Roustang, sj. Collection Christus no. 6. Paris: Desclée de Brouwer, 1961.

Salaman, Redcliffe N. *The History and Social Influence of the Potato*. Edited and with a new introduction by J.G. Hawkes, with a chapter on "Industrial Uses" by W.G. Burton. Cambridge and New York: Cambridge University Press, 1985.

Schmalz, Peter S. *The Ojibwa of Southern Ontario*. Toronto and Buffalo: University of Toronto Press, 1991.

Siggins, Maggie. *Bitter Embrace: White Society's Assault on the Woodland Cree*. Toronto: McClelland & Stewart, 2005.

Simpson, Leanne. "Keeping a Promise: Industrial Pollution and the Anishinaabek at Paa-kaa-aa-gaamoni (Quibel), Final Report of the Wabauskang First Nations Indigenous Knowledge and Contaminants Program." Ohsweken, Ont.: Indigenous Health Research Development Program, October 2007. Accessed 2016-06-05 at http://nationtalk.ca/story/final-report-of-the-wabauskang-first-nations-indigenous-knowledge-and-contaminants-program.

"St. FX to award two honourary degrees at Fall Convocation '98." *News@stfx.ca*, no. 17 (November 27, 1998): 1. Newsletter of St. Francis Xavier University, Antigonish, NS, accessed 2016-10-05 (pdf) at https://is.gd/sPvNV5.

Talaga, Tanya. "Dalton McGuinty Says He'll Study Report on Grassy Narrows Mercury Poisoning." *Toronto Star*, April 6, 2010. Accessed 2016-06-05 at www.thestar.com/news/ontario/2010/04/06/dalton_mcguinty_says_hell_study_report_on_grassy_narrows_mercury_poisoning.html.

Thesiger, Wilfred. *Arabian Sands*. London: Longmans, Green, 1959.

Thwaites, Reuben Gold, ed. See *Jesuit Relations* etc. above.

Twigger, Robert. *Voyageur: Across the Rocky Mountains in a Birchbark Canoe*. London: Weidenfeld & Nicolson, 2006.

Voltaire (1694–1778). *The Huron, or Pupil of Nature*. Translated from the French by William F. Fleming, 1889. Full text accessed 2016-06-01 at www.online-literature.com/voltaire/the-huron. Originally published as *L'Ingénu: Histoire véritable tirée des manuscrits du Père Quesnel*. Utrecht, 1767. Page images accessed 2016-06-01 at Gallica, the online archive of La bibliothèque nationale de France, https://is.gd/FIsKlT.

Willis, Jane. *Geniesh: An Indian Girlhood*. Toronto: newpress, 1973.

Wright, Ronald. *Time Among the Maya: Travels in Belize, Guatemala and Mexico.* Markham, Ont.: Viking, 1989.

Historical statutes and Royal Proclamations

An Act for the Better Establishment and Maintenance of Common Schools in Upper Canada. Statutes of United Canadas (1841–1866), 9 Vict., c. 20, 1846. Page images and transcriptions accessed 2016-04-05 at https://bnald.lib.unb.ca/node/4455.

An Act to Prevent the Further Introduction of Slaves, and to limit the Term of Contracts for Servitude within this Province. Statutes of Upper Canada (1792–1840), 33 Geo. 3, c. 7 (2nd Session), 1793. Page images and transcriptions accessed 2016-04-05 at https://bnald.lib.unb.ca/node/1560.

Constitution Act, 1867 (formerly British North America Act, 1867) 30-31 Vict., c. 3, s. 146 (UK). Accessed 2016-04-05 at www.solon.org/Constitutions/Canada/English/ca_1867.html.

"Royal Proclamation of 1763." HRH Geo. 3, October 7, 1763. Excerpt re First Nations at "Indigenous Foundations" (website). Vancouver: UBC, 2009. Accessed 2016-06-05 at http://indigenousfoundations.arts.ubc.ca/home/government-policy/royal-proclamation-1763.html.

Rupert's Land Act, 1868, 31-32 Vict., c. 105 (UK). Accessed 2016-06-05 at www.solon.org/Constitutions/Canada/English/rpl_1868.html.

Rupert's Land and North-Western Territory Order (formerly Order of Her Majesty in Council Admitting Rupert's Land and the North-Western Territory into the Union), at the Court at Windsor, June 23, 1870, art. 14. Accessed 2016-06-05 at www.solon.org/Constitutions/Canada/English/rlo_1870.html.

Temporary Government of Rupert's Land Act, 1869, 32-33 Vict., c. 3 (Canada). Accessed 2016-06-05 at www.solon.org/Constitutions/Canada/English/tgrla_1869.html.

OTHER BOOKS BY JAMES BACQUE

FICTION

The Lonely Ones
A Man of Talent
Creation (with Robert Kroetsch and Pierre Gravel)
The Queen Comes to Minnicog
Our Fathers' War

HISTORY

Other Losses
Crimes and Mercies

ESSAYS

Dear Enemy (with Richard Matthias Mueller)

BIOGRAPHY

Just Raoul

DRAMA

Conrad

INDEX OF NAMES

JAMES BACQUE was an editor at Macmillan for eight years and was a co-founder and partner in newpress. The author of nine works of fiction, history and biography, and even a very successful satirical play on Conrad Black (which Lord Black himself reportedly thought quite amusing), Bacque is widely known for his two bestselling books *Other Losses* and *Crimes and Mercies*, about the treatment of German POWs and citizens respectively by Allied Forces at the end of the Second World War. Together, these books have sold over 250,000 copies in 10 languages and 13 countries around the world. He lives in Penetanguishene, Ontario.